Journey To The Land Of Angels

Sophia Moon

BALBOA
PRESS

A DIVISION OF HAY HOUSE

Balboa Press books may be ordered through booksellers or by contacting:

Balboa Press
A Division of Hay House
1663 Liberty Drive
Bloomington, IN 47403
www.balboapress.com
1-(877) 407-4847

Because of the dynamic nature of the Internet, any web addresses or links contained in this book may have changed since publication and may no longer be valid. The views expressed in this work are solely those of the author and do not necessarily reflect the views of the publisher, and the publisher hereby disclaims any responsibility for them.

The author of this book does not dispense medical advice or prescribe the use of any technique as a form of treatment for physical, emotional, or medical problems without the advice of a physician, either directly or indirectly. The intent of the author is only to offer information of a general nature to help you in your quest for emotional and spiritual well-being. In the event you use any of the information in this book for yourself, which is your constitutional right, the author and the publisher assume no responsibility for your actions.

Any people depicted in stock imagery provided by Thinkstock are models, and such images are being used for illustrative purposes only.

Certain stock imagery © Thinkstock.

ISBN: 978-1-4525-8063-0 (sc)
ISBN: 978-1-4525-8064-7 (e)

Library of Congress Control Number: 2013915268

Printed in the United States of America.

Balboa Press rev. date: 9/16/2013

TABLE OF CONTENTS

CHAPTER 1————————————————AUG 1981
A New Beginning

I T WAS AUGUST, 1981 AND I was twenty four years old. I wished my friend had never given me the idea to move from Georgia to San Francisco. It had been a frightening and exhausting three thousand mile drive and I could not have done it without the help of my two travel companions. My friend had raved about San Francisco, saying it was the most European city in the country. Yet, there was something spooky about the fog floating around like apparitions, warning of impending doom. Holding my breath in fear, I gripped the steering wheel tensely as I drove around the vast city. Pushing the accelerator through the floor, I considered pulling on the emergency brake to keep us from rolling backwards down the treacherously steep hills. The whole place was like a huge roller coaster.

Arriving at Fisherman's Wharf, I parked my car next to a meter. Cold air ripped through me and I pulled on a sweater, longing for the warmth I was accustomed to in August. We walked around observing the sidewalk markets which overflowed with lobsters, crabs, oysters and shrimp. Seagulls flew overhead, screeching loudly and diving down to pick up a tasty morsel here and there. Multi-colored boats bobbed and swayed in the wind, their snow white sails fluttering freely.

My acquaintance, Jerry, who I had considered driving across the country with, had told me I could stay with him for a couple of nights when I arrived. He had given me a number where I could call him at The Brotherhood Of Truth. It sounded like some spiritual organization.

I dialed the number from a gas station pay phone. A stern sounding woman questioned me suspiciously. I was relieved when his gentle voice finally came on. My mind drifted back to the day I had met him for lunch after finding his name on a ride board in the health food store. His eyes had shone with brilliance as he talked about his spirit guides and The Course In Miracles. I had been impressed by the fact that he was a vegetarian. We had considered traveling to our new city together but, a few days later, he had told me that he felt too awkward traveling with a female and had decided to take a Greyhound Bus instead.

He welcomed us with a warm smile and respectful hugs when we arrived at his small apartment. He commented that we must be tired after our cross country drive. After we chatted for a while, he showed Helena and I to his living room sofa bed and helped us to fold it out. After peaceful slumbers, we took a walk around the neighborhood and had some tea in a café.

Golden sun streaming through the window woke us the next morning. Jerry cooked us pancakes with wheat germ which we smothered with butter and syrup. As we ate and talked, he suggested that we tour Berkeley.

When we arrived, I observed the panorama with curiosity. The spirit of freedom filled the air. I imagined that I had been transported back to the sixties as I watched long-haired men in paisley shirts and braless women in midriff tops walk by on bare feet. People rebelled against the government as they handed out pamphlets and petitions about various issues. Excited conversations and laughter poured from the many cafes as though a great, life changing revolution had begun.

Jerry bought us each an ice cream cone. My chocolate mint tasted indescribably delicious and I laughed as it dripped onto my shirt. After walking most of the afternoon, we climbed into my car and I drove home to Jerry's place. Collapsing onto the bed, I took a pleasant cat nap. Helena and I slept peacefully that night.

A cheerful mood came over me as Jerry cooked us pancakes the next morning.

"That woman who gave you my number was concerned that I might be involved with you. We have a rule in our Spiritual Order that we are not supposed to get involved with women". His eyes shone gently and a soft smile turned up the corners of his mouth

"Yeah. She did sound suspicious. She really intimidated me", I replied, lifting a forkful of warm, syrup smothered pancakes to my mouth.

"Well, you can stay here three nights. Maybe you can apply at some temporary services. A lot of them are hiring. That's what I did when I arrived", Jerry suggested.

"Are you going to live in San Francisco too?", he asked Helena.

"Oh, no. I just came on the trip to see America. I will go back East and eventually move back to Germany", she replied.

I listened to their conversation as I daydreamed about my future. After a while, he excused himself saying he had to take care of some business.

We pulled on some sweaters and walked out to the car. Curiosity filled me as I drove up and down the unbelievably steep hills. The colorful pastel houses were unique like my friend had said. A trolley car zoomed by, cheerily ringing its bell. When I saw a sign that said "Owl and Monkey Cafe", I asked Helena if she would like to go in and have a cup of tea. Waiters bustled around hurriedly as I studied the long list of herbal teas, intrigued by their unique names. After we had both gotten a cup of tea, and I had gotten an application, we began searching for a table. I filled out the application and gave it to a person behind the counter who told me they didn't need anyone. However, they would call me if they did.

A handsome man watched me, meeting my eyes with his dark, penetrating stare. His sun-bronzed, muscular body exuded magnetic energy and I couldn't refuse when he asked us to sit with him. I listened with rapt curiosity as he talked, in his appealing German accent, about being on top of a mountain in Tibet and his narrow escape from some savage men who had attacked him with spears. He had grown up in Germany and moved to San Francisco ten years ago to get into acting.

Suddenly, I remembered that I had promised my friend, Michelle, who had inspired me to move West, that I would call her ex-husband, Robert. I told the others I was going to call a friend and excused myself. A counter person pointed me toward a phone. Robert's familiar voice comforted me. He arrived about twenty minutes later. I waved when I saw him making his way through the crowd, his dark head moving above everyone. I introduced him to Helena and John and, as we got to know one another, a light celebratory mood filled the air. John suggested that we all take a ride to the countryside north of San Francisco.

Robert and I sat in the back seat of my car and John took the wheel. I spoke shyly with Robert, asking him how his Counseling Psychology studies were going. John and Helga spoke fluent German up front. I listened with fascination as I observed exquisite Eucalyptus trees, with endless branches twisting and turning into the sky. Wheat colored hills glowed in the bright sun as we came near to our destination.

John parked the car in a shady area under some trees. As I stretched my tense muscles and breathed in the pure air, I inhaled the intoxicating fragrance of Eucalyptus trees. I imagined living as a nymph of the woods, relying on nature to serve my every need. Living in a simple state of grace, unburdened by the complications of city life and unencumbered by material possessions, would be bliss. So much energy went into shopping at the supermarket and mall, bathing and dressing the body, going to the doctor, exercising, cooking and eating. I dreamed of transforming into a nature spirit who could flit from here to there and live on air. As we climbed to the top of a steep hill, Helena and Robert conversed with enthusiasm. I stared at the ground shyly as John reached for my hand.

"Why did you decide to move to San Francisco?", he asked, looking directly into my eyes.

"I graduated from college and I decided it was time for me to learn about life in the real world. A girl friend of mine told me this is the most European city in the United States. We talked about moving together but she changed her mind. I wanted to be independent of my family and to concentrate on finding myself", I replied.

"Well, maybe you never lost yourself", he laughed, revealing a tender, affectionate side of himself. I laughed with him, feeling grateful to be released from my dark prison of seriousness.

Trickles of sweat ran sensuously down my back as we reached the top of the hill. John took my hand gently as I sat down beside him. The blazing sun beamed down on us, licking us with a billion fiery tongues, igniting a blaze of passion in our young bodies. His eyes were full of brooding emotions, like a dark sky being split apart by lightning. I imagined him acting in some Shakespearean play, holding an audience spellbound.

"Let's go skinny dipping. Everyone who comes here swims nude in the pond. It's a blast. Come on", he said with childlike enthusiasm.

"What if we get arrested?", I asked.

"That never happens. Oh, come on. Don't worry. I won't even look at you. It's no big deal really. You've got to start living. Come on. Have some fun. I'll turn my head while you put on a towel", he urged persuasively.

"Oh, alright", I replied shyly.

My face burned as I slipped out of my clothes and wrapped a towel around me. I followed him down the hill. Fresh air nourished my lungs as we arrived at the lovely pond nestled in between the wheat colored hills. A tall, skinny man swung on a rope over the water. Suddenly, he let go of the rope. A loud noise echoed through the air as a huge splash of water scattered around. He slapped his arms on the water and called up at a child who was watching him from the shore. The child plunged playfully into the water. I watched with wonder as he came swimming up to the surface and then effortlessly turned a somersault.

John dove into the water. I watched him swim as I dipped my big toe in hesitantly. After a few minutes, I dove in. The coolness invigorated me as I explored its dense mystery like a mermaid. I broke through the surface gasping for air. John climbed out of the water onto a rock, then pulled me up beside him. I was deeply grateful that he was keeping his promise, not looking at my body. After sunning on the rocks for a while, we wrapped ourselves up in our towels and began hiking back up the hill. The towering green trees and robin's egg blue sky touched my senses and a blazing, bright sun warmed us. I went behind a tree to get dressed.

John suggested that we take a walk. He talked about life in Germany and how friendly people would wine and dine him there. After describing the Black Forest as a beautiful magical place, he told me I would love to live there. We hiked back up the hill and found Helena and Robert.

We all climbed into my car and John drove us to a pretty café which shone like a seashell in the moonlight. The mood was light as we all sat together and ate. I felt like a flower opening toward the sun as John gave me his undivided attention. Later, we walked along the beach under a black, velvet sky. I leaned my head back, gazing in wonder at the mysterious void that sparkled with diamond like stars.

As Helena and Robert explored the beach, John and I climbed up onto a rock. We sat and watched the crashing waves send white cascades of confetti foam flying onto the white sand. John reclined on the rock. Hesitantly, I nestled my head on his shoulder, hoping he didn't think I was too forward. My soul danced in ecstasy as I drank in the divine, spiritual energy of the cosmos and felt the warmth of his strong body soothing the ragged edges of my psyche. Stars and planets moved in their heavenly orbits, guided with miraculous precision by some divine power that I wanted to understand. I breathed in rhythm with John, enjoying the comforting sensation of his chest rising and falling underneath me.

"It's beautiful", I said, too overwhelmed with emotion to say more.

"Yeah. Every one of those stars is light years away and there are universes and universes expanding into infinity. Even the most advanced scientists can't measure the universe because it's so vast. I know these things because my father is a famous physicist", he replied, squeezing my hand affectionately.

He took my hand and we sauntered along the sand through the shimmering, magical night. Suddenly, he gave me a long, wet kiss. I blushed and felt overcome with shyness. I hardly knew him and I wondered why he liked me so much.

When we arrived back at the car, Helena and Robert walked over from a nearby sandy oasis. We decided it was time to head on. I turned the ignition key, the motor roared and I began driving down the open road, watching the moon shine luminously over the craggy cliffs.

The city lights accosted us harshly when we arrived back in civilization. I parked next to the sidewalk in front of Robert's apartment. John said he would call me. Then, he sped off on his motorcycle. I had no place to go and, luckily, Robert said I could stay with him for three nights. He spent time with Helga, while I read employment and apartment listings and waited anxiously for John to call.

He finally called at two in the morning three nights later. Robert was so angry at him he cussed him out. Later, when I asked Robert a question, he angrily told me it was a stupid question. I searched for his female room mate. She kindly showed me to the phone. With a trembling hand, I called John and asked him to come pick me up.

He smiled warmly as he arrived at the door. I thanked Robert for his hospitality and told him goodbye apologetically. As I pulled on my coat and hung my back pack around my shoulders, fear and homesickness gnawed my guts. Staring at the floor despondently, I walked down the dark stairway, mentioning gloomily that Robert had called me stupid.

"You should have just laughed at him when he put you down like that", John said, his dark eyes glowing with warmth.

"Oh, easier said than done. It really hurt my feelings. I thought he really cared about me", I lamented.

"People like that aren't worth getting upset over. You just can't let them get to you", he said.

"Yeah. I know", I replied glumly.

"We can help each other out. Well, I don't know. That will be like the blind leading the blind, right?" He laughed with abandon.

I laughed faintly, trying to hide my wounded feelings as I followed him silently into the dark night. He drove my car to an empty place on the beach and said we could sleep there. My mind raced restlessly as I tried to sleep on my reclined seat. I worried because I had lost the phone number of the café I had applied for a job in.

The next morning I had a pounding headache. My muscles stiffened with tension when John scolded me for not having the common sense to leave the windows cracked. He complained that he had not gotten any fresh air all night and that it was very unhealthy. He yawned and brushed his fingers through his hair. With a grumpy sigh, he started the car and drove to a filling station. I watched him walk to a pay phone and make a call. His face brightened as he talked energetically for a few minutes. Then, he hung up the phone and walked back to the car.

"Let's go see a friend of mine. He's a great person. You'll like him", he said with excitement. He pressed the accelerator to the floor and sped through the streets. Streetcars carried people up and down the hills as pedestrians walked dogs and admired fancy shop windows. Soon, we arrived at a charming cafe. A cup of peppermint tea and a blueberry muffin consoled me as I sat at a table with them and listened to them talk .

John looked at me. "Brian is an artist. He does incredible paintings", he said, beaming with genuine happiness over his friend's achievements.

"Really? That's great. I paint too. I got my B.A. in Art History and I went to Rome, Italy and studied the art of the great masters of the Renaissance", I replied, admiring his shiny, blond-streaked hair and sparkling blue eyes.

"Yeah. I get out the Michelangelo and Botticelli books and do copies of the great masters' paintings. It's a great way to learn and keep your skills sharpened", he said with enthusiasm.

I listened to them catch up on old news as I worried in silence about finding a job. After a while, John left with his friend saying he had to take care of some important business. I swallowed hard as an uncomfortable lump formed in my throat. I wondered why he had not given me his phone number.

As I drove around the city, searching bulletin boards in laundries and cafes for a place to live, fear held me in a merciless grip. God only knew what strange and decadent characters posted the various scraps of paper that advertised for room mates. I had had fantasies about San Francisco being a friendly, welcoming place—like the summer of love. Looking at photographs of the hippies, I had observed that they were empowered by kindness and a cooperative community spirit.

Soon, night fell and my heart sunk into the dirty gutters that lined the strange streets. I longed to feel John's arms around me as I worried about where I was going to sleep. I couldn't afford to stay in a hotel. My three thousand dollars my grand father had given me had already dwindled by one third. I parked my car on a street near the Golden Gate park. Then, I pushed back the front seat and stared into the dismal, black night, holding my breath with fear.

CHAPTER 2 ——————————SEPTEMBER, 1981
Lost in a Strange Land

THE BRIGHT SUN RISE AND the hopeful singing of birds comforted me. Yawning widely, I ran my fingers through my hair. Restless energy surged within me as I locked my car and began to walk. Strange characters ambled by as I walked quickly up and down many hilly blocks. I found myself on a street lined with attractive shops and restaurants. A bright blue and gold sign that said The Grand Piano beckoned me. I held my breath in anticipation as I walked toward it.

An assortment of unusual characters approached me. A tall, blond man smiled as he handed me a long stalk of rhubarb he pulled out of a paper bag. A woman with a mane of frizzy, gray hair wearing a psychedelic purple dress handed me a pamphlet urging all brothers and sisters to unite against nuclear arms. A rotund, short man wearing a shawl around his shoulders and loads of Native American Indian necklaces handed me an invitation to a healing circle.

A row of rowdy, horny men sat on a ledge in front of the Grand Piano. I became weak at the knees as a chorus of "hey babies" and suggestive leers bombarded me. My face flushed as I walked nervously through the front door. A tall, dark man smiled sweetly as I ordered a cup of chamomile tea. The earthy, soothing aroma calmed me. My eyes darted around the room and landed on a pretty woman sitting alone. I walked over and sat at the table near her.

"I just moved to San Francisco and I'm looking for a place to live" I said, admiring her beautiful face and eyes.

"Oh really? Where did you move from?"

"From Georgia", I replied, scanning the room curiously, then looking back at her.

"There's a place called room mate referral down the street that has listings of people who are renting rooms. They screen people so you can find a good room mate."

"That's good to know. I'll give them a try." I brushed my hair back nervously, listening to bits and pieces of conversation humming around me. Suddenly, the sound of music rippled through me in sensuous, delightful waves. I turned around and saw a strikingly beautiful, blond woman playing the violin. A handsome man accompanied her on the piano. I had loved piano music ever since I started taking lessons at the age of eight. The sweet, middle aged lady who taught me had treated me like I was special.

"Do you know of any place that is hiring people?", I asked shyly.

"No. I don't. I wait tables but they aren't hiring anyone where I work". She brushed her shiny, dark hair back, revealing a sparkling earring.

The thought of waiting tables again paralyzed me with fear. I had had several jobs waiting tables that had turned into disasters. I had run like crazy, trying to please impatient customers who scolded me callously. My mind would race frantically as I tried to remember-- this one needs ketchup, this one needs sugar. No matter how hard I tried, my forgetfulness did me in. I wondered if I would ever be able to take care of myself in this dog eat dog world or if I would end up handing out pencils on a street corner. Clinging to the warmth of my pretty acquaintance, I wished she would ask me to live with her. However, not wanting to frighten her with my neediness, I told her goodbye without asking for her phone number.

As I scuttled down the street in a tired daze I observed people. I pretended to not notice when I saw a dirty, tattered man urinating on the street. Then, another man came walking toward me rubbing his breasts and making lascivious motions with his tongue. He stared at my breasts rudely saying, "Nice tits."

When I saw an art supply store I ducked in quickly, glad to escape the perils of the street. I dreamed of various ideas for paintings as I scanned the brightly colored tubes of paint. My creative self had been stagnant for a long time. I looked into the eyes of a tall, thin man behind the counter. When I said "hello" to him he responded coldly as though he thought I was rather strange. Anxiety crashed through me like a wave as I studied a big bulletin board on the wall which was covered with scraps of paper of various sizes. I looked at one which was written in a sloppy scrawl.

"Creative household seeking creative room mate. Large Victorian house with high ceilings".

My hand trembled as I wrote the number down on a scrap of paper. My shoulders rose tensely as I walked outside to a phone booth. I dialed the number slowly, looking at passing pedestrians nervously. A man with a deep, resonant voice answered. My nerve endings crackled as he gave me directions.

My muscles tensed like knotted ropes as I drove into the foreboding neighborhood. Burglar bars stood out ominously on the windows of dingy, rundown row houses. Desperate looking black men hung out in front of dirty laundries drinking from large Vodka bottles. Every now and then they made catcalls at passing women.

I wished John was there to protect me as I drove cautiously, gripping the steering wheel and straining my eyes to read the numbers on the houses. Beat up cars sped by as tough looking characters gunned the motors forcefully. Savage sounds and rhythms that my mother used to call "Missionary cooking" music deafened me. Finally I spotted the big, blue Victorian next door to a Baptist church. Wincing at the smell of carbon monoxide I looked up at the white cross reaching into the sun drenched sky. I parked my car on the curb and pulled myself hesitantly out.

As I made my way up the steep stairs of the blue Victorian on rubber legs, I craned my neck back to ogle the thick, black burglar bars. I'd never seen such ugly window coverings and I swallowed nervously as I knocked on the door. An exceptionally tall, black man wearing sunglasses and a hat opened it. I leaned my head back to meet his eyes and introduced myself shyly, hoping he couldn't see I was shaking all over.

"Hi. I'm Rob. You must be the person looking to rent a room. Come on in and you can talk with my room mate, Mark." As I followed him, I looked up at the high ceilings which were decorated with flowers, leaves and flying cherubim.

"Mark is a painter and I'm a jazz musician. I'll let you two talk for a while and Mark will tell you everything you need to know about the room." His black skin shone like ebony and his large eyes glowed.

Mark sat on a plush, blue chair, his seemingly endless legs crossed at the ankles. His face was lined with wrinkles and his thinning, dirty blond hair was salted with gray. A half-finished oil painting stood on an easel in the middle of the room. A mattress covered with tousled covers lay in the corner. I wondered why he didn't get a frame for his bed, thinking that it must make one feel like a dog to sleep so close to the floor. As I sat down on a small sofa across from him he looked at me with scrutinizing eyes. Their pale blue shone in the sunlight coming through the window.

"What are you looking for in a living situation?", he asked.

"Well, I mainly want a place that is quiet and where I get along with everyone", I replied, fidgeting nervously.

"Well, it's not always quiet here. Rob is a musician and he plays his bass and we listen to music. We're looking for someone who will add to the creative energy we have going here. This house really has potential. Do you do anything creative?" He searched my face with a look of curiosity.

"Yeah. I've painted since I was eight years old", I replied.

"Oh really? I'd like to see your work". His voice made a shift from scrutiny to acceptance.

"I have some in my car. I'll bring them in." I ran down the hard, concrete stairs and pulled my paintings out of my car with trembling hands. With a burst of hopeful energy, I carried them to him and watched him study them.

"You are really talented. You should do more with this", he said.

"Thank you. I'm going to as soon as I get settled", I replied.

"Well, Rob and I both like you and we've decided you can move in tonight", he said. He stretched his arms up over his head and yawned.

"Is there any way I could pay less rent? I have very little money."

"You're trying to get bargain basement prices. Two hundred dollars a month is already much cheaper than most places. I can't make it any less than that", he said firmly.

"Okay. I'll move in tonight", I said.

I held my breath with fear as I carried my suitcase and boxes into my room. I gazed out the small window at the cross on the roof of the Baptist church. Scenarios of people being dunked into huge vats of water and speaking in tongues flashed through my mind. The thin mattress that lay on the floor looked tattered and dirty. The room was tiny but, at least, I had a tiny closet and my own toilet and sink. As I started to stack my books on a wooden bookshelf, I found a torn, red photo album that contained a few snapshots of myself as a child. I looked deeply into the eyes of my three year old self, bundled up in my snowsuit, standing on the white blanket of snow. I longed to get back that feeling of enchantment, to view the world as a wonderful place again.

I knew I had to forget the pain of my past and move toward something positive, yet I didn't know what to move forward to. I didn't know who I was, where I was going or even if I could keep myself alive after my money ran out. I would never forget the fear I had felt when I heard that I was "schizophrenic" and "catatonic". I was institutionalized two months before my eighteenth birthday. My doctor had said that I would need to take medicine for the rest of my life because I had an incurable mental illness. I had taken pills every day, gone to therapy three times a week and lived on a ward with twelve other patients for an entire year. Even after I was released from the hospital, my father often hounded me about taking my medicine. However, I loathed the cotton mouth, drowsiness and vegetable brain it gave me so I went for long periods without it.

I prayed to the good spirits to bless me as I hung up my clothes. I had collected some very nice outfits. I ought to be able to attract a loving boyfriend with them. I jumped nervously when I heard a loud knocking on my door. It was Rob asking me to go with him and Mark to a concert of

John Coltrane's music. We all piled into my car and I drove us to a nearby church.

We sat on wooden pews and watched a strikingly beautiful, blond woman, in a long, black dress, dance with abandon to the soulful jazz music. A drummer beat out a lively rhythm as saxophone and clarinet players filled the room with harmonious sounds. After the concert, we went to a restaurant and talked until late. I listened with interest as Mark talked about his trips on acid and Rob reflected on his love of God.

Later on, my blanket was no comfort as I tossed and turned on my lumpy mattress. Living in a house of men I didn't know was quite unsettling. I had been deathly afraid of them ever since my alcoholic father beat me with his leather belt when I was a child.

Two years ago, the painful experience of being raped, when I traveled alone with my Eurail pass after my Art History study abroad program, had devastated me. Then, I had given a homeless man and his girlfriend shelter in my shabby rented room, a few blocks from campus, just a month later. The woman had said that her boyfriend would like some alone time with me and I was flattered. I had trusted him enough to let him sit on my bed, my only furniture. He had forced himself on me suddenly. As his penis entered me I floated out of my body. I remained disassociated for the thirty or so seconds that seemed like eternity. I didn't kick or scream because I felt embarrassed and didn't want to disturb my landlords, a busy, working couple. I had never told anyone because I was so ashamed.

But, that was the past. I had moved to begin a new life for myself. I yawned and wiped seeds of sleep from my eyes as I shuffled into the kitchen the next morning. A thin woman with short hair was standing there dressed in a tank top and short shorts that revealed a bit of her buttocks. I greeted her and took my last container of strawberry yogurt out of the refrigerator. As I mixed some peanuts into it, Mark walked in.

"How did your night go last night?", he asked the young woman in a friendly tone.

"It was really rough. The customers were a bunch of savages. There was one obnoxious guy sitting on the front row. I had stripped down to my G-string and I walked across the stage to get my violin out of the case. Suddenly he started yelling really loudly, 'Make that pussy bark'". Her eyes were puffy and surrounded by worry lines.

"God that sounds like hell. I don't know how you put up with it", Mark replied with a compassionate expression.

"It's really tough being a stripper. If I wasn't making so much money I never would have started. I'm going to keep saving money for a while and then get out of it permanently", she said in a weary voice.

I watched Mark sway back and forth energetically on his long legs.

"I'm going roller skating today. Would you like to go?", he asked, looking directly at me with a child like excitement on his face.

Since I could barely open my eyes, the thought of speeding down the treacherous hills of this strange town on roller skates didn't exactly appeal to me. I shook my head to tell him "no."

"Oh, come on. You need to start living. Roller skating is great fun. I do it all the time. You'll have a blast. Come on". His enthusiasm was contagious.

"Well, I really need to spend the day looking for a job but I'll go for a little while." I ate my last spoonful of yogurt and walked to the trash can to throw the container away.

We rode the bus to a roller skating shop. As I pulled my skates on, I remembered how I had loved to roller skate when I was a child. I watched with amusement as Mark whooshed by in a tornado of energy, his long legs and arms swinging back and forth wildly.

I realized I would never be able to catch up with him so I started out on my own solitary adventure. The sound of metal rolling across concrete vibrated through my ears as I glided along the sidewalk, remembering my childhood roller skating adventures. The window of a bakery on the corner shone invitingly, displaying colorful, freshly baked treats. A pleasing aroma tantalized me as I turned the corner.

I gasped with horror as I stared down a long, steep hill at the four lane street below which was rushing with speeding traffic. I tried leaning forward on my skates to stop myself but I couldn't. I grabbed a mailbox and then some tree branches but they slipped through my fingers and I continued rolling. Images of being hit by a speeding car and dying a bloody death raced through my mind.

Finally, I steered myself toward a mailbox and ran into it with a painful thud, wrapping my arms around it gratefully. Self-consciousness overcame me as I sat down on the sidewalk and took my roller skates off. I looked around nervously as I walked up the steep hill to the Grand Piano. As I drank a cool glass of iced tea, the Brandenburg concertos calmed me. After a while, I walked down the street to return the roller skates, cursing them for being the sinister objects they were.

I needed to start looking for a job. Combing my hair with my fingers and straightening my clothes, I slithered past the aloof pedestrians. When I saw a bookstore, I walked in purposefully and asked a tall, handsome man at the front desk for an application. I filled it out and handed it to him, smiling cheerfully. He told me he would keep it on file and call me if they had an opening. I crossed the street and filled out applications in a bakery, an ice cream shop and a bookstore. No one needed me.

My mind raced with worries as I walked back to my new home, cringing and staring down at the sidewalk. Rough looking men drinking from bottles covered with brown paper bags stared at my body lecherously.

The sounds of Rob playing his bass filled my ears as I walked in the front door. A shiver ran up and down my spine as I walked into my room and locked the door behind me. An evil presence seemed to hover around me.

I was surprised beyond words when John knocked on the front door the next day. I introduced him to Mark and they became instant, close friends. I longed for John to pay attention to me as I listened to them talking and laughing late into the night, night after night.

One lonely night when I was pining for my parents and home, John asked me to go to a jazz club with him. I climbed onto the back of his motorcycle and wrapped my arms around his waist, feeling the magnetic energy ebb and flow between us. A cool breeze rippled through my hair as he sped through the city.

Conversation hummed through the air as we walked into a smoky, dimly lit jazz club. We found a small, candle lit table and sat down. I watched in fascination as a tall, skinny, black man swayed on the stage, playing jazz music on his saxophone. John drummed on the table self confidently. He talked expressively as he drank gin and tonic until about two in the morning. Then, we slept together on the fold-out sofa bed near the kitchen in my blue Victorian home. He hugged me gently, non-sexually and I relaxed into his affectionate warmth, feeling elated.

We sat and talked with Mark in the golden sunlight the next morning. John asked me to sit on his lap and he playfully arm-wrestled with me. I laughed nervously, feeling my cheeks burn with a blush as I reveled in the glory of his attention.

As the days passed we began to see less of each other. I wondered if he loved me as I rode the bus around the city looking for a job. He and Mark hung out together in the day time and went to a bar every evening. Again and again, at two a.m., John lumbered into my room and lay down beside me, jerking the covers off and waking me with his Vodka breath.

I remembered my father when he got drunk. Sometimes he could be quite amusing, walking around the house singing opera or talking about his plan to raise a thousand poodles on his farm. Sometimes he would yell, "I'm tired of being the enemy around here." He would vehemently exclaim that we needed to get an army together to storm the White House and padlock the Pentagon. He also said that the astronauts had not actually walked on the moon in the 1968 moon landing. Other times he would be unbelievably cruel, threatening to throw all my belongings out into the street. When I made C's and D's he said he was going to send me to a convent. If I dared to raise my voice to him, he threatened to beat me to within an inch of my life. Often, he would become very demanding, ordering me to cook his supper. I wondered if he imagined himself to be a plantation owner in the Old South with me as his nigger. Maybe he had studied humiliation tactics with the

KKK. He certainly was an expert at intimidating me. I would rush around like a terrified servant, cooking a meal for him. Then I would hand it to him with a stoic, smiling face while, inside, my heart was breaking.

My mind drifted to thoughts of my parents, my sister who was two and a half years older, my sister who was two and a half years younger, and my brother who was four years older. We were a complicated family which was now scattered around the country. My brother lived in southern California and my older sister had moved to Maryland with her college sweetheart as soon as she graduated. I missed my younger sister and parents back in Georgia immensely.

There had been immense tension between my parents. My siblings and I had individual ways of coping with the constant impending disaster in our home. My younger sister had been playful, dramatic, funny and sociable. My older sister had submerged herself in her violin playing in the Youth Symphony. My brother had stayed in his room writing constantly. I wanted to call them all and talk to them. However, I often felt like they did not want to take the time to talk.

John took my breath away with his handsomeness, confident vibrancy and intelligence. I kept reliving our walk along the enchanted beach and his incomparable kiss. Now, however, his dark side was closing in on me like a threatening storm cloud. A drunk had destroyed my childhood. I wasn't going to let another one destroy my adulthood.

He had given me the number of a psychic. Hope bubbled inside me as I called her. She started the session with a meditation which relaxed me deeply. She instructed me to visualize orange and green energy moving through my body. Soothing sensations flowed through me. Then, her expression became distant as she went into a trance.

"I see several past lives before this one in which you were always struggling to survive. I see you carrying a heavy bundle of sticks on your back and working long, hard hours. You chose to come into a difficult situation in this life to bring this struggle situation to a head. You picked your parents out." She paused.

"You have to break out in this life as far as really coming out with a lot of power. You have really been changing the energy, moving to a new place and opening yourself up to new experiences. There is a certain amount of power for you to have now. Don't worry that you will misuse it. Just bring it in because you need it and you deserve it."

"You were really taught to be a quiet girl and, when you're inside yourself, you have this tiny, little voice. You're really afraid of saying something. I see this comes more from your father's side of the family. It was pretty important to him for you to be seen and not heard."

"I would like to heal my parents and help them be happy but I feel so rejected by them", I said, pain throbbing in my heart.

"You can't heal them. Heal yourself by coming into your body more. Right now you really have no conception of your body. You know, when you see people wandering along the street looking spaced out it's because they're not in their bodies. Your mother really tried to get you to be more "normal". She would get frustrated with you, you know, and say, 'Stop being such a space case.' What a way to come into your body. It makes you want to go right back out again, doesn't it?" She laughed as she looked at me with warm eyes.

"Yeah", I laughed.

"See, your love for your mother has nothing to do with her personality which you just cannot stand. Jesus really loved Judas but Judas was just a little worm, you know. The idea that your body is unclean and unattractive--that's something she really threw at you. She felt very threatened by you. See, you really came to heal one another. The two of you are similar in that fact that she is not together herself."

"I see her growing up in a rural community, somewhere where there was just no support at all for being a woman. She felt that your father was not around enough. She was fine with having her first child. With the second one there was a little hesitation, but by the time you came along she really wasn't sure if she wanted to have you. Abortion was something she couldn't even think about. I mean that was something only whores in the city did."

I was shocked beyond words. So that explained her hostility toward me. Now the pieces of my lonely, painful childhood were starting to fit together.

"She felt very tortured inside. She had ambitions which had never been supported in the way she wanted. She felt 'I'm a woman. I have children. I have no power.' She only looked at it one way like, 'This is the earth life. Life is a struggle.'" She dramatized the words with her voice.

"What she could have done was open her seventh chakra to get direct spiritual information and asked, —'What am I here to learn?' But she chose to not do that so she brought through you, with a really open seventh chakra. I want to stress to you the fact that you really have a lot of spiritual information."

"You picked up a lot of her feelings of not wanting you while you were in the womb. And, when you were an infant, she left you alone for long periods of time. What a mother usually does is bring the creativity through and give it to the child but, since she never did that for you, basically, you felt like you were her mother, as little as you were, to help her out."

A wave of emotion overcame me as the blurred confusion of my past became a crystal clear pool of understanding. I had always seen my mother as helpless, unable to protect herself from my violent, crazy father. I couldn't stand to hear them argue and to listen to her cry in agonized sorrow.

"I see you in a past life in the Renaissance in which you were a woman with very high ideals about art and beauty. I see that you fell in love several times but, every time you did, the person moved away and you never saw him again or you only saw him rarely. You brought that with you into this life and so, now, you cut off a lot of love to yourself and to whoever you're relating to because you think, 'I'm not going to stick around and he's not going to stick around'. You have a tendency to get involved with someone who you perceive as being intelligent, who has an ability with words but who lacks the warmth you long so desperately to find. And you're really angry about the way men have treated you. The thing to do in the future is, when you see those qualities in someone, don't get involved."

"It's FEELING for you because no one has ever believed anything you've ever felt so you go out there and you look at it. Whenever you thought someone was trying to manipulate you they would say, 'Oh, yeah. She's a real bitch'. You have been told you're wrong a lot and singled out as the scapegoat in your family. You have this tendency to contract your energy and keep it very close and dim around you. What will be helpful for you, when you feel this way, is to imagine your energy expanding. You have a golden light that you bring in very briefly, but begin now to let it expand and fill up the whole room so you're not always like this little bedraggled dog, you know, that just came up out of the white caps of the waves at the ocean."

"I recommend that you have a ceremony. Make your intentions known to the universe--OK. No more shit. Tell it that you intend to start having more loving, joyful experiences. I suggest that you burn a red candle and have a silent meditation. Ask good spirits for their help. They are there. When you ask for their help it opens the door to positive change. It's about to be a full moon. Around that time there is heightened energy coming from the universe. Really open yourself up to the forces of good because the spirit world is ready to bless you. You have such a touch with it."

"As you make the change, things are going to come up to test you to see if you've really made the change. So make the resolution firm in your mind that you are now going to start creating more positive experiences for yourself. This is the time to focus on yourself. You have always been very sensitive to what other people want but you really carry that too far. You are stronger than you know and you will survive. Just get a job washing dishes or something. Forget about all the disaffirmation you received in the past. Just look at it as a past life because things will change."

"It is very important for you to have the choice about whether or not you have children. If you do want children it must be when you're ready to have them and, if you don't want children, that doesn't mean you're selfish. It means that that is what you want."

"I see that you have a fascination for music but that is not developed yet. You have great creativity and what I sense as positive for you is to use this creativity in a way that can somehow be supportive, because for you to have a job that brings you money that is very routine can be very depressing for you. You have beauty and strength and now is the time to get to know you. You can be the warrior and fight off any creepy people who try to get to you."

My session came to an end. She invited me to a channeling session she and her husband were having a few nights later.

CHAPTER 3————————————————OCTOBER, 1981

Searching

OCTOBER ARRIVED WITH COLD WINDS and I longed for home, as I drove around the confusing city full of heart attack expensive parking traps and one way streets. After a fruitless day of job searching, I arrived at my blue Victorian home and parked my car in the driveway. As I climbed the stairs I worried and sensed the sadness moving through me. I peaked through a crack in the door of Rob's room and saw him sitting on his mattress on the floor drinking a bottle of Ballerina Vodka. I knocked timidly, standing on jelly legs. His voice boomed out loud and strong.

"Come in and talk to me", he said.

I walked in, barely breathing, and sat down on the floor in front of him.

"How have you been doing?", he asked. He sat on his bed in a lotus position with his Bible beside him.

"I've been okay. I've been driving around getting to know the city. It's the most beautiful place I've ever seen. I love the scenes of the bay with sailboats sailing", I said.

"I've been reading the Bible. It gives me faith when the cruelty of people in this city brings me down". His ebony skin shone and his large eyes conveyed deep faith.

"That's good. I've just read bits and pieces of the Bible but it's hard to understand", I replied.

"I read it every day. It fills me with the love of the Holy Spirit. There's nothing we can't do with the power of God." His face glowed with conviction.

"I don't know if there's a God or not but I hope there is and I hope he loves me", I replied, smoothing out my long, rainbow colored skirt.

"Knowing that God loves me is the only thing that keeps me going. People have become so hardened they won't let God into their hearts. A man got shot down on Market Street yesterday and no one did anything to help. People are so selfish and wrapped up in their own worlds they won't take the time to care about someone. God's love is so pure and powerful it can transform even the worst sinner. I pray every day for everyone in the world to experience God's love." He looked at me reflectively as though he wanted to know what was going through my mind.

"I've been hurt by John. I thought he had real feelings for me and, now, he doesn't seem to be in love", I said sadly.

"Oh, he loves you. He said he treated you like a young virgin. He didn't think you appreciated it. He's a good person and his father is a great man. He's a world famous physicist. You two are a great couple."

"It doesn't seem possible. He just doesn't seem interested." I stared at the floor despondently.

"You are a very special person. I remember the day you came to rent the room. I was feeling really angry about a lot of different things and, the minute you walked through the door, all the anger vanished. You have great energy."

We talked a while longer and, then, I began yawning. I told him I would see him in the morning and then walked to my room. A full moon glowed above the Baptist church as I got undressed. John and Mark were out at a bar. I crawled onto my mattress on the floor and pulled my cheap sleeping bag over me. The peace of sleep cradled me softly until two in the morning, when John stumbled in drunk.

Four people from France suddenly started living in the house the next day. When I expressed my anger about it to Mark he acted as though I was being unreasonable. He and John quickly made friends with the visitors. They spent days touring around the city while I sat on my bed wasting time and worrying.

One sunny morning, a couple of weeks later, John told me he wanted to take me to a place that had a sauna where we could sweat all of the toxins out of our bodies. I agreeably climbed on the back of his motorcycle and wrapped my arms around him tightly. He flew up and down the roller coaster hills and, soon, we were there.

A woman with shiny, dark hair greeted us and told us to sign in. She smiled as she handed me a fluffy, white towel. I followed John into the locker room. As I took my clothes off I stared at the floor in embarrassment. In a daze of emotion, I followed him into the steam room. I almost jumped three feet in the air when I sat down on the scorching bench. I put my towel underneath me. Sitting in silence, I avoided looking at John who sat wedged between two fat, black women across from me. Drops of sweat started rolling down my face and body. The moist steam softened my skin and I felt pure, like an orchid in a hothouse. The womens' skin shone like ebony. They didn't seem bothered by the fact that John was a man.

John suggested we go soak in the hot tub. I clutched my towel tightly around me as I followed him. Removing my towel, I slid nervously into the warm, circulating water. Bubbles of warm water gurgled around me, massaging away my worries. Soon, I was in a profound state of relaxation as though I was floating in a never-never land. Ripples of sensuality pulsated through my body as John took my hand and helped me climb out of the whirlpool. He held my hand as we walked to the sun deck. We stretched our towels out under the sun lamps and lay down. Just when I felt like a strip of bacon frying in a pan, John said we could go cool off in the shower. Intoxicated with his gentle strength and warm charisma, I held his hand gratefully as he led me there.

After we showered, we wrapped ourselves up in fresh, fluffy towels. John patted me on the shoulder and said he wanted to take me on a tour of the club. Holding hands, we walked down some long, wide stairs and into a big room which was full of black, leather seats hanging by long chains from the ceiling. A feeling of horror rolled through me as I wondered if people sat in them to have sexual intercourse. I thought about the Bible verse about the city of Sodom and Gomorrah.

John looked at me and laughed. I looked back at him blushing, feeling too shocked to speak. He took my hand and led me into another room where shiny glasses and liquor bottles glowed behind a bar. A thin, spectacled man polished glasses as we sat down on a sofa. John put his arm around me affectionately. I looked into his deep, glowing eyes, admiring his perfectly chiseled face, dark eyebrows and full lips. His brown, wavy hair shone with copper highlights.

We looked at a large movie screen on the wall in front of us. Foggy, blurred pictures began to move into focus. I became numb with shock and felt my cheeks burn as I watched groups of people laying together, emitting moans of pleasure as they masturbated each other. Men and women, women and women and men and men lay intertwined, stimulating each others' erotic appetites in a communal sexual feast.

Confusion swirled like a whirlpool in my mind as we left the club. As we flew up and down the steep, perilous hills, I held John's waist tightly. Tall skyscrapers loomed threateningly on all sides of me. Everything was so different here in this strange, new land.

"Mark and I have been talking about going to Europe. You should come with us. You shouldn't stay here. People in this city are really cold. You need to start enjoying your life. You're not happy like you should be", he said with compassion.

"I know. I don't have the money to take a trip though and I've got to find a job", I replied hesitantly, tightening my hold around his waist.

"Let's tour around the city. I want to show you Lombardy Street". He slowed down to make a right turn.

Interesting looking people walked up and down the steep sidewalks carrying shopping bags and leading dogs. Clouds drifted lazily in the sky. Sailboats sailed effortlessly in the sparkling, blue bay and, soon, we arrived at Lombardy Street. The cobblestone street wound around and around like a corkscrew as John drove down it. Down below, buildings sat in peaceful repose, shaded by flowering trees. Fancy sports cars sped by haughtily as we turned onto the busy main street. Staggeringly steep hills plummeted dramatically, ending in a crescendo of color at the blue, sparkling bay.

"I've got to go downtown to pick up some stones", he said as he came to a halt at a red light.

"What kind of stones are they?", I asked, my voice rising with curiosity.

"Emeralds and rubies. I started dealing in them about a year ago. See, I'm an entrepreneur."

His voice was strong and proud. There were so many interesting facets to him. A frenetic energy assaulted my nerves as cars sped by and people hurried along the streets. Street performers sang and played instruments. A tall, wiry-haired, black lady in mismatched clothes played an electric bass in a style like Jimi Hendrix. An old, frail looking, gray haired woman played an accordion and sang in front of Woolworth's. John parked his motorcycle and told me to wait.

I clenched my jaw in anger as I watched him disappear into the tall, gray building. It was very disrespectful of him to dominate me the way he had been doing since we met. He had talked me into taking my clothes off, then kissed me romantically and asked me to go live in the Black Forest with him. Then, he had abandoned me and let me scrounge for shelter, alone and frightened. Then, he had treated me like a casual friend who happened to have a free bed to sleep in. He had come in drunk at two a.m. and pulled the covers off of me. Now, he had shocked me into speechlessness by taking me to a porno movie in a strange steam house. Fury suddenly erupted in me, like lava spewing from a volcano which had been dormant for eons. I got off of his motorcycle and charged down the street to the bus stop. When it arrived, I climbed on and sat down. I was tired of being used and disrespected by men.

I sunk into a bottomless ocean of the most painful loneliness I had ever experienced as I rode the bus to the creepy Victorian house. Like an alien from another planet, I felt distant, detached. Fear and anger consumed me as I stepped off of the bus, down onto the unfriendly sidewalk. An aura of fatigue emanated from people who walked by. My legs felt weak with fear as I dragged toward my home. Someone revved their motor and I jumped nervously. Climbing up the stairs of my blue Victorian home, my mind raced with worries and depression seeped into my veins. Mark was in the kitchen making bologna sandwiches with Deardra and Tom, the couple from Paris.

"How's everything going?", I asked cheerfully, trying to hide my feelings of despair.

"Great. We've had a great day. I went roller-skating and the three of us went to the beach. It's a thrill a minute here in the big, blue house. Where have you been?", Mark asked. He took a big bite out of his sandwich and wiped his mouth with a napkin.

"I've been touring around getting to know the city", I replied.

"We're all going to go to Europe. You should come with us", Mark said.

"I would love to but I have to find a job", I responded. I had applied for about twenty jobs over the past month with no results. I was having trouble keeping up with phone numbers so I could check back with them. Shyness overcame me when I asked people if they were hiring. I did not have a resume so I must not look very organized. Feelings of worthlessness crashed through me as I heard my father's voice saying I was a hopeless case. It must be true, I thought, full of self hate.

"You can find a job when you get back. Why don't you let yourself live? You're always worrying about something", he replied.

"Well, it sounds great but I don't want to travel around Europe with no money and then come back here with no money", I replied, sadly.

My body went rigid with shock when, suddenly, Mark threw the brown crust of a piece of bread at me. I walked into my room and crumpled down onto the bed. Tears came to my eyes as I rearranged some photos I had displayed on my shelf. I stared at a photograph of myself as a child standing in a snowdrift, bundled up in my winter coat, smiling happily.

Suddenly, John walked in. "What happened to you? I came out after my appointment and you were gone. I rode around looking for you", he said in an exasperated tone. With nervous concern, he tucked in his shirt.

"I got tired of waiting and decided to ride the bus home", I replied, feeling embarrassed when I heard the childlike sound of my voice. It was as though I was explaining myself to my punishing father.

"Well, next time, let me know before you just disappear", he said, with an authoritarian tone. If he would tell me where I stood with him I might want to keep following him around. But one minute I was his heart throb and the next minute I was his buddy and bed mate. He looked at the photograph I was holding. Then, he touched me on the shoulder gently.

"You looked like a happy child. What happened?", he asked.

I couldn't respond so I just looked at him self-consciously, wishing I was more talkative. Tears filled my eyes and a lump of pain formed in my throat.

"I'm going to take a nap. Will you wake me up in half an hour?"

"Sure", I replied, admiring him as he stretched out on my bed.

"I want to introduce you to a friend of mine after I rest. The two of you are a lot alike. I think you will get along really well. You can talk with her about metaphysical things and terrestrial things."

I stood and watched him roll over. His toned, muscular, perfectly proportioned body was a work of art like Michelangelo's David. Electrical attraction moved through me, like sparklers burning on a dark night. I turned and tiptoed out of the room, closing the door quietly behind me.

"Come on in", Rob's deep voice resonated as I tapped timidly on his door.

He was sitting cross-legged on his bed holding his Bible. A bottle of Ballerina Vodka stood against the wall.

"How are you doing?", he asked. He wore no shirt and his dark skin shone in the sunlight.

"Not very well. I'm confused about my relationship with John and I'm worried about not having a job", I replied.

"Yeah. You better find one fast or this city will eat you alive. You'll end up taking the midnight train back to Georgia. It's tough to make it here all by yourself but you can do it. I have faith in you", he said. His eyes shone as he radiated a peaceful vibration.

"I've applied for a few jobs but no one has wanted me", I said, looking at him forlornly.

"You've got to keep trying. What sign of the zodiac are you?" His eyebrows rose with curiosity.

"Aries", I replied.

"Aries is the fighting sign, the pioneer. If you're a true Aries you don't let anyone or anything hold you back. My mother is an Aries and she's a bad motherfucker. She doesn't let anyone mess with her. She's not afraid of anyone. You've got to be self-confident and not let anyone intimidate you."

"Yeah, I know. I wish I had more self-confidence", I replied, fiddling with my hair nervously.

"I get so much inspiration from the Holy Spirit when I read the Bible. I feel like I can do anything. It fills me with power. God made us in his image. He wants us to believe in ourselves. We are no weak, worthless beings. We are the children of God, full of power and wisdom."

Time seemed to stand still as he spoke about how cold people in the city could be and how he wanted to move to the country and live a simple, peaceful life close to nature. His spiritual attunement created a magnetic force field around his body. It oscillated in waves of light, sending peace and love through the house. The rapture of having his attention filled all my senses.

I was surprised when I realized that half an hour had flown by and it was time to wake John up. I told Rob that I had enjoyed talking with him. His white smile shone against his ebony skin as I closed the door.

Sunlight illuminated John's face and body as he stretched and yawned.

"I slept really deeply. I was tired. Let's go visit my friend, Sheila", he said languidly. He pulled himself out of the bed and ran his fingers through his sun-bronzed hair. My eyes lingered on him insatiably as he tucked in his shirt and tightened his belt. I followed him out of the house and down the stairs. The cool breeze caressed my hair as he began speeding down the street.

CHAPTER 4 ——————————OCTOBER, 1981
Lost and Alone

"YOU SHOULDN'T STAY HERE. PEOPLE in this city are really cold. All the sixties type people went to Hawaii." A chill ran up my spine as I observed fog hovering above like haunting ghosts. The October air felt cold and unpleasant and there were no leaves turning orange and red like the ones I loved back in the East.

John parked his motorcycle on the corner of a quiet street. I followed him down the sidewalk and watched him ring the buzzer to his friend's apartment. Her voice came over the intercom telling us to come on up. I was awed by her beauty when she opened the door. She had light, blond hair that fell softly below her shoulders. Her high cheekbones, large, blue eyes and full lips gave her the look of a fashion magazine model. I sat down on a soft sofa and John settled back into a big, padded armchair, stretching his legs out. She asked us if we would like something to drink and, after our affirmative response, disappeared into the kitchen. Soon, she emerged carrying a silver tray of drinks.

"Well, Sheila. Long time no see. This is my friend Janet. She just moved here from Georgia, after graduating from Emory University." John looked at me with affection as he took a colorful drink.

"Boy. That takes a lot of courage to move to a new place", she said warmly.

"It was a real adventure. I drove across the country with a woman from Germany. We went to the Grand Canyon and Mesa Verde. We had a great time. I love European people.", I replied, sighing with sadness as I realized how much I missed Helena, the German woman who had helped me drive across the country.

John opened his case of gemstones which sparkled brilliantly in the golden sunlight. My eyes widened with delight as I gazed at tourmalines, emeralds, rubies, opals and sapphires. I listened to them talk, catching up on old news. As John talked about his plans to visit his parents in Germany, I fantasized about going with him and being introduced as his bride. Sheila's coffee table was covered with books about metaphysical subjects. I picked one up and started reading an interesting paragraph which stated that we create our everyday reality with the thoughts we think. The conversation between Sheila and John buzzed cheerfully in my ears as I read.

Later in the day, John suggested that I could buy an opal from him for ninety dollars. I bought it, even though I couldn't afford it. I hid my pain as I secretly hoped that he would give it to me because I was the woman of his dreams. Nonchalantly, I said goodbye to him as he left to go out bar hopping with Mark again.

Stumbling into the room at three a.m., he woke me. My teeth gritted with anger as he pulled the covers off of me. My mind raced with frightening images as I held my breath with fear, longing for some deep sleep.

A paralyzing depression overcame me as I walked into the bathroom the next morning. This was the most humiliating experience I had ever had. I was nothing to him I lamented as I grimaced in disgust at the ugly, puffy bags under my eyes. I wasn't getting any younger and most women my age had husbands.

When Helena showed up at the front door the next day I felt like dancing with joy. We hugged one another warmly. She sat on Mark's sofa and talked about what she had been doing since I left her at Robert's apartment and sped away on John's motorcycle.

"I went sailing with some friends I made in Berkeley. We sailed down to Mexico and saw a lot of ruins that are thousands of years old. It was beautiful. The water was the most gorgeous color I have ever seen. We went fishing and had fish for dinner. I had a fantastic time", she said enthusiastically.

"Wow. I wish I had gone with you. That sounds great", I replied.

"It was. I'm so glad I did it. I'll be heading back to Georgia tomorrow. I found a ride on the ride board in Berkeley", she said.

"Well, good luck with everything. I'll miss you. You've been a great friend", I said, hugging her. I watched her walk down the stairs, feeling my heart skip a beat in bewildered angst.

Loneliness fell on me like a dark cloud as I sat down on my bed and started looking through the employment listings. Everything sounded so deadly boring that I threw down the paper in despair. I went into my bathroom and washed my face and brushed my hair. Silence wrapped me in a golden bubble, soothing my ragged nerves. A mood of excitement suddenly came over me when I realized that I would be going to the channeling session that night. Finally, my years of curiosity were over and I would experience the mystery I had read about.

The city spread far and wide, like a vast, mysterious maze as I drove to the psychic's apartment. Dusk fell like a blanket, lulling the struggling earthlings into a peaceful state as they retreated into the safety of their homes after a day of hard work. After a frightening drive, I parked my car in front of the small apartment. The beautiful brunette who had given me the amazing psychic reading opened the door and welcomed me and a few other people. We walked into the small living area and sat on cushions on the floor. Her husband meditated on the sofa, his shoulder length, dark hair shining. A purple amethyst earring dangled from one ear.

The psychic led everyone through a relaxing meditation. Then, unfathomable silence filled the room as the medium, her husband, closed his eyes. His expression became completely blank as if he had entered another dimension. Then, suddenly, his body jerked convulsively. An otherworldly voice started to speak in an English accent. He introduced himself as a bodiless entity from a higher plane of reality.

People asked him questions, one by one. Intelligence resonated in his dignified, English voice as he concisely delivered thorough, articulate answers. My palms sweated and a lump of emotion sat in my throat as I started talking.

"I just moved here and I feel afraid a lot. Sometimes I think about moving back to my parents house", I said as my heart beat rapidly.

"It would be foolish of you to move back there. They have cast you out. You represent sin to them", his voice boomed powerfully.

"What would be the best way to use my creativity?", I asked.

"Doing acupressure massage and setting stones. Your hands shine with the light of the sun. Even though you do not show them to me I can see them shine. You will not be very dramatic in this life. You've been very dramatic in past lives. The most pressing issue you have to deal with now is the fact that you have no feeling of self-worth. You must have that to be happy. You need to go back to the beginning, to working in a group", he said.

"I feel bothered by thoughts of hatred towards myself. Sometimes I hear a voice in my head calling me disrespectful, degrading names. How can I stop this?", I asked.

"In a past life in the eighteenth century in England you were a prostitute. People used to call you "slut" and other derogatory names. That is where those feelings come from. Do not feel guilty any more. You are forgiven", the entity said with calm command. I thought about what a wretched person I must have been. A wave of sorrow crashed through me as I grieved for all people who had been ostracized.

"I want to change my name. What would be a good name for me?", I asked.

"It should be a name that has something to do with the sun", the entity replied.

I listened in rapt fascination as the remaining people asked their questions and got replies. Soon, everyone's questions were answered and the medium came back to normal consciousness. An affectionate gentleness graced his face as he opened his eyes.

"When I go into a trance everyone looks blurry and soft like a Renoir painting. When I come back I start noticing all these details like…..you have a pimple on your nose", he said, looking at the man in front of him and laughing playfully.

The room began to hum with conversation as people divided into twos and threes. I stood near the trance medium, listening to him talk with a pretty girl. When he introduced himself to me, I glowed like a pearl being held in the palm of his hand. He asked me if I would like something to drink and led me into the kitchen. I sat down on a stool and watched him as he opened his refrigerator and poured me a cool glass of lemonade.

"You have trouble with math, don't you?, he asked as he handed me my lemonade.

"Yeah. It's always been my worst subject", I replied, my face burning with a blush as I remembered all the times my father had yelled at me for not getting good grades.

"People get angry at you because they think you're playing dumb", he said with compassion.

"Yeah. People get angry at me a lot. It hurts my feelings", I replied.

"You come across as this lost, unsure, defenseless person and men respond with, 'I'll take care of you', fluffing up their big, male egos. And that's not what you want", he said, with sincere understanding.

A warm glow soothed my sorrows away as I drove home. Deardra and Tom, my French house guests, greeted me. I listened to them talk with excitement about their plans to go visit Yosemite. Deardra was a short, petite woman with shoulder-length, brown hair. Tom was taller than her, thin and brunette, with small, wire spectacles that covered his dark eyes. Deardra spoke in bursts of childlike effervescence as her face sparkled with innocence. Tom was quiet and reserved. She worked as a secretary and he worked as an accountant.

When they asked me to go to Yosemite with them I quickly agreed. We laughed and talked playfully as Tom drove my car. When, we arrived, the gorgeous grandeur took my breath away. We sang old songs from the sixties as we hiked up the long trails and looked up at the brilliant, azure sky. Lofty mountain peeks stretched into the heavens as clouds floated magically. Stately trees stood in quiet dignity, dressed in a variety of lush foliage, blessing us. As we stood on the brown, dirt trail we looked out over the wide valley which shimmered in the golden sunlight. We held our breath in silent reverence as we admired the ethereal radiance of a rainbow glistening in the sun.

"Did I tell you I had been to Paris once? I went to the Louvre and the Jeu de Pommes. I walked around the Left Bank at night and heard singers performing in the cafes. I saw the Eiffel Tower and Place De Concorde and Montmartre and Sacre Couer," I said, relaxing into their kindness.

"You should come with us and visit again. We'll show you around. We know the city well and can give you a great tour", Deardra said affectionately.

"I would love to but I don't have the money for a ticket. But it was great being there. I walked all around the city with my camera and took pictures of people and their dogs. They were really friendly and enjoyed posing for me. I watched children play and sail little boats. I loved sitting in the gardens full of fountains and pools and I love those pastries. They are beautiful to look at and fabulous to eat. It amazes me how you Europeans make everything you do a work of art."

"You should come and live there. We will help you find a job and you can learn to speak French. Have you ever studied it?"

"Well, I took two years in high school and a couple of quarters in college but I never got good at it. I'd like to speak it fluently." I looked up into the soft, green trees and the dazzling sky full of peacefully drifting clouds. Then, I gazed dreamily at a pool nestled between some large boulders, sparkling like diamonds in the sun.

"Let's go skinny dipping", Deardra said, her eyes shining with mischievous fire.

"Hey, that would be a blast but what if we get caught?", I responded, stiffening with anxiety as my fear of authority figures gripped me.

"No one will see us", she reassured me joyfully, pulling her T-shirt over her head and dropping it onto the ground. Then, with free-spirited charm, she pulled off her blue jeans and underwear.

I was inspired by her lack of self-doubt and I wriggled playfully out of my clothes. We laughed with each other as we sat down in the pool of clear water and gazed into the shining sun. Tom pulled off his clothes and joined us. Warm light caressed us with a pearly glow as we played and splashed, watching the water sparkle like fire opals in the golden, radiant sun.

We had just dried off and were getting dressed when a park ranger walked by. I held my breath in suspense. Luckily, he didn't see us. After he was gone, we laughed hysterically, feeling smugly triumphant about getting away with our misdemeanor. Majestic mountains towered around us like harbingers of peace as we began climbing the steep slope toward Half Dome. Singing old sixties tunes with wild abandon, we celebrated our freedom. The day seemed eternal and our energy endless as we communed with ever loving mother nature.

Dusk was beginning to fall as we arrived at a pretty, wooded area and walked toward a glistening stream. The sun descended, casting streaks of pink and lavender across the sky. Golden beams of light danced upon the water. Tom took the lead as we pitched the tent, working quickly and efficiently. In no time, our nature home was standing. The sound of breaking twigs snapped through my ears as I helped gather sticks to build a fire. Tom stacked them and then crumpled up large wads of newspaper and threw them on top. Then, he struck a long kitchen match and held it up to the wood.

In a matter of seconds, a fire blazed brilliantly sending colorful, powerful ripples of fire up into the dark firmament. The orange-red heat of the fire contrasted the blue coldness of the sky with its crystal-like stars. I gazed in awed fascination. All the elements and chemical compounds I had learned in high school chemistry did a wild, phenomenal dance through the vast, multi-faceted universe. Galaxies expanded into new universes as new galaxies were created. Black holes, nova stars and red dwarfs moved in a fantastic cosmic orchestration through the endless, light-filled expanse some mysterious power had created. It must be God, I thought, remembering Rob's poignant reflections.

I had worked up quite an appetite. My mouth watered as we toasted hot dogs over the fire. I ate two hot dogs, and then satisfied my sweet tooth with toasted marshmallows. Later on, we had fun acting silly. We danced around the campfire like Indians, whooping and hollering. Tom and Deardra teased me, saying they were going to tie me up and cook me over the fire.

When the radiant sun came beaming in the next morning, I stretched and yawned, shaking off the dark cocoon of slumber. Pure, clean air nourished my lungs as I walked out of the tent and into the canopy of lovely, nurturing trees. Arriving at the stream, I listened to it babbling. Diamonds of light sparkled as I leaned over the softly rushing water, cupping my hands and splashing it onto my face.

Deardra and Tom had woken when I got back to the tent. We packed everything quickly and started off down the trail again. An adorable baby bear peeked out from behind a rock. We watched him with awed affection. Our spirits rose high as we hiked half of the day, enjoying the phenomenal beauty.

As dusk began to fall, Tom drove us from our mystical land back to the caustic lights of the freeway. The city looked like a crumbling, corrupt, concrete zoo as we arrived there late in the dark night. John was sleeping with his long arms and legs sprawled across my tiny mattress. I crawled into a miniscule space beside him

CHAPTER 5 ———————————— OCTOBER, 1981

There's a Job for Me

THE NEXT MORNING, I SAT up and stared out the window. Emotion flowed through me as I picked up a Eucalyptus bud I had saved from the glorious day John and I had run through the forest holding hands. I picked up a pen and pad and started writing a poem. It flowed from me automatically, effortlessly.

Sun streams through my window
I hold a small seed in my hand
The beginning and the end is but an illusion
It is all contained in one small seed

I rest my head on nature
We feed each other
Protect me God and help me
become one of your infinite rays of transformation

As I read my poem, I longed for a person or force that loved me unconditionally. There must be some divine force in the universe that could raise me to a higher state of consciousness. I wondered if Rob's talk about God was true. Who was God and where was he? Did he sit up on a cloud? Did he wear royal, purple robes? When he looked at humanity down below did he laugh or did he weep? Did he exist at all? I wondered.

The man in my life left much to be desired. He wasn't warm or reassuring and he didn't tell me why he was spending time with me. I needed his affection, yet I worried and wondered about where I stood. I was too shy to ask him. I felt completely under his power. He was handsome and interesting and had the ability to make friends that I yearned for. Yet, I felt like I was unraveling emotionally, losing control of myself and my life.

Weeks and months passed and then, the reality of my situation suddenly crashed down on me like a brick wall. John wasn't in love with me and he had no thoughts of marriage in our future. He was just using me for a free place to sleep, fluffing up his male ego by having his power play over me. I was caught like an innocent fly in a spider's nest on the verge of being eaten alive. Another night of being rudely awakened by him stumbling in drunk would send me back to the mental institution--permanently this time. I would spend the rest of my life sitting twiddling my thumbs, in a vegetable state, knocked dopey by various pills. I had to find a way to escape and I had to find it fast.

A heavy rock of depression sat in my chest as I made my way into the kitchen. I opened the refrigerator and saw that I only had two containers of strawberry yogurt left. I ate a cup slowly, wishing I could go out on a shopping spree but knowing I had to save most of my money so I could pay rent. Returning to my room, I observed John sleeping off his hangover. I got dressed in my most business like job hunting outfit. As I walked past Rob's room and Mark's room, I wondered if they were sleeping off hangovers too.

I pulled open the front door with a surge of determination. The October air chilled me and filled me with longing for the beautiful Indian summers I enjoyed in my home town. My shoulders rose tensely as I observed winos hanging out at the corner laundry. I bought a newspaper, trying to not breath in the cigar smoke coming from a tall black man who ran his eyes up and down my body.

When the bus arrived, I climbed on listlessly and sat down by a window. I held my breath in fear as I read through the job listings. Buildings flashed by in a haze of colors as sirens and car sounds jostled me out of my sleepiness. In no time, I arrived in the Haight Ashbury. I tried to appear confident as I filled out applications in a grocery store, an ice cream parlor and a bookstore. They told me they would call me when they needed someone.

A charming trio of musicians were playing guitars and singing on the sidewalk. I stopped to listen and, when I looked beside me, the dark, gentle eyes of an enormously attractive man met mine. His hands rested on the handles of a stroller. I looked down into it and admired his adorable, little, dark-haired boy.

"Hello. I'm Janet. He's adorable", I exclaimed, looking down shyly.

"Hello. I'm Brian. Nice to meet you", he replied in a confident, smooth voice.

"This is a really lively performance. I just moved to San Francisco and I've never seen anything like this. It's great." I tried to put a lilt into my monotone, depressed voice to make myself attractive. Men had always liked vivacious girls.

"Would you like to go have a cup of tea?", he asked, gripping his baby stroller tightly.

"Yes. I'd like to."

Various emotions of people talking and laughing in The Grand Piano poured through me as I followed him slowly through the café. We sat down at a table covered with a white cloth in the back room. I smiled at the baby. He smiled back at me. Then I gazed into Brian's large, dark, glowing eyes.

"How do you like San Francisco?" Strength and intelligence emanated magnetically from him.

"I love it. It is really pretty. I've been exploring around getting to know it."

"What were you doing before you moved here?", he asked as his calm, controlled demeanor put me at ease.

"I was going to college. When I graduated, I decided it was time for me to learn about real life so I moved", I replied.

"What did you get your degree in?" His voice rose with curiosity.

"Art History", I replied.

"Is there anything you can do with that?", he asked.

"Not much. I could work in a museum passing out tickets or something", I replied.

"Well, it very much stands in your favor that you had the perseverance to get your degree", he replied.

"Yeah. I don't know how many doors it will open for me but I'm glad I went to college. I love to learn", I replied.

"Well, go ahead and get a job as soon as you can. Don't wait until you get down to your last four hundred dollars. I teach English as a second language at San Francisco State. I have a lot of students from Russia. They are really great. It is remarkable how quickly they get adjusted to a foreign country. They are very strong", he said.

There was a long pause as I sipped my tea nervously, trying to think of something to say. I had applied in shops up and down the street we were on and I had applied in about ten shops on Market Street downtown. I had not written down their phone numbers because the managers I had spoken with had said they would call me. The guys I lived with were on the phone a lot and I worried that an employer might be trying to reach me and getting a busy signal. My head raced with confused, fearful thoughts.

"I have to take David home now. Would you like to go hiking at Mount Tamalpais on Saturday?", he asked.

"Yes. I'd love to", I replied, knowing how nature always lifted my spirits.

I wrote my address on a piece of paper and handed it to him.

I jumped out of bed with my heart racing when I heard his horn honk outside a few days later. Watching John sleeping off a hangover, I pulled on my clothes quickly. Combing my fingers through my hair, I walked out the front door, locked it behind me and hurried down the stairs.

"I was about to leave", Brian said, looking deeply into my eyes and smiling.

"Oh, thank you so much for waiting. I've been looking forward to this so much. I'm sorry I overslept." I pulled my seat belt around me and locked it into place.

"That's alright. We're going to have a great time. It's a gorgeous day", he replied, pushing the gearshift energetically.

I sat in frightened silence, wanting to blurt out my desperation to him but not wanting to burden him with my problems. Finally I gathered the courage to tell him that I hated the house I lived in.

"I never would have moved into a place like that. It is not a good situation", he replied with understanding.

He stopped at a grocery store and bought bread, cheese, fruit, trail mix and wine. Men gave me a feeling of security with their amply filled wallets. Money flowed to them like a water fall. As his sturdy, solid Toyota climbed the steep hills I gazed in wonder at the Golden Gate bridge glistening in the sun, partially concealed by long swaths of clouds. They hovered like a walkway for angels over the sparkling, blue ocean.

Brian parked the car. We began to hike up a hill which was covered with tall grass that looked like wheat. Vigorous, youthful vitality surged through me as sun poured over my face and body. We came to the edge of a quiet, enchanted forest. As we walked into the forest I gazed up into the lush canopy of emerald green trees. Birds sang in the branches high above in melodious, exuberant sounds.

"Listen. There's a lot of wisdom in there", Brian said, taking my hand as we walked deeper into the forest. I fought self-consciously with my silence, wishing I could be more talkative.

"I must say, I find you to be a very attractive woman. I would like to be sexually involved with you but I do have a close, loving relationship with my wife and I wouldn't want to jeopardize that."

Visions of an ugly confrontation with a jealous wife who called me "slut" and "husband stealer" ran through my mind.

"Oh no. I am not interested in that. I just want companionship", I replied, staring at the ground. After a while, we emerged from the forest and looked out over the endless valley below.

"Tell me about yourself", he requested, looking at me with sincerity.

"Well, I like to paint and I love music", I replied, looking down shyly.

"Oh, that's interesting. What type of paintings do you do?", he asked, looking into my eyes with genuine interest.

"Well, they're mostly realistic but I'd like to do things that are more abstract", I replied.

"Are you ready for lunch?", he asked.

"Yeah. That hike really stimulated my appetite", I responded.

I watched him spread out a blanket and fill it with bananas, grapes, cheese, French bread, trail mix and wine. I took a bite of French bread and cheese and began to chew slowly, savoring the pungent taste. He touched my shoulder gently and pointed down to the road below. I turned my head and saw a white tailed deer running swiftly.

"Poor thing is in a bind. Probably running away from some stud. It's mating season", he said. He stuck a corkscrew in a bottle of red wine and turned it forcefully. The cork made a popping sound as he pulled it out.

"Would you like some wine?"

"Yes". He put a plastic cup in front of me and began to pour wine into it. I took a sip, swallowed too fast and started coughing convulsively. He slapped me on the back a few times and, soon, I could talk again.

"What did you like most in school?", he asked, listening attentively as he took sips from his cup.

"I liked psychology and philosophy a lot", I replied vacuously, remembering how much I had abhorred school.

"What did you learn in psychology?"

"Oh, I studied a general overview of theories--Freud's theory of the unconscious, superego and libido and Maslow's hierarchy of needs. I'm striving for self-actualization. I'm on the bottom rung of the ladder. I have food and shelter but I haven't reached my full potential or achieved peace."

"What is it that brings lasting peace of mind? I wonder."

After a pleasant, relaxing conversation, we started to walk down the steep hill in the sweltering sun. Suddenly, he stopped and wrapped a towel around my head. I started to laugh, thinking about how I must look like Lawrence of Arabia in my turban.

"You laugh now but you'll see you need it. Lean your weight against my hand."

He held his flattened hand behind his back. I leaned my weight against him and let him guide me down the staggeringly steep hill.

Lightness filled me as we chatted while he drove. When he dropped me at the big, blue Victorian he asked me if I would like to go to Stinson beach with him and his son in a few days. I eagerly accepted.

I walked up the precarious stairs, grimacing at the hideous, black burglar bars. The house was empty. I shuffled despondently into my room and collapsed on my bed. I didn't like my tattered, patchwork life. I lived on bits and pieces, surviving by taking leftover crumbs of kindness from married men and disrespectful alcoholics who could never give me the security I needed. My head ached like it was going through a grinding machine as I dreaded the impoverished future before me--sleeping in an alleyway, begging for spare change. Soon my money would be completely gone and I would be like a piece of rubbish to be tossed any which way by the cold winds of the city.

Suddenly, I remembered the psychic had advised that I do a ceremony with a red candle to make my intentions known to the universe. Excited expectation rolled through me as I pulled on my long, purple, silk dress I had bought in a fancy shop. I lit my long, red candle and began meditating quietly, asking the forces of goodness in the universe to bless me with happiness, love, peace, joy and success. As the red candle flickered in the darkening room, I gazed through the window at the cross on the Baptist Church, remembering the lesson Jesus taught about having the faith of a mustard seed.

The moment I finished my meditation, John walked into the room and reclined on the bed. I crawled into bed beside him, nestling my body close, hungering for affection. Erotic desire flowed like a cresting wave inside me as I gazed in wonder at his firm, strong, beautifully sculpted body. I started rubbing his chest. Then, I pulled up his shirt and moved my tongue tenderly over his soft skin, continuing down to his belly button. I didn't know if this was the way to win his love but I hoped, with the fervor of a saint in ecstasy, that it was.

He looked at me with complete disinterest and turned over. I lay beside him in humiliated silence. By the time the moon rose above the cross on the Baptist church, I gave up all hope that we would ever get married.

A chorus of singing birds woke me the next morning. I got dressed and read through the employment adds, admiring John's handsomeness as the sun shone on his slumbering body. Then, I walked down to the corner and bought a newspaper. A black man standing at a payphone watched me, running his eyes up and down my body. He motioned with his arm toward another black man who was sitting behind the wheel of a huge, black Cadillac. I climbed up onto a bus, analyzing his strange behavior. Hugging myself around my waist, I sat by the window watching cars, houses and pedestrians flash by in a dizzying blur.

Soon, I arrived in the Haight Ashbury. I walked down the empty, early morning streets scanning the shops for Help Wanted signs. I filled out several applications. The managers told me they would keep them on file and call me if an opening came up. I was soon too weary to continue so I went to the Grand Piano and drank a cup of chamomile tea. After turning in a job application, I sat for a while and observed people talking around the room.

When I arrived back home, John was still sleeping. A sudden fury exploded inside me as I watched him reclining casually in MY bed. He hadn't even given me an engagement ring. I pulled a shirt and a pair of pants off of their hangers. Then, I ducked into the closet sized bathroom to change.

"What are you doing?", John asked in a critical tone which reminded me of my accusing father.

"I'm going to visit Sheila", I said, my voice quivering as I looked down at the floor like a guilty child.

"Well why don't you stay here? I want to go out and get something to eat", he asked.

"I don't want to stay here with you", I responded, slicing the air with a knife edge of anger.

"Take a hike", he yelled with a rage that tore through me.

My legs wobbled like rubber underneath me as I went to the phone and called Sheila. Her voice sounded motherly and sweet as she invited me to visit.

I ran down the stairs and drove, in a lost fog of tears, to Sheila's apartment. The street was quiet and empty when I arrived at the entrance. Ringing the buzzer with anxious anticipation, I drank in her voice gratefully when it finally came clearly through the funny looking box. Green floor numbers flashed as I rode the elevator up to her floor. Her peaceful face relaxed me as she let me in. I sat on the soft sofa, staring at the floor forlornly.

"How is everything going?", she asked.

"Not very well. I can't relax in the place I'm living in. John wakes me up in the middle of the night, coming in drunk. I really liked him at first and thought we were falling in love but, now, I don't know where I stand with him", I said.

"Yeah. He's got a lot of problems. His girlfriend got fed up with him and moved to Hawaii. She decided she wasn't going to take any more of his shit. He's an alcoholic. Everyone who knows him thinks he's very difficult. He has problems with his ego. That's why he acts like he's better than everyone else and tries to dominate people."

"Well, I've had enough of him dominating me. He just expects me to let him sleep in my bed. He yelled at me when I left to come over here. It really scared me. I'm too scared to tell him to leave. I still hope he will fall in love with him", I said.

My need to be loved felt intense and all consuming. I had felt utterly unloved when my parents didn't ask me why I had had to drop out of college for a year to live with the Christian couple. I had been emotionally shattered by the two men who raped me yet I had been too ashamed to talk about it and had not told a soul. I had resented my female psychologist who humiliated me once by ordering me to go wash my hair in the sink. She had forced me into the treacherous clutches of the drug pushing counselors at the mental health day program. The Navane, Stelazine and Mellaril they had given me had rendered me unable to think or remember anything. In my frustration, loneliness and rage, I had eaten cookies and ice cream in huge quantities and had become hideously obese.

I had had no friends when I returned to college after my deep sleep in the bedroom town. I was angry at the psychologist who had recommended a "corrective family experience" to me. I also resented the psychiatrist she had referred me to before I traveled abroad. He had convinced me to take Tofranil, Stelazine and Mellaril. They had turned my mind to mush. I would not have made the life altering decision to travel alone in Europe if I had not been forgetful, excessively sleepy and unable to make sound judgements. I gritted my teeth in anger getting lost in memories, staring at the floor. Then, I looked up and came back to the present moment, knowing I had to move forward with my life.

"The male ego is the ugliest thing. They can be very difficult, there's no doubt about that. I prefer women. I don't get involved with men except for prostitution." She spoke in a self-accepting, matter of fact tone. I hoped my face didn't reveal my shock. She had seemed so holy.

"I want to go out and dance tonight. There's a gay womens' hangout place I go to a lot. It's not far from here. It's always a lot of fun. Do you want to go?" Her voice rose with charming, childlike enthusiasm.

"Yeah. That sounds like fun", I responded.

We rode the elevator down to the street level and walked outside. I climbed into her car nervously. As I watched her turn the key, I fastened my seatbelt. She talked lightly as she drove through the streets and, in no time, she pulled into the parking lot. I followed her into the crowded club. Brightly colored strobe lights flashed in my eyes as I followed her to the middle of the dance floor. Her blond hair shone like gold as she began to sway and spin to the pulsating, rhythmic music. I began to move my body self-consciously, looking around the room nervously.

A feeling of nausea overcame me as I noticed a hefty, tough looking lesbian with dark, short hair and large bones leaning against a wall, staring at me. She was dressed in a black leather jacket and black boots with gleaming silver spurs. I stared at the floor tensely as she studied my body more and more aggressively. To ground myself, I focused on Sheila. We looked like sisters as we swayed gracefully under the colored lights.

When we got back to her apartment at two a.m. she said I could spend the night. She put clean sheets on a thin mattress on the floor for me. Yawning sleepily, I reclined on my back. She pulled the soft sheets over me in a motherly way as I relaxed into the soft, fluffy pillow. Suddenly, she touched my breast. I pushed her hand away and, luckily, she stopped without seeming offended. I wished it was that easy to say "no" to a man.

The next morning she cooked me French toast for breakfast. A golden glow enveloped me as I sat by her window at her charming table covered with a colorful cloth. I admired her small apartment filled with paintings and sculptures, thinking about what a talented decorator she was.

"What are you going to do about your living situation?", she asked, pouring syrup onto her French toast.

"I don't know. I'm trapped because I don't have first and last month's rent to move into my own place", I replied despondently.

"I've been looking for a room mate. I would say you could move in with me but I have to interview more people. I have a very different lifestyle and I will only live with someone who accepts it. My friends and I do drugs together. I believe in drugs. When we use them, we party in the higher realms together. They are a God given gift that we can use to experience the higher states of consciousness. We're supposed to be enjoying life but everyone has forgotten that. People are trapped into negativity because they've forgotten that the purpose of life is to have fun. See, none of this world is real. All the violence and negativity and ugliness is illusion. The real world is full of beauty and joy and peace. There's no struggle in the real world. People are out there struggling because they refuse to believe that life can be different." Her big, blue eyes shone with intelligence.

I was impressed by her metaphysical knowledge. It seemed to me that the suffering in the world was very real. Yet it made sense that, if we focused on the positive things we wanted and ignored the negative, we would magnetize happier experiences toward us. I finished my French toast and drank the last drop of my orange juice. I thanked her for her hospitality and told her I needed to go find a job.

The bus arrived in the Haight Ashbury and I told the driver goodbye. I walked from store to store, filling out applications, straining to remember manager's names and phone numbers. Various people told me they would notify me if they had an opening. Frustration and anger over peoples' detachment from my needs filled me. They took their money and security for granted and seemed unwilling to put themselves in my shoes, though I never told them I was desperate. My days were filled with curt replies from busy people who I meant nothing to. I began to feel invisible and totally unloved and alone. At times, I thought about walking in front of a bus so I could die.

After searching for a few hours, I decided to go to the Golden Gate Park. The art museum was showing an exhibit of Tiffany stained glass. I drank in the beauty, feeling my mood being lifted by the exquisite shapes and gorgeous colors. After a while, I walked across the street to the outside amphitheater. I sat in a chair and admired the bonsai trees and flowers surrounding the stage which was framed with Greek arches and columns. I tried to recall the Art History terms I had learned in college--Corinthian, Ionic, Doric, Greek, entablature, pediment, Gothic etc. but they had faded from my mind.

I became restless and began to walk again. Soon, I arrived in the Japanese Tea Garden. I walked up some stone stairs, admiring the flowering trees and bushes. A large, elegant stone statue of Buddha exuded deep tranquility as it sat in deep meditation. Maple trees, brightly colored flowering bushes, tall pine trees, azaleas, camellias, roses and captivating bonsai trees touched me with their beauty. I explored in the golden silence.

As I walked home, I admired the sun slowly descending--a fiery, orange ball getting smaller by the second. I racked my brain for a way to escape the trap I was in. Suddenly, I remembered John introducing me to a friend of his named George. We had talked with him briefly at his apartment front steps. He was tall and stocky with shoulder length, dark, wavy hair. He wore a gold earring in one ear that made him look like a gypsy. He had invited us both to go to the Renaissance Fair with him. Maybe he could save me from John. Stopping at the corner near the blue Victorian, I put a quarter in a newspaper box and pulled out a newspaper. After quickly scanning the employment adds, I decided to call George.

He responded to my telephone greeting in a surprised voice. In an upbeat, friendly way, he said he was going to the Renaissance Fair with his female room mate on Saturday. He would like for me to go along. I wrote down the directions on a scrap of paper.

Soon, Saturday arrived. I watched John sleep off yet another hangover as I got dressed in the purple, silk gown I had bought in a fancy shop downtown. He turned over, yawned and looked at me through puffy eyes.

"Where are you going so early?", he asked.

"I'm going to the Renaissance Fair with George", I replied, hoping I looked good in my elegant, purple silk dress.

"You better be careful. He's really fast." He ran his fingers through his thick, sun streaked hair, looking at me with concerned empathy.

Evil eyes seemed to be watching me as I drove out of the dirty, desolate neighborhood. Only a few cars passed on the street as people slept peacefully inside their houses, warm and cozy, enjoying their freedom from the toil of the week. As I passed the Grand Piano, I looked into the window, longing for company. A few short blocks flashed by and I arrived on George's street. I parked my car across the street from his apartment. A pink and peach Hare Krishna temple stood next door to his apartment. My nerves bristled as I walked up the stairs and knocked on the door timidly.

George opened the door and smiled. He was wearing a black cape, frilly, white shirt and black pants. His big, black hat had a long, white and gray feather in it. I followed him through his narrow hallway and sat on the edge of his bed. He made adjustments to his outfit, preening and admiring himself in the full length mirror. Suddenly, he raised his arm and flashed his sword like a pirate in an Errol Flynn movie. I wondered apprehensively what sort of person he was. When he knocked on his room mate's door, a mousy woman with brown hair emerged.

She drove us to the fair in her car. I sat in the back seat listening to the two of them talk easily, like a brother and sister. We arrived and I thanked George several times as he bought my ticket. As we walked through the entry gate, I admired beautiful women wearing long, flowing skirts with flower garlands in their hair. Strikingly handsome men walked by wearing short, multi-colored, striped knickers and frilly shirts. Cod pieces accentuated their genitals as they walked proudly, gesticulating dramatically as they recited Elizabethan poetry.

The loud beating of drums and ringing of bells cascaded through my ears. I watched a parade of characters dressed in elaborate costumes pass by. People shouted "God Save The Queen" as a group of servants carried the queen in a jeweled, gold-curtained carriage. She was dressed exquisitely in silks, lace and jewels. Fanning herself with a peacock feather, she waved at the fascinated serfs, enjoying her proud splendor. George talked in a lighthearted way as we continued down the road. When we saw some puppets performing on a tiny stage we sat down to watch. Like Punch and Judy, they jabbed at each other slowly at first. Then, they accelerated into a knock-down, drag-out fight. Delighted people roared with laughter.

After a hearty laugh, we ambled down the dirt trail again and came upon a big pit of mud. Large, muscular men and women with oversized bellies were wrestling with each other. Looking ridiculous, covered from head to toe with slimy mud, they threw big handfuls of it at each other. We laughed as we watched them slipping and sliding, falling down on top of one another like clowns in a slapstick comedy. As we walked on, I observed the interesting displays surrounding us. Psychic readings, astrology charts, crystals, portraits, incense.

My stomach started to grumble with hunger as I inhaled the pleasing aromas from food stands. As I ogled a colorful poster advertising waffles topped with ice cream and fresh strawberries, my mouth watered. George asked me what I would like to eat and I told him I would like a waffle. He suggested that we split one.

The rest of the day was wonderfully buoyant as we explored the various intriguing sights and activities. Jousters and jesters played their games as acrobats, jugglers, fire eaters and actors dazzled their captive audiences. When we came upon the cage of a unicorn, I stared at the mystical creature in amazement. George explained that scientists had created him with an operation that caused the two horns of an ordinary goat to grow into one. I reached through the metal bars of his cage and touched his cute chin.

George talked about his experience working as an engineer. He had had to stop because the long hours were too demanding and the work was stifling. He now worked delivering magazines and spent the rest of his time taking it easy and enjoying life as much as possible. When we got home to his apartment, I told him about the trouble I had been having with John coming in drunk and waking me up in the middle of the night. He expressed genuine concern.

CHAPTER 6————————OCTOBER, 1981
Where Is Love?

PINK STREET LIGHTS GLOWED IN the dark as I drove home. I crawled into bed and pulled the covers over me. When John staggered in drunk at two a.m., I realized I couldn't take it any more. Rage boiled in the depths of my guts and I wanted to curse at him. Yet, I felt too frightened to express anything I was feeling.

Panic overcame me more and more as each day crawled by miserably. I felt helpless and stuck. I had no money to rent an apartment and no one wanted to hire me. People who had not studied hard at college like I did were getting jobs and it did not seem fair.

A few days later, George called and asked me to ride to Monterey with him. I instantly agreed and we left early the next morning. We talked lightly as he drove his large van. He had packed lunch for us and was well-prepared with maps and tourist books. Soon, we were moving fast down the open road. My lungs expanded as I breathed fresh air and let it ripple through my hair. I sighed with happiness as the sterile, ugly concrete gave way to natural, rolling hills covered with graceful trees.

We arrived at Cannery Row after driving half the day. As we walked along the pier, holding hands, George talked about his sister who was married with a child. He said he went to visit with her on the east side of the bay sometimes. I watched long winged pelicans fly overhead and swoop down to catch fish with their enormous beaks. Landing on the water with a great splash and bobbing up and down on the waves, they were comical, charming creatures. Playful otters frolicked in the water, doing somersaults. Sometimes, they floated on their backs eating, using their chests as a dinner table.

We had lunch in an Italian restaurant which was decorated with brightly colored paintings. Hanging on the wall was a very large bra that belonged to Sophia Loren. He handed me a picture book of the houses on a tour we were going to. I studied it with envy, thinking that his apartment was a rat hole in comparison.

I greatly enjoyed the tour. The last house we explored was the one that John Steinbeck grew up in. His original manuscripts were on display in glass cabinets. I surveyed them with awe, thinking about what a genius he had for expressing the feelings of people who struggled. George and I mingled with happy, well-dressed people, drank lemonade and ate cookies. Their humming conversation rolled through my ears as I wondered what they did for a living and how they had met their spouses.

Later on, we walked along the beach and watched the sun set. The sand felt soothing as my bare toes dug into its wet softness. The sky grew darker by the minute and soon became a limitless, black void which sparkled with enchantingly radiant stars. He helped me climb up onto a huge boulder jutting out over the ocean.

"I love you", he said, holding me around the waist and pulling me close.

His long legs wrapped around me. My skin tingled with pleasure yet I didn't feel in love.

"There's the Big Dipper", I replied, ignoring his emotional confession.

He was refreshingly open and free compared to the conservative dentist and accountant types I had known in college. He seemed sensitive to women as he talked about his female room mate and how she had been a family friend when he lived in Ohio. And he seemed to like me. Still, l felt tense.

We retreated to his van to rest for the night. I would be wise and take plenty of time to find out if we were right for one another, I thought, reclining on the floor of his van. Suddenly, he unzipped my jeans and pulled them off. My body felt pleasure but my heart felt pain as the uninvited sex happened.

The two men who had raped me two years ago had robbed me of my ability to set boundaries. I simply froze, when I needed to say "no" and became a helpless mute. I wondered if it was a facet of my sickness and if my mental illness had been formed when I was young and afraid of not pleasing my father. I had been deeply hurt by the way my father ignored me and I had a constant neediness for love, so I would accept any man who showed the slightest feelings. Their desire for me gave me value it seemed.

Anger and humiliation simmered within me the next day as we explored the Cannery. The sun shone sensuously and seagulls squawked as we explored the amusement park. People walked by happily, munching cotton candy and popcorn. Horses on a brightly painted carousel moved up and down as delighted children rode them. Happy music played as they waved at their parents. Their innocence touched me and I grieved that I had lost mine.

Ambivalent emotions flowed through me as George drove the van to a place he had found on his map, talking with enthusiasm about how scenic it was. Men were so grounded, so capable of handling car problems and maps. I wanted the stability that only they could provide me with. Yet, my guts churned in anger over the way he had not respected me.

I watched George park the van. My body trembled as I opened the door and let myself out. We walked down a path through some rocks to a beautiful cove filled with pure, white sand. The ocean shimmered in gorgeous, royal blue. Seagulls flew around and perched on craggy rocks. I picked up a piece of driftwood and studied its interesting, twisting shapes as I walked toward the water enjoying the warm caresses of the sun. The ocean waves lapped around my body and the warm, nurturing cove felt like a womb inviting me to return to its primordial security. We walked down a path into a vast forest of redwoods which were covered with bright orange lichen. I envisioned living serenely in a tree house in the midst of this spiritual serenity. The sound of chirping birds lifted my spirit into the heavens.

Later on, we walked through white sand dunes. The sound of the sea and the sensuality of soft sand massaging my bare feet exhilarated me. Patches of tall sea grass brushed my skin and I breathed in the ocean mist and fresh air. We slept in the van on the beach.

A glorious sun woke us. We toured the Hearst Castle and a haunted Victorian mansion. A tour guide told amusing stories about the eccentric lady who lived there and the frequent visits she got from ghosts.

I dreaded facing the task of finding a job as we headed back toward the city. A malevolent energy lurked in the air as George and I walked up the long steps and into the strange, male-dominated, blue Victorian house. I opened the door to my room and saw John sleeping in my bed. George raised his voice in anger and ordered him to leave. John ran fearfully out of the room with my sleeping bag clutched around him.

When George asked me to move in with him I quickly agreed. We loaded all of my earthly possessions, which consisted of books, clothes and a guitar into the van and headed to his apartment. I hung my clothes in his hall closet and stacked my books on the floor.

He told me he needed to pick up some things at the store. A foreboding feeling came over me as he closed the door behind him. My mind raced with chaotic images and my heart pounded. John had warned me that he was fast and he was. I had given him complete control over me and I felt trapped.

I picked up a newspaper and flipped through it until I found the employment section. I gave myself a pep talk. I had my illustrious college degree. It was time for me to now start commanding mega bucks. Watch out world. I was a graduate of the Harvard of the South. Anxiety tightened my shoulders as I read the listings. Pathologist, Nurse, Legal Secretary (must type eighty words a minute). I couldn't do any of those jobs. Physical Therapist, Counselor (Master's Degree required). Maybe I should enroll in school, but with what? It would be expensive and I only had about three hundred dollars in the bank.

I read on desperately, wondering where I would ever fit in the working world. A glimmer of hope ran through me as I read the listing for Graphic Artist. I loved to draw and was good at it. My hopes were dashed as I read on. Must have degree from a commercial art school, excellent computer skills and at least five years experience. I couldn't do a thing on a computer.

I read on. Accountant—I had nearly killed myself studying for college math tests, hoping for approval from my ever-distant father. Ds were the best grades I could ever achieve. My shoulders rose with fear as I read on--Science teacher, Math teacher. My grandmother had told me I would be a wonderful teacher. I'd have to go to graduate school though and I had no money for that. Bank teller--a good, secure position but would I be fast enough? Waitress--I had done my best at those jobs but customers were rude and my managers had ended up firing me. Proof reader--Must have experience. I didn't have any. Lawyer-- I had imagined fighting for peoples' rights. Nuclear Medicine technologist, Anesthesiologist—those were out of the question. I had graduated from the Harvard of the South but I had entered the world with no survival skills whatsoever.

My eyes fell on a listing for a creative arts teacher. I had always been creative and enjoyed being with children. Excitement bubbled within me as I dialed the number and made an appointment for an interview. I got one for a few days later. As I boarded the bus, I asked the bus driver to tell me when he arrived at my exit street. My body trembled as I hurried through the streets. I breathed a deep sigh of relief when I finally found the school.

The woman who interviewed me was friendly, yet I sunk in shame when I realized the stiff competition I was up against. She talked about various people who had worked with the children. One of them had a Ph.D. in music and was a successful composer. Another one had instruments from all around the world and could play all of them. She told me she would call if she could use me with a tone of obligatory politeness. I worried that my mental illness must be apparent to people.

That night, George was gentle as I leaned my head on his shoulder and told him how I had struggled with jobs and been fired a lot. He gave me an add he'd cut from the paper about a one day job helping at the polls. I enjoyed working with some elderly ladies the following Saturday and earned fifty dollars.

Early the next morning, we talked lightly as we packed a cooler with sandwiches and drinks. We crawled into his van and, soon, the hectic confusion of the city gave way to breathtaking vistas of blue ocean and sky. Craggy, majestic cliffs towered over the ocean which rolled with frothy, cresting waves. Magnificent redwood trees stretched into the sky.

A pure, pristine blanket of snow covered the ground when we arrived in Oregon. We explored through a cave full of stalactites and stalagmites which hung from the ceiling like icicles, shimmering with radiant rainbow colors. We walked around in awe enjoying the mystical vibrations of our natural, magical cathedral.

The next day we walked through an enchanted redwood forest. Lacy, light green ferns brushed my body as we trekked energetically along the path. I leaned my head back to look at the breathtakingly gorgeous trees climbing to the heavens. Sunlight shone luminously through mosaic shapes in the leaves. I breathed deeply, filling my lungs with clean, fresh oxygen as we hiked vigorously for hours.

Hunger overcame me as we walked back to the van. We sat and ate bologna sandwiches and brownies which George had baked. Drinking a cool cup of milk, I watched the sun descend, casting streaks of dazzling color across the sky and water. We slept peacefully in the van.

When a glorious sun woke us, I shuddered with anxiety as I contemplated facing my challenges in the city. George started the motor and, soon, we were heading onto a crowded freeway. The concrete chaos of the city folded over me like a suffocating nightmare when we arrived at home.

George got back into his routine of delivering Hustler and Playboy magazines and I went out job hunting. After a few days, I landed one in a dating service in a tall building downtown. The name of the company was Yellow Phone. It was run by a short, fat Greek man. He was warm and friendly and said he could use me to address and stamp envelopes and answer the phone twenty hours a week. The pay was eighty dollars a week—not enough to get my own place. But it was a start.

As I rode the streetcar to work every day, I realized I was becoming increasingly disturbed by feelings of panic. I didn't trust George and I felt prodded from within to escape fast but I did not know how. When George told me I had screamed very loudly in the middle of the night, I thought seriously about making an appointment with a psychiatrist. However, I had many other things to do and I didn't have the money for one.

The October air sent chills of loneliness through me. I longed to spend Christmas with my parents but did not have the money to buy a plane ticket. George told me he was going to start sleeping in his van. He said he couldn't stand the noise the people in the upstairs apartment were making. I wondered if that was the real reason.

The next day, when I got off of the streetcar after work, I decided to walk around his neighborhood for a while. Suddenly, I saw Brian, the married man I had hiked on the mountain with. He looked vibrant as he jogged along energetically. I had missed his warm attention. No man had ever made me feel so special and respected.

"Hi. How are you? I've thought a lot about you", he said.

"Oh, I'm fine. I took a trip to Oregon", I replied, looking down in shame, hoping he didn't find out I had a live-in boyfriend. I didn't want him to think I was a slut.

"That's great. I've got to hurry home and get ready to go teach class. Why don't you come over tomorrow morning and have breakfast with me? I live just down the street", he said, writing his address and phone number down and handing it to me.

I felt like a bird in flight as I accepted. I couldn't wait until the morning came and I could sit and soak up the soothing waves of his presence.

That night, George came in late from his delivery job. I didn't feel happy to see him. I had stuffed all my anger toward him into a deep, hidden crevice. He was big and domineering and disrespectful and had taken total control of me. It felt as though I was losing any idea of who I was and what

I could do and becoming a thing that he owned. Like a cobra, I wanted to strike at him.

The next morning, I jumped out of bed, eager to spend time with Brian. He was so gentile, so refined. I pulled on my jeans and nicest shirt and practically ran up the steep hill to his place. His row house apartment was immaculate and beautifully decorated with plants, paintings and sculptures. Expensive looking furniture, light filled windows and colorful cushions gave it a soft, homey look.

"Come on into the kitchen and sit down. I'm cooking French Toast." His nurturing kindness felt like soothing balm on my frayed nerves. He put a large glass of orange juice in front of me as I sat down at the pretty glass table which shone in the sunlight.

"Tell me about your trip to Oregon", he said, handing me a plate full of French Toast, covered with butter and syrup.

I froze into embarrassed silence for a few moments, then shyly said that I had gone with a friend and explored the mountains and a beautiful cave full of stalactites. My taste buds swelled with pleasure as my mind relaxed, enjoying the peaceful, aesthetic surroundings. His handsome face glowed in the sunlight and his eyes shone with warmth and intelligence as we talked for a little over an hour. He gave me a respectful hug as we said goodbye. When he asked me to go to the beach with him and his son I accepted his offer gratefully.

Cool crispness filled the air as the sun shone brightly the next day. It was getting close to Halloween. George's face lit up with anticipation as he told me about the annual Exotic Erotic ball.

"It's really outrageous. People go all out and dress up in really wild costumes. They have a lot of different bands. I had a blast last year. You'll really enjoy it". His eyes sparkled with enthusiasm.

I decided I would go as a devil. I got on the phone and called department stores around town to find out if they sold a red bra. None of them did. I ended up wearing a short, red jacket and red pants. A friend of George's lent me some red horns, a red tail and a mean looking pitchfork.

George got dressed as a flasher in a big raincoat as his friend sat on the edge of his bed. Big, green, gossamer wings extended from his friend's shoulders. He looked like a fractured fairy tale as he leaned over a mirror and snorted a long line of cocaine with a rolled up dollar bill.

We all piled into my car and I drove through the frenzied night, admiring the full moon. I waved my pitchfork playfully as we walked into the vast, noise-filled ballroom, surveying the eclectic crowd with curiosity. A man who was dressed like the Empire State building strode by with cool elegance. Four women who were dressed as a table and chairs edged their way through the noisy crowd. Martians in silver space suits walked by, the colored antennas on their heads bouncing up and down. A man and woman who were both dressed as bright, red devils walked by. She looked vulnerable as she clung to her tall, handsome husband.

Suddenly, I realized that George had disappeared. I looked through the crowd trying to find him. Three men started jeering at me, pulling at my tail and laughing. As I pushed my way through the crowd, watching lights flashing up on the stage, I smelled fragrances and hair sprays wafting from spruced up ladies. A sensation of dizziness overcame me as my senses became overloaded by the loud music and voices. I held my breath as my rubber legs trembled underneath me. My eyes scanned the room searching for George.

Suddenly, my eyes fell on him. He was standing in front of a woman who was sitting in a chair. A big grin covered his face as he held his raincoat open. With stunned disbelief, I watched her take his penis into her hands and lower her mouth to it. He smiled with unabashed pleasure as she moved her tongue deftly around it.

I turned away and walked into the high spirited crowd. People laughed happily, enjoying their togetherness. I was completely alone. Wandering to the refreshments, I looked around at the fascinating characters. Then, I stuffed myself with snacks to numb my pain. The minutes crawled as I spent several hours alone. When George found me, long after midnight, I didn't even want to look at him. My feelings for him had died. As I drove the three of us home, I listened to him brag about all of the women he had flashed and the woman who had licked his penis.

"I really liked that woman. She wants to have an orgy with you and me and her husband ", he said with anticipation.

"Oh no. I'm not interested", I replied, boiling with anger, concealing it completely.

A week later, we took a trip to Big Sur in my car. His van was not working. I gazed out of the window dreamily as George drove. I leafed through his tour book and read about the architecture, trying to recall the various terms I had learned in Art History classes. He pointed to houses that had beautiful wrought iron lookout places on the very top. Women used to stand on them to look out to sea to see if their husbands were returning from voyages he explained.

After several hours of driving, our stomachs were grumbling with hunger. We stopped and ate lunch in a charming little café. Then we wandered along a pier looking with curiosity at various trinkets that were displayed in shop windows. When we got to the end of the pier we gazed out at the vast ocean.

We drove further down the coast and came to a beautiful cove filled with shimmering white sand. The aqua water sparkled iridescently in the sun as I picked up a piece of driftwood and observed its gnarled, twisted beauty. I took off my tennis shoes and let the fine sand massage my feet as I walked toward the water. Warm waves lapped around me soothingly. Later on, we parked on a secluded beach to watch the sun go down. George wanted to have sex in the back of my car but I wasn't interested. We didn't say much as he drove us back to the city.

CHAPTER 7————————NOVEMBER, 1981
If You Meet Mr. Wrong Run

THE NEXT MORNING, I SAT on the sofa in the front room. Suddenly, great sadness moved in a wave through me. Great, gut-wrenching sobs came endlessly from the depths of my being as I drowned in an ocean of sorrow. An excruciating feeling of alienation and loneliness was eating me up inside. I wanted to call my mother and ask her to send me a plane ticket. Even though my parents were abusive at times, it was far better there than it was here. I hated the West coast.

Suddenly, George walked in. "What's wrong with you?", he yelled in a harsh tone that cut me like a dagger.

"I don't know. I just feel really afraid", I responded, fidgeting nervously.

"Why don't you go talk to a counselor?", he asked impatiently, gritting his teeth with anger.

"I guess I should. Maybe I need some medication", I responded. I stood up and walked toward the hallway.

"You mean you haven't been taking your medication?" he yelled, stabbing me with angry eyes.

I wanted to shout at him that I had not been taking medication since I left my substitute parents (the Christians in the bedroom town) and went back to college. Even the counselor, at the mental health center I had attended while living with them, had agreed that those careless professionals had been over drugging me. The medications had never helped me feel less depressed. They had only caused me to waste my youth sleeping.

Suddenly, he grabbed me by my arm and shoved me against the wall.

Pain shot through my shoulder and little lights danced in front of my eyes.

"I'm going to take you somewhere. I can't put up with this shit any more", he growled, his face burning red with rage.

I followed him out to his van and sat in frightened silence as he drove through the traffic packed streets. I watched people walk along the sidewalks and heard sirens screaming in the distance. After a fast drive, he stopped in front of a small crisis clinic in a dangerous looking section of the city.

"Go in there and get a counselor to help you", he yelled with a look of utter contempt. I crawled out of the van and told him goodbye in a humiliated voice. My legs trembled as I walked across the street and through the front door of the small free clinic. I had been in two treatment hospitals since I was seventeen and the counselors had always insisted that the patients take their mind destroying pills. However, I'd never needed pills, I needed love.

This was the first clinic I had been to in San Francisco. I was getting hooked back into the deadly system that I had tried so hard to escape. I walked to the check-in counter and wrote my name in the sign in book. A pathetic, gray haired woman shuffled around babbling nonsense to herself. I picked up a House Beautiful magazine and drifted off into dreams of home and marriage. When a counselor tapped me on the shoulder, I followed him to a small room.

"What has been going on with you?", he asked, his face conveying genuine concern.

"I've been feeling frightened and confused and crying a lot", I responded sadly, searching his eyes for comfort desperately.

"Do you know what you're frightened of?", he asked, knitting his brows together and looking deeply into my eyes.

"I feel afraid because I'm new in San Francisco and I don't have any friends. My boyfriend has been helping me but I don't think I want to be involved with him any more", I said numbly.

"I'm going to give you some medication so you can get a good night's sleep. Things are going to work out fine. Try not to worry", he said with a soft, caring tone.

He led me into the isolation room, then put a tiny, plastic cup containing the deadly, blue pill I hated into my hand. It was called Stelazine. I had read in the big drug book that it was an anti psychotic drug. It was the first drug I ever took when I was admitted to the hospital at the age of seventeen. The memories of counselors punishing me for falling asleep in the middle of the day came back. I needed to stay awake in this big, complicated city for God's sake. Stelazine was the last thing I needed. A silent scream wailed out of me and moved in waves across the universe as I hurled it to the floor.

He looked at me with disbelief, then turned and walked quickly out of my dismal cell. No one ever came to let me out of that depressing, sterile room. I was trapped for the night. As I brushed my teeth, washed my face and put on my hospital gown, the four walls closed in on me. I crawled onto the uncomfortable cot, curled into a fetal position and hugged myself. Finally, around five a.m., I was released to the land of sleep—the only peace I ever had.

After slumbering a while, I stood up suddenly, like a bull ready to charge a toreador. I wrapped my blanket around me, picked up my purse and strode defiantly out the front door of the clinic. My hospital gown flew flimsily in the wind as I ran across the street, dodging honking cars. Cringing, I hurried past the people and noisy confusion and ducked into a small café. The sound of sizzling filled my ears. I inhaled the aroma of fresh coffee, sausage and buttered toast as I sat down on a wooden chair. A waitress smiled sweetly as she took my order, not raising an eyebrow over my strange attire.

As I ate my sausage, eggs and toast, I wondered what my next best move would be. With no friends to talk to I felt lost in a stormy sea. I ate ravenously, enjoying immensely the one pleasure I had. Whenever the waitress looked my way I smiled so I could get her comforting smile in return. As I paid my bill she wished me good luck and touched my shoulder in a loving, reassuring way.

My voice trembled as I called George on the phone. He agreed, begrudgingly, to come pick me up. When he arrived, I told him I had worked everything out with a counselor and he would not have to put up with any more crying spells. I sat in silent pain as he drove to his apartment.

He got ready for work while I rested on his water bed. Then he headed out to deliver dirty magazines. I stretched out on the water bed, trying to relax. However, dark, malevolent energy swirled around me threatening to drive me over the edge. I was not taking medications and had no intention of taking them. It was ridiculous for psychiatrists to think that the answers to my problems were in a pill.

I walked into the kitchen and looked with anger at the stack of Hustlers and Playboys on the kitchen shelf as I drank a quick glass of water. Then, I picked up my shoulder bag and walked out of the front door, slamming and locking it behind me. I was nothing but an object to him.

I needed someone to talk to. When I saw a sign pointing to a psychic fair, I followed the arrow. Soon, I arrived at a gathering of kind looking people. A motherly looking, overweight woman with curly, dark hair met my eyes. When she asked me if I'd like a reading I instantly accepted. She asked me to hold my palm out for her to study.

"You have a boyfriend don't you?", she asked.

"Yeah. I haven't known him very long", I replied, feeling ashamed.

"He's a lot like your brother. Another man would be better for you. You've got to get stronger. You let them have their way too much." Her dark eyes glowed with motherly concern. She squeezed my hand and gave me a warm hug.

Suddenly, I remembered I had seen a counseling center a few blocks away. It looked like a much friendlier place than the free clinic in the poor section of town that George had discarded me into. I thanked the psychic, then ran down the sidewalk, watching couples walk along hand in hand, their adoring dogs running beside them. Longing to be a mother, I admired adorable babies being pushed in strollers.

In desperation, I pushed the front door of the counseling center open.

A brunette receptionist looked at me with concern as I signed the waiting list. She told me a counselor would come and get me after a while. I sat on a sofa and read Good Housekeeping and Homes and Gardens, dreaming of the joys of marriage.

A tall, handsome counselor appeared in front of me. The gentleness in his face was like a rainbow after a hailstorm. I followed him back to his office and sat down on the brown, worn sofa.

"What has been happening with you and what is your reason for coming here?", he asked, his large, dark eyes shining with compassion. His thick, dark hair framed his handsome face and his well-built, toned body looked good in his green cotton shirt and blue jeans.

"I'm new in the city and I feel frightened all the time. I'm living with my boyfriend who was very kind and helped me but, now, he's yelling at me and criticizing me a lot", I said in a low voice.

"How long have you known this guy?", he asked, his eyes widening with protective concern.

"About three weeks", I responded, gripping my hands tightly together.

"Has he hit you?", his voice rose with emotion.

"No. He's really helped me a lot. But, now, I've got to get away. I'm really afraid of him", I replied, wringing my hands anxiously.

"I sense that you're feeling a lot of anger", he said, his solid, composed presence presenting a clarifying mirror for me.

"I am. I don't know how to stand up for myself. I made friends with a guy who had a drinking problem and he ended up sleeping in my bed and completely dominating me. He was very handsome and intelligent and I wanted to be in love but I always get overwhelmed by men. He ended up yelling at me. Then, I got involved with my current boyfriend and he has been yelling at me too", I said, shyly.

"I want to do an exercise with you. I want you to pretend that the guy you were just talking about is standing in front of you. Tell him you're angry", he said.

"Look. I feel angry at you. I want you to find some place else to stay. I don't like the way you just expected me to share my bed with you. You wake me up in the middle of the night coming in drunk and have no respect for me", I said timidly.

"Is that the angriest you can get? It didn't sound like you meant anything you were saying. You're not going to be taken seriously if you talk like that", he said.

"It's hard for me to express anger. I'm afraid of it. I want to get along with people. I'm dying of loneliness. I've been sitting in Denny's restaurants and starting conversations with strangers. I talked with a man who was drunk yesterday. His nose was swollen and red", I said.

"I don't think you ought to be talking with drunks. They're not the nicest people in the world you know. You've got to learn how to take care of yourself. I'm going to arrange for you to get into a halfway house" That sounded better than that horrible cell in the clinic in a dangerous area of town. I had felt safe and loved when I lived in the halfway house when I was eighteen.

My counselor listened with empathy and reassured me that I was going to be alright. I didn't want to leave as the session ended. I walked down the street to the Grand Piano. The room hummed with conversation as I ordered a cup of chamomile tea. The earthy aroma and taste soothed me as I observed people. I took my notebook and pen out of my bag and began writing a poem:

My eye falls in a beautiful dream on blood, red fuscia hanging pendulously, falling slowly, gently toward the mother. I walk along the street. The puddles are muddy and dark and I no longer enjoy jumping in them. I pause along the way when I notice a few that are filled with rainbows. A tulip blooms like a bleeding heart being sold on the corner for a dollar.

I was totally absorbed in my thoughts when, suddenly, I felt the presence of someone standing near me. My entire being melted into rapture as I gazed into the lovely, dark, liquid eyes of a strikingly handsome man with dark hair and a mischievous smile. He introduced himself as Stan and shook my hand warmly. Then he asked about my writing. I told him I enjoyed writing poetry and had started when I was eight. He told me he was an actor and was rehearsing for a play. In a funny, childlike voice, he invited me to come see it. I had been delivered from my loneliness by a jester. He wrote his phone number and address and drew a map on a scrap of paper. Smiling with warmth, he handed it to me. He said he would like for me to have dinner with him that night.

An elated feeling moved through me as I told him goodbye and headed down the street toward the Golden Gate Park. When I saw a sign that pointed toward the Conservatory I followed it. People looked happy as they glided by gracefully on roller skates and skateboards. Adorable dogs trotted loyally beside their good looking masters. The Conservatory shone like silver in the sun. It was geometrically shaped like a Christmas ornament. A lush, green tropical forest welcomed me warmly as I walked through the front entrance.

Orchids and birds of paradise stood like welcoming friends, calming me with their bright, vibrant colors and heavenly perfume. Like Alice in Wonderland, I wandered as if in a dream, blissfully observing all the incomparable beauty surrounding me. A warm, tropical mist hung in the air, creating the vibration of an enchanted jungle. Blue pools full of bright orange and yellow fish glistened in the sunlight. Pendulous petals of lavender, pink, white and yellow hung gracefully from luxurious trees and bushes. Time seemed to stand still as I drank in the lovely serenity and enjoyed the fragrance.

Looking outside, I noticed the sky starting to grow dark. Hurrying outside, fast walking toward the Grand Piano, I looked around nervously. I pulled the map Stan had sketched for me out of my pocket and studied it in the pink glow of a street lamp. I held my breath with hope as I walked through the dark, deserted streets. A wonderful sense of relief rolled through me when I looked up and saw his number printed in bold, black letters on his row house. I walked up the stairs and knocked on the door.

"Hi cutie", he said warmly, giving me a quick hug. "Remember. Don't go around horny", he laughed, slapping his thighs in a slapstick way. I laughed along with him admiring his short, yet muscular body. His dark eyes shone like nova stars in his expressive face.

My jaw clenched with jealousy when he introduced me to his gorgeous girlfriend, Dot. She was tall, slender and voluptuous with long, blond hair and huge blue eyes bordered with thick, dark lashes. Her dark eyebrows arched gracefully under her blond, shiny bangs and a hint of lipstick made her lips look like a rose. Plants, books and occasional pieces of furniture which looked like they had been found in junk piles stood haphazardly around. I sat on a black mat on the floor which was piled with big, overstuffed cushions.

Stan walked toward me and handed me my plate, smiling cheerfully. The aroma of turkey, collard greens and potatoes filled my nose as my mouth watered. As I began eating he poured me a glass of grape juice. I basked in the warmth of newfound friendship as I listened to him and his girlfriend playfully joke with one another. The evening passed in a carefree way like a summer afternoon in childhood.

I died inside as I told them goodbye. The street lamps glowed an eerie pink and a streetcar rumbled by as insecurity trembled within me like an earthquake. I wanted to call my mother. However, my shoulders tensed as I remembered the last time she had yelled at me and ordered me out of her house. She didn't like me at all.

My breathing stopped as I turned my keys in George's front door and opened it. I walked down the hall, past his room mate's room. Her voice murmured through the door as she talked on the phone. I took a metaphysical book out of my back pack and stretched out on his water bed, wishing we could have the close, carefree relationship that Stan and his girlfriend had. Painful memories of the men who had raped me lashed at me like shards of broken glass.

I had thought I could trust the man who had asked me to travel with him when I was penniless in Paris over two years ago. However, he had taken advantage of me. Then, the homeless man who I gave shelter to in my rented room a few blocks from my college had forced himself on me.

His girlfriend had taken advantage of my hospitality too by talking me into letting him into my bedroom. I had never told anyone because the shame was so unbearable.

I needed some deep sleep but did not want to take sleeping pills. Mellaril had helped me sleep in college yet it had stolen my precious time, causing me to sleep twelve hours and wake up foggy and late for class.

One day, a month or so before my European travels, I had been so spaced out on drugs I had forgotten to put the emergency brake on when I parked my car. I had heard a sudden loud crash and looked down the driveway at my car which had rolled down and smashed into the garage. Shame over my inability to be present had tortured me and I had longed to talk about the drugs and find out if they were causing my forgetfulness. However, the psychiatrists who wrote my prescriptions had never had the time to talk.

I came back to the present. George came into the room briefly, wished me a good night's sleep and then retreated to his van. We were hardly talking and I felt as fragile as glass and afraid that he might smash me. I wished I could call my father and tell him I needed to go home and live with him again. However, fear and anxiety filled me when I thought of talking to him. He usually hurried off the phone like he didn't want to listen.

The next morning, I read a book as I waited for the Grand Piano to open. George came in briefly, chatted distantly about some errands he had to do and then left. I got dressed in a bright, purple shirt I had sewn myself, a pair of green shorts and a blue belt. I cringed with fear as I walked down the strange sidewalks. Soon, I reached the chatter filled café. A tall, handsome man observed me as I ordered a cup of chamomile tea.

My hand shook as I carried my cup and saucer to a table and sat down. A young man and woman who looked about my age, twenty four, walked in and sat down near me. The man was tanned, muscular and healthy looking, his wavy, blond hair streaked with highlights. The woman was petite and innocent looking. Her light blond, fine hair cascaded below her shoulders. They introduced themselves, saying their names were Becky and Tom.

As I listened to them talk about how they had moved to San Francisco from Boston, I was touched by their pure simplicity. They behaved the way I imagined real sixties flower children would behave—friendly and humble. Floating in a golden bubble, I listened to them talk about traveling around the country in their van. Tangy ketchup satisfied me as we shared a plate of potato wedges.

A tall, slender man shook our hands warmly and told us his name was Randy. After we had talked for a while, he suggested we all go somewhere and get high. We all walked down the street to Becky and Tom's van. I watched people passing by, walking dogs or jogging along briskly. When we arrived at the weathered, green van we all crawled inside. I folded myself up as small as I could and leaned against the back door.

Tom lit a joint and they each took a long drag of it. I remembered my psychiatrist who treated me for schizophrenia, when I was seventeen, for a year. His voice echoed in my mind as I remembered him telling me I should not smoke pot. I passed it back when it was handed to me. Marijuana smoke curled through the sunlight, twisting and swirling in billowing shapes as I listened to my friends talk. After a while, Randy said he had to leave. Tom and Becky said they had gone a long time without a shower and they couldn't stand it a minute longer. I told them they could take one at my place. Tom drove his van carefully and parked across the street from the apartment.

We walked up the stairs and opened the door. George and his room mate were gone, luckily. All three of us got into the shower. Becky and Tom were buck naked but I wore my bra and underwear. Like happy children, we rubbed shampoo into our hair, working up a rich, full lather. Laughing lightheartedly, we spread the frothy bubbles over our bodies, then took turns standing underneath the warm stream of water. Steam floated around us. When we felt as clean as newborn babies, we stepped out of the shower. We dried ourselves off with George's big, fluffy towels and got dressed.

Suddenly, George came storming in, glaring at me with fury.

"What are they doing here?", he yelled, cutting through me with dagger eyes.

"They're friends of mine and I told them they could take a shower. They've been staying in their van and they haven't been able to shower for a long time", I replied, my voice trembling with fear.

"Well, I don't want you bringing your friends over here. This is MY apartment. You can't expect me to open my place to your friends who I don't even know. Ever since we returned from our trip you have shut me out", he yelled, clenching his fists with anger as though he wanted to hit me.

I looked at Tom in a silent plea for help as George stormed off to his room.

"Come on. Let's go. You can do better than him", he said. I followed him and Becky out to their van. As he started to drive down the street, a torrent of tears began flooding down my face.

"I keep settling for too little because I'm desperate for love. I've got to get away from him. I don't have anywhere to go though. I don't have any money to rent my own apartment", I cried, wiping tears from my face.

"I thought his behavior was inexcusable. He shouldn't have yelled at you like that. He is a real asshole. You've got to get away from him. He's just a creep. You can do better than him. Stay with us tonight. I don't want you going back there. He's such an asshole he might hit you", he said.

We went to the Grand Piano and ordered a plate of lasagna. The waiter kept refilling our basket of bread, smiling at us warmly. The moon shone brightly as we walked down the street to the van. I curled up into a ball and pulled a blanket over me.

The next morning, I walked back to George's, trembling with fear. I was greatly relieved when I found out he was not there. Gratitude flooded me when, suddenly, I got a phone call from my counselor. He told me that he had found a halfway house for me and that he would pick me up at my boyfriend's place.

My eyes darted around the place nervously as I started to pack. Visions of George storming in and beating me up raced through my mind. I grabbed my toothbrush, toothpaste and other toiletries and threw them into a paper bag. Next, I took a huge armful of clothes off the rack and carried them to the sofa where I dropped them. I opened my suitcase and started throwing clothes into it frantically. I sat on top of it to force it shut. Then, I started grabbing armfuls of books, jamming them into boxes and bags as fast as I could.

When I heard a car horn honk outside, I felt like a slave who had just been set free. I picked up my suitcase and walked out the front door and down the stairs. My counselor helped me load my few earthly belongings into his car.

"How are you?", he asked. In my three sessions with him I had grown to trust him completely.

"I've been panicking all day. I was afraid he might come in and beat me up", I said.

"Well, that was not a healthy relationship you were in. I'm taking you to a halfway house where you'll be able to talk with a counselor as often as you want. You need a safe, supportive place to live", he said compassionately.

I enjoyed my counselor's gentle vibrations as he drove through the afternoon traffic. He parked his car on a steep hill. I followed him up the stairs into a beige, brick row house. We walked up a long, narrow staircase and down a hall to a small office. A man with dark, blond hair and a gentle face was sitting at the desk.

"Hello. How are you?", he asked, looking with concern into my eyes.

My counselor spoke for me, explaining that I was new in San Francisco and was experiencing a lot of difficulty. I listened to the two of them speak for a while. When my counselor left, I gave him a quick hug. Then, I began talking with the halfway house counselor telling him I didn't know who I should trust.

CHAPTER 8 ————————————NOVEMBER, 1981

Shelter from the Storm

"THE OLDER YOU GET AND the more experience you have with people, the better you will get at choosing who to trust and who not to trust. You can't trust everyone", he said. "Welcome to your new home. The frightened little girl who walked in here is nothing like the empowered woman who will walk out."

After we had talked for a while, a female counselor introduced herself to me and led me down the stairs to my room. I sat down on the bed and played my guitar listlessly until I was called to dinner. After dinner, everyone sat in a circle of chairs. The counselors listened with serious expressions on their faces and wrote notes on large pads. Various patients whined about their problems, going around and around in pathetic circles. The meeting was very boring and I was relieved when it was over. My body tensed in angry dread as a counselor handed me a large, bullet-shaped Navane pill with a cup of orange juice. It was just another one of the thousands of "Miracle" drugs. It was enough of a knockout on its own. Yet, the counselor then handed me Stelazine. I was becoming a walking drugstore. I swallowed it obediently and then walked down the stairs and crawled into bed. My eyelids drooped and I went deeper and deeper every second until, suddenly, I checked out.

The next morning, I felt like Rip Van Winkle as I looked at the clock and realized I had slept fourteen hours. I got dressed slowly and walked up the stairs in a fog, on wobbling, jelly legs. Sun shone through the window as I poured a bowl of Frosted Flakes and sliced a banana on top of it.

Eating had become my only pleasure in life. I ate slowly, savoring the sweet crunchiness.

I finished eating breakfast and walked down the hall to the T.V. room. As I sat on the sofa and stared blankly at the T.V., my head began dropping down to my chest. Every time I lifted it up, a great drowsiness would overcome me and it would drop back down again. Before I knew it, I had gone out like a light.

I woke up a few hours later, still sitting upright, with an irritating pain throbbing in my neck. As I stared at the wall I felt like I was falling into oblivion, losing all sense of myself, my dreams and my goals. I had lost all my desire to live. There was simply no joy inside me. It seemed like the assaults I'd suffered in childhood were meant to follow me all my life. I couldn't trust myself and felt doomed to forever give my power away to abusers. My parents had convinced me I was not good enough. I kept trying to find the key to happiness by turning my life over to some boyfriend who would give me a gold star of validation. Yet, they only exploited me. A deadening depression descended on me as I wondered if this existence was all I had to look forward to. Wasting the rest of my life, sitting and staring at a wall or pacing a dark hall. Existing as a reject of society, unloved and not respected, just another number taking up space in the sterile rooms of mental health hell. If this was the mental health system, I wondered what the mental unhealth system was like.

After a while, I got bored with my analysis of myself and came back to the present moment. I went outside to remove the clothes from the back seat of my car. My window was smashed and all my clothes had been stolen. John had been right when he told me people in this city were mean.

I played my guitar but soon got frustrated over my limited knowledge of it. I wished I had the money for a good teacher. I read books or watched T.V. but quickly got tired of that. I was pleasantly surprised when I found a record player and a stack of records. I sat and listened to music for hours, completely tuning out the world. My favorite old Beatles tunes and other hits from the sixties lifted my spirits.

That night at the hall meeting, the patients talked about their various woes and the counselors listened with empathy. I wanted to complain about the drugs they were giving me but I didn't dare. The meeting finally ended and I sat and watched Apocalypse Now, sharing a big bowl of popcorn with a patient who wore flannel pajamas and had dark, curly hair. She spoke in a disjointed, vacuous way. I longed to be with people who were intelligent and successful. I dreaded taking on the behaviors of the eccentric, awkward patients. After the movie, a counselor handed me my nightly Navane and Stelazine pills. She talked with me for a while, encouraging me to relax and be good to myself. I told her about my background and how frightened I was to be alone in the city.

After a few days of sitting around doing nothing, watching T.V. and eating popcorn I felt very restless. It was a cruel world like my father had warned and I wanted to go home. I didn't have the strength to make that long cross country drive again though.

The one place which picked up my spirits was The Grand Piano. I would walk there I decided. Sun shone down on me, warming my face and body. I looked up and watched fluffy clouds swim freely through the dazzling blue sky. A light springiness came forth in my step as I crossed the street which rushed with loud traffic. The aroma of Indian food came from a restaurant when I arrived in the Haight Ashbury. I breathed deeply as I walked briskly up a steep sidewalk which was lined with charming shops. I avoided the eyes of a group of rough looking characters hanging out on the corner. Several sad looking beggars asked me for change with woeful eyes. I handed five dollars to the last one.

I arrived at The Grand Piano and walked to the counter to order some chamomile tea. My favorite friendly waiter handed me my tea and I sat down at a table. Curiosity flowed through me as I observed various characters around me. A drunk man rambled on and on about his girlfriend who worked as a stripper in a downtown joint. An old woman with a grotesquely lined face and swollen red nose listened to him with a perturbed look on her face. A man with dark, wavy hair that reached down to his waist was completely absorbed in drawing on a pad of paper. I drew for hours with some colored, thin tipped markers he gave me. Then, I wrote in my journal about how I had escaped from a mean boyfriend. When I returned the markers to the man he smiled warmly and introduced himself. I shook his hand shyly, feeling his warmth spread like a nurturing sun ray throughout my inner being. Then I turned to leave. I daydreamed as I rode the bus back to the halfway house.

Dinner with the counselors and residents calmed my agitated nerves that night. Black beans, vegetables and baked chicken filled the emptiness within me. I ate two huge plates, knowing that it would add pounds to my derriere but not caring. If I became hideously overweight all the sex obsessed, predatory men would leave me alone.

Later, I gorged myself excessively with popcorn and stared listlessly at a movie, totally unable to concentrate. When a counselor handed me my Navane and Stelazine, I swallowed it willingly, longing for the sweet release of sleep. No one heard me as I told them good night and began groping my way awkwardly down the stairs to my room. I wasn't being cured it seemed, though I tried talking about my emotional distance from my parents and the fact that my sister got all the attention. I couldn't talk about the rapes because I felt too ashamed. Something was missing. Nothing any of the counselors said removed my feelings of self-disgust or depression.

Morning came in a fog of uncertainty, after I'd slept fourteen hours. I staggered upstairs to the kitchen and made myself some breakfast, wondering what I was going to do with my life. My mood lifted as I sat and talked with the male counselor who had admitted me. He kindly suggested that I write a few pages about fear. He said he had heard me playing my guitar and that he could tell that I played to get away from my feelings. He wanted me to feel my feelings more. With his wavy, dark blond hair and compassionate eyes he was soothing balm for my fractured heart.

I thanked him for his time and excused myself to go write in my room. I tried writing but could not concentrate. Restless energy surged within me so I called my friend Sheila. I was still in a state of shock over the fact that she was a prostitute. Yet, Jesus hung out with prostitutes I reasoned.

Her gentle voice calmed me as she invited me to go over and spend the night with her. I walked to the office and told the male counselor that a friend had invited me for an outing. He responded that I could go this time but, in the future, there would have to be more discussion about my activities. I liked the halfway house because it was helping me feel like a human being again. I got lots of praise for cooking dinner for everyone once. The patients and counselors were kind and respectful.

I threw a toothbrush and flannel nightgown into my back pack, feeling like a child again, going to a spend the night party. Then I tiptoed up the stairs and out the front door. The bus driver gave me directions in a kind, caring tone. I observed my fellow passengers as I rode to Sheila's apartment.

Sheila's beautiful face glowed with serenity as she opened the door and welcomed me in, looking soft and feminine in her cream-colored outfit. She introduced me to her friend, a tall, tough-looking, dark-haired lesbian dressed all in black. Her silver belt buckle shone brightly like the silver spikes on her heels. Her dark eyebrows rose dramatically as she said hello in a deep tone and shook my hand. I felt dizzy as I suddenly remembered she was the one who had eyed my body as I danced with Sheila at the club. Sheila walked over to the record player and put some rhythmic, fast music on.

"We've been partying in the higher realms. We snorted some amyl nitrate. Here. Give it a try. It will heighten your consciousness so you can experience the joy of the angelic world", Sheila said, looking at me with tenderness as she handed me a small bottle.

"You just take the cap off and sniff it up your nose", she said encouragingly.

As I inhaled it, a burning sensation seared my nostrils. I asked Sheila for a cigarette. My hand trembled as I tried to light a match, striking it again and again. I couldn't hold it steadily and, when I finally got it lit, it brushed my nose and burned it. Soon, my brain felt like it had been fried on a five hundred degree griddle and pounded with a hammer. My friends chattered non-stop, chain-smoking, drinking Martinis and smoking marijuana until two in the morning. I tried futilely to sleep on a mat on the floor, feeling like a scared rabbit in a trap.

When the morning sun came through the window, I glanced at the two of them sleeping in Sheila's bed. I tiptoed out the door, grateful to be released from my party in hell.

Back at the halfway house, the protective look of the counselor cast a calm over the stormy seas churning within me. For the next few weeks, I sat watching T.V., eating popcorn, drinking hot chocolate and listening to music. I didn't understand what the drugs and the talks with counselors were doing for me. I was deriving the benefit of security, safety, good food and companionship. However, I felt less and less competent as I slept long hours and daydreamed the days away. I used to be a good file clerk and I envisioned finding a job doing that and renting an apartment. Feelings of hopelessness and helplessness overwhelmed me though.

The crazy street people fascinated me so, sometimes, I left without telling the counselors a word of goodbye and rode the bus around the city. Walking home from Woolworth's one night I got lost. When I asked a security guard for help, he unzipped his pants and looked at me threateningly, like he was going to force me to perform oral sex on him. Sheer terror hit me like lightning and I ran and ran praying to stay alive as the dark night shrouded me like a death shawl. After what seemed like hours, miraculously I recognized the street the halfway house was on.

Tears ran down my cheeks as I ran up the front stairs and pounded on the door frantically. When a counselor let me in I wanted to cry in her arms. My face must have been as white as a ghost because she looked at me with protective concern. Not able to talk, I ran past her, up the stairs and into the bathroom. I turned on the bath tub faucet and poured foaming gel under the gushing torrent. Bubbles frothed up beautifully, building white cushions of comfort before my grateful eyes. I slid into the warm bath and soaked. Sleep was welcome release as I drifted off, after tossing and turning for a long time. My soul flew freely far beyond the troubles of the heartless world.

Life seemed too dismal to face and I wanted to stay in bed all day when I woke up. I forced myself to get up and go to the kitchen. As I poured myself a bowl of cornflakes, I told the blond counselor that a security guard had unzipped his pants and looked at me threateningly.

"You should have gotten his badge number", she said matter of factly. Then, she asked me what I was going to do about my financial situation and told me my rent was due. When I told her I had no money at all (I hid the fact that I had three hundred dollars) she suggested that I take the bus downtown and apply for general assistance. I had never heard about getting free money from the government and it sounded like a good idea. My eighty dollar a week job, stamping envelopes for the dating service, had only lasted three weeks. I would have to set my alarm for five o'clock in the morning to allow myself enough time to get there.

My alarm rang shrilly the next morning. I crawled out of bed despondently. A faint desire to die trembled through my bones as I pulled on my clothes listlessly. Rain pitter pattered on the windows as I buttoned up my rain coat. The house was as silent as a tomb as I walked up the front stairs and out the front door. A feeling of doom grew within me like a bitter, poisonous vine as I climbed up the hill to the bus stop. I was like an icicle hanging in an empty, cold sky. No one ever touched me. Like an alien from another planet, I walked through life deadened by isolation.

Soon, the bus arrived and I rode in silence for about a half hour. Rain poured down in torrents as I stepped off the bus onto the crowded sidewalk. A line of people huddling under cardboard boxes and plastic bags stretched for blocks and blocks. As I splashed through puddles, cold water soaked through my tennis shoes and socks. I wished I was wearing the tight rubber galoshes I observed on some people. At least I had a working umbrella I thought gratefully, watching miserable people hanging onto inside out, broken umbrellas. I listened to a man ramble on and on in a disjointed monologue about the number 666, which represented the Anti-Christ who was planning to destroy the world. I remembered my mother calling me an unnatural child and accusing me of trying to destroy her house. I wondered if I was the Anti-Christ. Finally, a somber faced man let me into the building, handing me a ticket with a number on it. I sat down in a tiny, wooden desk and waited and waited and waited.

A caseworker took me into his office. He looked over my application with scrutinizing eyes. After a few minutes of silence, he told me that I could not get welfare because I had a car. Not knowing what to say, I left his office.

I rode the bus to the Grand Piano, my safe refuge. As I scanned the job listings, I felt incapable of doing any of them. My attention span was short and I couldn't concentrate or remember much. I listened to the beautiful piano music and humming of conversations.

I caught the eye of a slender, brunette man and we exchanged names and greetings. His name was Taylor and he talked enthusiastically about a book about Egyptian mysteries he was reading. When I stood up to leave, he asked for my phone number.

He called the next day and asked me to fly in a helicopter over the bay with him. He sounded delighted to be talking with me so, when he suggested that we go to his favorite restaurant together, I accepted happily. He was charming and full of life as we talked over shrimp creole and champagne. Boats chugged by and I watched them with wonder through the huge, glass wall. The ocean sparkled right beside me and I savored living with seagulls and pelicans. A tuxedo dressed waiter filled my water glass and asked me if I needed anything as I admired the flowers, paintings and sculptures.

Taylor convinced me to leave the halfway house, saying that the drugs they were giving me were harmful and that I would never make any progress as long as I was under their control. I believed him and immediately stopped taking my medicine. I paid him a month's rent and began sleeping on his sofa in his living room.

One afternoon, I invited a group of friends over. They passed a joint around and I inhaled a small puff of it. I cried with deep sorrow for a while as I imagined that I was floating in space looking down on the suffering blue and green planet.

Suddenly, I began laughing hysterically. The phone rang and I picked up the receiver and laughed uncontrollably into it. George's angry voice came through, demanding that I give him his keys back. I gave him the directions to Taylor's apartment. About fifteen minutes later, he arrived at the door and banged on it loudly. When I opened it he yelled that I better not be laughing at him or he would break my face. Terror crashed through me like a tidal wave as I handed him his keys.

"Who was that? He was horrible", a kind man from England I had met at the Grand Piano said. I let Randy, who I had gone to Shawn and Dawn's van with, stay for the night because he was homeless. Randy talked me into taking a bath with him, which Taylor heard from his bedroom. It infuriated Taylor that I would let a stranger sleep in his place and that I would behave so loosely.

Taylor had been my hero, I had felt, when he told me the evils of the halfway house and offered to save me. He had called me a diamond in the rough. However, I died inside as he yelled "I thought you were a special person when I met you but now I realize you belong in a nut house. I want you to leave here now."

Randy stayed with me in my car a couple of nights and took me to sleep in a cheap room down town one night. He promised to take me to live in a house with some of his old friends. Then, he disappeared one sunny morning, after we had croissants in a café. Deep sadness and confusion came over me. Various bus drivers told me how to get to the Grand Piano. I spent my days there reading job listings and drawing pictures in my sketchbook. None of the listed jobs sounded right for me.

For the next few nights, I slept in my car. During the day, I asked for work in shops and bookstores I had applied in a month or so before. I couldn't remember what manager had told me what or what day it was. It was getting harder every day just to get through the day because I felt constantly threatened, like some disaster might happen. Sudden panics came over me often and I had nightmares. I dreamed that I was crashing down to the ground in an elevator with broken cables. And my recurring dream, that I had had for years, of being hit and killed by a tornado happened again. I was not taking any medications and was feeling extremely confused and anxious.

One night, about five days later, I was walking to my car to go to sleep when, suddenly, a friendly black man who had bought me a cup of hot chocolate in the corner doughnut shop approached me.

"How are you?", he asked, his eyes glowing in the light of the pink street lamps which shone under the full moon.

"Horrible. I have no place to sleep tonight", I replied.

"You can stay at my place. I'll make sure you're alright", he replied with an innocent, compassionate expression.

I wondered if I should accept. I didn't know him from the man in the moon. A bus rolled up with a screeching sound and I followed him on. The full moon glowed like a pearl, captivating me with its lustrous beauty. We rumbled through the desolate streets to his neighborhood. The ugliness of his building appalled me as I followed him through maze like corridors full of smashed out windows, trash lined halls and grimy, graffiti covered walls.

"Don't talk to anyone here. The man who lives next door is very rough. I don't want him to know you're here", he said protectively.

"Okay. I won't", I replied. I followed him into his small, grungy ghetto. One of his windows was broken. A cold draft sent a shiver through me as I stared at the glass scattered on the ugly, cement floor which was caked with layers of dirt. I had no one else to call, to visit, to talk to. I couldn't remember how to get back to the halfway house and I had enraged everyone who had tried to help me. I had had the same effect on my parents and siblings and was beginning to believe that I was the stupid, crazy person people had said I was. If I could just survive through the night, maybe I would find something to smile about the next day.

"You can use my jacket as a blanket", he said with concern as I sat on the soiled, thin mat on the grimy, hard floor.

Handing me a pillow, he wished me pleasant dreams. Then, he turned off the bare, glaring light bulb. My mind raced with thoughts about my mother.

I longed to call her and sob and have her listen. But she always hurried off the phone.

Now that she had bought herself a condo at the beach with my trust fund money, I hoped she was happy. It gave me great joy to help her with the three thousand dollars my grandfather had given me. I wanted her to find freedom from my father and his cruel domination. She could paint and get back some self esteem which she needed. I imagined her eating her grits and omelet, drinking coffee and basking in the sun which streamed gloriously through the stained glass windows of the opulent hotel a stone's throw away from the ocean. After she finished her sumptuous, leisurely breakfast she would drive to her pretty condo and paint watercolor masterpieces for the rest of the day.

Now, however, I wanted to pour my troubles out to her. Yet, fear kept me from calling her. As I shivered in the cold, longing for sleep, an agonizing desperation screamed deep within me.

A choir of cheerful singing birds woke me the next morning.

"I've got to go find a job", I blurted, jumping up suddenly. I'd been too timid to talk to any managers for several weeks because I felt haggard and disgusting. My friend followed me as I walked outside through the empty, alienating halls of the concrete zoo. We walked down the long flight of stairs and out into the sunlight. Suddenly, I caught the worried, protective gaze of an older, overweight black woman. "You shouldn't be staying in there. They'll eat you alive", she said, her eyes moist with concern.

I hadn't even thought about the danger, though I felt the creepiness of the desperation emanating through the night. Somehow, meeting the threshold of death was leading me somewhere though I didn't know where.

My friend and I continued to walk toward the street which screamed with the sound of passing traffic. My entire body became wooden when I noticed a police officer standing in front of his car, staring at us sternly. His accusing eyes looked through us as he stood arrogantly, his silver badge gleaming in the sunlight.

"What were you doing in there?", he asked, looking up and down our bodies with scorn.

"My friend needed a place to stay so I let her stay with me", my friend replied, not able to conceal the fear in his voice.

"Let me see your I.D.", he demanded.

His eyes cut through me with intimidating authority as I fumbled nervously through my purse. I found my driver's license and handed it to him. I did not tell him that I was new in town and using my car for sleep while I searched for work.

"You're under arrest", he growled, locking steel handcuffs around my wrists and the wrists of my friend. I gritted my teeth in anger as I resisted the urge to kick him.

"Get in the car. We're going to the police station", he ordered callously, slicing through me with his cold eyes.

We sat down in the back seat. I watched the surly officer through the metal grilling that separated us. My friend turned his head and gave me a sympathetic look. Sirens wailed through the sinister streets and traffic rushed chaotically. I stared at the ground as I followed the police officer into the station. He ordered me, in a brusque voice, to have a seat. Gritting my teeth with anger, I sat down on a hard wooden bench, observing the alienating concrete, glass and steel. A muscular, tall police officer led my friend away. He waved goodbye, with a look of helpless despondency.

A black lady led me into a room where a fat man pressed my fingers one by one into an inkpad and rolled them over white paper. Then I was led down a dreary hall into a sterile cell which glared caustically with fluorescent lights. A masculine looking woman with bleached, blond hair sneered at me cruelly.

"Take all your clothes off", she ordered, looking up and down my trembling body.

As I removed my pants, shirt and underwear my cheeks burned with embarrassment.

"Stand on the line", she ordered like a Nazi, pointing to a line of tape on the floor.

"Lean over from your waist. Lower. Lower. Okay, now spread your buttocks", she demanded. I shook like a leaf in the wind as I leaned over and spread my buttocks open.

"Wider", she barked angrily.

I strained to spread them wider, remembering a magazine article I had read about drug smugglers who carried heroin in their rectums.

"Okay. You can get dressed." Her eyes cut through me in arrogant satisfaction over the way she had stripped me of my dignity.

A tall, male police officer was waiting by the door for me. He led me to a huge, steel cage and locked me inside. Two fat, angry looking, masculine women moved their eyes up and down my body. A volcanic rage rose within me and I wanted to yell and pound my fists on the steel bars.

"Let me out of here. I don't need to be here. I need a medical test. I feel faint. Someone get me a medical test", I screamed at the top of my lungs, pacing like a caged tiger as time crawled. Three or four hours passed and I feared I would never escape the hell I had been so cruelly tossed into.

Finally, an obese, black woman with mean eyes unlocked the door, her large collection of keys clattering. For hours, I had been just an invisible insane person. No one had responded to my medical requests and now, they were glad to get rid of me. I walked down the hall to a pay phone on wobbly legs.

Suddenly, I remembered that Stan had introduced me to a nice couple in the Grand Piano. I had been living with George at the time and I wished I had asked them for help back then. I had not wanted to impose on anyone though. I kept hoping I would find a job and not be trouble for anyone. However, I had to call them now. Their names were Jim and Martha. Jim had given me their phone number and asked me to call if I ever needed anything. Luckily, I had saved his number. My hands trembled as I searched through my bag and, finally, I found it in my wallet.

I dialed the number nervously, looking around the police station. Jim's gentle voice comforted me as he said hello. I told him I had been handcuffed and locked up. Hope rose within me when he told me I could stay with them until I found a place. I walked out into the daylight, feeling grateful I was still alive.

CHAPTER 9————————————DECEMBER, 1981
I'll Get by with a Little Help from My Friends

JIM AND MARTHA GREETED ME warmly when I arrived. That night, Stan, my comedian friend, and his gorgeous girlfriend, Dot, came over. Stan looked at me with a special expression of affection which melted my heart.

"I'm going to name you tragedy. I heard about what happened. I think a dark cloud follows you around", he said, holding my hand gently.

I laughed for the first time in what seemed like eternity as we sat together eating salad, spaghetti and French bread. Martha talked about political issues and womens' problems. Both she and her boyfriend had degrees from college but neither had been able to find good jobs. They were practically starving as they barely survived on "General Assistance", a welfare program that gave people two hundred and fifty dollars a month to live on. I couldn't understand why they had been granted this benefit and I had not, only because I owned a car. Stan talked enthusiastically about a play that he and his girlfriend were rehearsing for. She smiled warmly and everything seemed to fade as I became drowsy from the wine.

I asked Martha if I could take a hot bath. She showed me to the bathroom and gave me a fresh, fluffy towel. The rush of water relaxed me as I poured some bath gel under it. Soon the tub was filled to the brim with frothy, foaming, white bubbles. I slid underneath and watched a rubber ducky float in front of me, singing "I'll get by with a little help from my friends."

Stan suddenly appeared and asked if he could get into the tub with me. My boundaries instantly dissolved and I said he could. I wondered why I had no self-respect and presumed it was just a facet of my mental illness. All I knew was that I wanted his company and his innocent face and gentle voice relaxed me.

Pulling off his clothes quickly, he slid into the tub. As we sat facing each other, a childlike innocence emanated from us and we pushed a rubber duck back and forth and played with the white, frothy bubbles. He made absolutely no sexual advances and I felt safe with him. He didn't even look at my body at all. We got out of the tub and dried off with soft, fluffy towels. He joked lightly as we pulled on our clothes. Magic filled the air for the rest of the relaxed evening as everyone talked and laughed. Stan and Dot said goodbye around midnight. I hugged them and told them I was looking forward to their play.

The next week, I went to see Stan and Dot perform in the famous Sartre play "No Exit" in a high school auditorium. They both did remarkable acting jobs, captivating the audience with their charm and good looks. People laughed and talked in the cafes as I walked back to Jim and Martha's. They were sleeping so I reclined on my thin mat on the floor quietly. I tossed and turned through the night as worries ran through my head.

The next morning, I passed a blond woman on the corner as I walked toward the Grand Piano. She handed me a piece of paper with directions to a party. Then, she offered me a puff from her marijuana pipe. The pungent aroma overpowered my senses as I inhaled. Soon, I began to fly like a balloon rising above the world. I floated down the hill and up the stairs into the apartment where Martha sat quietly on her bed reading a book. My mind swam with disjointed thoughts and scenarios of dramatic dialogues between imaginary characters. An unreal feeling came over me as though I had stepped into a different dimension. Thoughts flitted like fireflies across my blazing brain until it felt like it was on fire.

"Why do brown cows fly?" I asked Martha in the child like voice I used to use when I was seven and called strangers to heckle them on April Fools' Day. As she looked at me in bewilderment I laughed hysterically.

That evening, Jim confronted me and said that my behavior had been upsetting Martha. Part of me died as he shoved me against the wall and demanded that I leave immediately. My eyes filled with tears as I walked to the closet and picked up one of my boxes. I carried it down the stairs, opened my trunk and dropped it in. As I looked up I saw Jim charging down the stairs, his face contorted with rage. He slammed one of my boxes down into the front seat of my car. Then he strode quickly up the stairs. I followed behind him in frightened silence and finished removing my few earthly possessions from his apartment.

Tears streamed down my face as I drove down the street toward the Grand Piano. Suddenly, the sky opened up and torrents of rain started gushing down, pelting my windshield. I could barely see as I inched down the street cautiously and parked my car. Heavy, drenching rain soaked my clothes, hair and skin as I walked along the sidewalk.

The rich aroma of garlic, spices and freshly baked bread drifted into my nose as I sat at a table across from a thin, brunette woman who was stringing colorful beads together. I watched her intently as she worked diligently, completely engrossed in her task. Finally, I gathered my courage and told her I was homeless.

"You're in a crisis situation aren't you? I'll help you. You can spend the night with me", she said with warm concern.

I followed her in my car to her apartment, straining to see through the blinding rain. We walked together up her steep stairs and I sat down at her round, black kitchen table. Looking at me with motherly tenderness, she handed me a tall glass of orange juice. A pleasing aroma floated into my nose, filling my grumbling stomach with anticipation, as she brought a big, black pot of soup to a boil.

"Have you ever had miso soup?", she asked, sweetly, stirring the steaming pot.

"No. I haven't", I replied.

She set a steaming bowl before me. I ate in grateful silence, feeling my heart soften and my stomach gurgle happily. The delicious, unusual flavor satisfied me as I listened to her talk,

"I make jewelry and sell it on the street. I got a license from the city. I set up a table on Fisherman's Wharf. I don't make much money but people love my jewelry", she said. Her face was thin and drawn and her wet hair was plastered close to her head.

"What an interesting way to make a living. Where do you buy your supplies?"

"I order them from different catalogues I get in the mail. It's hard being a street artist." Her voice rose with a frustrated sound of weariness as though she missed the carefree days of childhood.

"Maybe I can sell my paintings on the street", I said hopefully.

"Yeah. You can do that. It takes a while to get a license. You have to fill out a lot of paperwork", she replied, drumming her fingers on the table restlessly.

"I'm sleepy. I need to take a shower and go to sleep", I said holding my hand over my mouth as I yawned widely. She took my hand and led me into her light, pink bathroom.

"Do you have lice?", she asked, sweeping the length of my body with her eyes.

"Oh, no", I replied, looking down as my cheeks burned with shame.

"You can stay in my daughter's room. Here's a nightgown and a towel. You can take a shower and relax. The shower head adjusts to make the pressure stronger", she said, pulling back the curtain and showing me how to turn it.

"I almost feel like you could be my daughter. My real daughter is a cocaine addict and our relationship is very strained. I hardly ever see her", she said sadly. Then she turned and walked out of the bathroom, closing the door gently behind her. Soon, she returned and handed me a soft, flannel night gown.

As I stepped out of my clothes and turned the shower on, I contemplated about how protected by the law of grace I was. The warm steam floated around me in an ethereal embrace like the soft touch of an angel. My muscles relaxed as warm water massaged my aching head and shoulders. The shampoo glowed light green as I poured it into my hand. I rubbed it into my hair, working up a rich, luxurious lather. Serenity flowed through me as I rinsed it out.

I stepped out and dried myself off with the fluffy, baby blue towel. Pulling on the soft, flannel nightgown, I felt like a child again. The bed soothed me as I settled into the cluster of pillows and the firm, wide mattress. I pulled the fresh smelling, white sheet over me and drifted off into a deep, peaceful sleep. I floated through the night in a blissful nirvana.

I awoke the next morning to the sound of my new mother knocking on the door. She invited me to come into the kitchen and eat breakfast. I yawned and stretched my arms to the ceiling. As I dressed slowly, I relived the peaceful sensations that had carried me through the night. When I arrived in the kitchen, I smiled at a tall, sturdy looking man with dark brown hair sitting at the table.

"This is my friend Bob. He is a research scientist", she said, putting her arm around his shoulder.

"Nice to meet you", I said, extending my hand to shake his.

"What would you like for breakfast? I've got granola and corn flakes and I will cook you some pancakes if you'd like that." She patted her friend's shoulder. He touched her hand.

"I'd like some granola", I replied, feeling deeply touched as I watched her pour my cereal.

"How long have you been living in San Francisco?", I asked the man, looking at him with curiosity.

"I've been here five years. I don't know if I'll stay or not. I don't really feel like I've found my niche yet", he replied.

"Yeah. I'm trying to find that too. I don't know if this is the place for me. I just moved here because a friend of mine told me it was a great place", I said, twirling my hair nervously.

My friend smiled as she set a bowl of granola in front of me. She asked if I'd like some herbal tea or orange juice. I responded that I would like some orange juice. My eyes widened with delight as she pushed a big glass toward me. She sat down next to her friend.

"I've been thinking about your situation and I've decided that I would be willing to rent you a room here for two hundred dollars a month. You can come and go as you please. I stay busy myself, working as a street artist and making jewelry. It's not easy being a street artist. I work very hard."

"I appreciate that. I would like to move in. I'd really like to play the piano. Would that be alright?", I asked beseechingly, feeling like a child.

"Do you think I would let you live here and not let you play the piano?", she asked, her voice rising in exasperation.

My shoulders tensed in anxiety. I hadn't meant to offend her. My hand trembled as I raised a spoonful of granola to my mouth. After a long, uncomfortable silence my friend looked at me with an expression of mistrust.

"I think your behavior is strange. I don't think that you are really honest", she said, looking at me with narrowed eyes like a mother reprimanding a naughty child.

"Well, everyone who has ever known me has told me what an honest person I am", I replied in self-defense.

"I think you're cash register honest."

I sat in silence, listening to her talk to her friend as I ate my granola. When I finished eating, I went into the next room and played the piano. After a while, she and her friend came in. I stood up and sat down on a beanbag chair and looked at them. Enjoying their company, I relaxed into the moment as we all sat and talked. I hoped that her feelings toward me would change but, after a while, she told me that she had decided it would be better for me to not live there. I wondered what I had done wrong. As I left, I thanked her for her hospitality and wished her the best of luck.

I drove to The Grand Piano, my only oasis of hope in my gypsy life. A tall, slender man with blond hair that fell below his shoulders looked at me and said "hello" as I approached the entrance. He seemed particularly glad to see me and I wondered why. His gentle, calm nature put me at ease as I told him my name and he told me his. We shook hands warmly. When he asked me to walk down the street to McDonald's with him, I quickly agreed.

People behind the counter scurried back and forth, scooping French fries and making change, as my friend ordered a cheeseburger, fries and a coke. I ordered fries and a strawberry milkshake and he kindly paid. As we sat down at a table by a large, plate glass window I watched people pass by on the street. My friend unwrapped his cheeseburger slowly. I watched his rainbow colored rings sparkle beautifully in the sunlight.

"Those are beautiful rings you're wearing", I commented, raising a handful of fries to my mouth.

"Oh, thank you. They're opals", he responded, taking a bite out of his cheeseburger and looking at me with eyes that glowed with the deep blue of the ocean. With his long, blond hair, his delicate way of moving and his shining jewelry he radiated femininity.

"I've been sleeping in my car. I'm looking for a place to live", I said, blushing with shame.

"Oh, you can come stay with me. I live in Berkeley", he responded.

I stared at the table in frightened silence.

"I haven't been to the ocean in a long time. Would you like to ride the bus to Stinson Beach?", he asked.

"Yeah. That sounds like fun. I can use some positive ions", I responded.

He took a long sip of his coke and looked with compassion into my eyes. He reminded me of a flower child from the sixties with his open, caring nature. It was as though I had known him forever. We finished eating and dumped our trash into the trash can.

The sidewalk bustled with energetic dogs with wagging tails and roller skating youngsters. A radiant sun blazed down on us as we crossed the street to the bus stop. His calm, loving vibrations soothed me as we rode the bus to Stinson beach.

The driver wished us a good day as we departed. We chatted with lightness as we walked down a long flight of concrete stairs. I pulled my shoes off and sunk my feet into the warm, soft sand. Crashing waves and squawking seagulls vibrated through me. Pleasure rolled through my body as the sand massaged my feet. We walked into the water, splashing it and watching it glisten as it flew up in arcs.

After a while, we walked to some concrete bleachers and sat down. I reclined on my side and leaned my head against my hand. As I stared out at the ocean, tears began rolling down my face.

"Are you alright?", he asked.

"Yeah. I'm alright", I replied, wiping the tears away self-consciously.

"I know things are going to get better for you. Everything will fall into place. I have a sort of intuition about people and I know that you are a good person. You are going to be successful. My powers of perception come from having taken a lot of acid. I have seen some incredibly fantastic visions while I was tripping. I can see DNA strands. I make my living selling heroin. I would like to have a room mate. I haven't had one in a long time. I have lived with men and women in the past. I go both ways. We could live together. We could be friends or lovers, whichever you choose. I'm sure we would get along fine", he said.

I was indecisive. I had never known anyone who was involved in crime but I had read stories about people who got locked up just for being a friend of a drug dealer. I walked silently with him across the sand and up some long stairs. We walked into a building and down to a basement room which glowed with the lights of pinball machines. Ringing sounds filled the air as we played and the enchantment with life I had known as a child emerged within me.

After a while, we rode the bus back to the Haight Ashbury. As we walked down the sidewalk near the Grand Piano, I observed various eccentrically dressed characters. Suddenly, he rolled his hair up in a bun, put a hat over his head and began walking faster

"Whew! He didn't recognize me. He's been on my case for a while. He wants to get me arrested", he said triumphantly, after passing a gray haired, serious looking man..

Maybe drug dealing was a crime, but he gave me nothing but peace, love and the reassurance that I was important. I bit my lip, trying to decide whether or not to follow him to his home. We walked and talked a while. Finally, I said that I better not live with him.

The sun descended as he told me good-bye. I wrung my hands in regret as I watched him walk away down the long, lonely sidewalk. A strong urge to run and catch up with him rose in me like a wave but I remained glued to the ground, unable to make a decision.

My mind raced and the ground seemed to move beneath me as I walked to the Grand Piano. As I listened to people converse, I felt alienated and isolated. I'd made a fatal mistake to not take my kind friend's offer. Sadness sapped all my energy as I analyzed myself. I couldn't accept help because I felt undeserving. I felt undeserving of love or joy. Time crawled slowly until the sky turned black. The staff members began putting chairs up on the tables and closing for the night.

I longed for my friend as I walked down the empty sidewalk. When I reached my car, I crawled into the front seat and locked all the doors. The seat made a thudding sound as I pushed it back. I worried through the miserable, sleepless night.

The clatter of passing traffic rattled through my eardrums the next morning. My stomach grumbled with hunger. I wished I could afford to buy an omelet as I walked to The Grand Piano, staring at the sidewalk. Sitting at a table, looking forlorn, I listened to people and searched them with my empty eyes. Someone gave me a left over plate of potato wedges.

I went into the bathroom and washed my face. Then, standing tall, I walked through the streets, asking managers in various places if they could hire me. They still didn't have any openings. The day passed quickly and, as it was beginning to grow dark, I met the eyes of a thin, brunette man sitting on the sidewalk playing a guitar. I stopped to listen and I met his eyes shyly.

"My name is Darryl. How is everything going?", he asked me.

"Horrible. I've been sleeping in my car", I replied, hugging my arms around my waist protectively.

"Sleeping in your car?" His mouth dropped open in disbelief.

"Yeah. It's very uncomfortable", I replied, looking down at the grimy sidewalk.

"It's not only uncomfortable. It's dangerous. Why don't you come stay with me?" He rested his arm on the top of his guitar as he gazed at me, his eyebrows knitted together in concern. I imagined some poor person finding my murdered carcass in my car after I slept there another night. His offer might be my last one.

"Thank you. I appreciate that." He did not convey the warmth that Brian had. Yet, he seemed to be my last hope for survival. I was unable to think of any alternative choice. Powerless feelings filled me as my mind chattered chaotically. I followed him down the dark street and up a steep hill to his place. We walked up several flights of stairs into a tiny, drab room with a dingy, brown carpet. He showed me his "library" which consisted of a row of books on the floor. A run down dresser stood by the door and a small, thin mat lay underneath a window covered with a torn, black, pull down shade.

I sat on the floor and he sat on his mat. Then, with morbid seriousness, he talked about the decline of the country until the wee hours of the morning. His monotone voice droned on and on. I observed his skinny body, balding head and small, hard eyes framed by wire-rimmed glasses. He was hardly the man of my dreams. I was relieved when he finally stopped talking and turned out the light.

I crawled into my sleeping bag and pulled the zipper up to my neck, like a tortoise withdrawing into her shell. After going through endless, awkward contortions to wrestle my jeans off, I finally got free of them and put them out on the floor beside me. Longing for sleep desperately, I worried through the night.

CHAPTER 10————DECEMBER 1981, JANUARY, FEBRUARY, MARCH 1982

Rabbit in a Trap

THE NEXT MORNING, DARRYL STOOD up in his underwear. He pulled a pair of beige pants on as he hummed a tune to himself.

"I'm going out to work. I show tourists views of the sea lions through my telescope." He ran a comb quickly through his hair.

"Oh, that's interesting", I replied, holding my sleeping bag up around my neck.

"Yeah. My office is a cliff overlooking the Pacific Ocean." He pulled on his coat and lifted an orange bag containing his telescope over his shoulder. His footsteps echoed in the stairwell as he walked down to the street. I stared in the mirror lost in thought for a while. Humming to myself, I walked into the rundown, tiny shower stall and pulled off my clothes. Warm water massaged me as I rubbed shampoo into my hair and worked up a rich lather. I stepped out and dried myself off with a fluffy, thick towel.

I walked back to Darryl's room and sat down in front of his mirror. As I brushed my hair, I wondered what I should do next. Noticing he didn't have a telephone, I wondered if he was a hermit. Sitting on his mat gazing out the window, I watched people walking by on the sidewalk, carrying shopping bags or leading adorable dogs. A crystal hanging in the window made rainbows dance on the white walls. A stack of tapes caught my eye. When I found one of George Harrison, I put it in the tape player eagerly. As I listened to him sing My Sweet Lord time stood still.

Darryl came in late in the afternoon. His sunburned face exuded anger as he complained about how snobby the tourists were. He suggested we walk down the street to a restaurant. Fresh air filled my lungs as I breathed deeply, following him down the hill. A man with a foreign accent asked what we wanted from behind a glass case filled with various foods. Darryl recommended the piroshky, a Russian piece of dough filled with meat and sauce. We carried our wrapped dinners to a table. Listening to the rushing sound of speeding cars and honking horns, I watched people in colorful clothes walk by outside the huge plate glass window.

"San Francisco is an energy center. People come here from everywhere looking for an alternative lifestyle. I come from a very conservative background. My father was a lawyer and we had the house in the suburbs, two cars and two chickens boiling on the stove always. But I could see that my parents were not happy. They were deadened by the artificiality of that life. The only way to be free is to be really rich or really poor. The government in this country has become so corrupt it is unbelievable. They're trying to make slaves of everyone." A serious expression filled his lined, sun reddened face as his dark, beady eyes pierced through me. The bald part of his head shone in the setting sun.

I didn't believe what he was saying about the government. I wondered why he was so suspicious when he lived in the best country in the world. Yet, I feigned interest and listened to him talk about the downfall of the country until the early morning again. When I started yawning, he asked me if I was ready for him to turn out the light. I said that I was and, sheepishly, I slid inside my sleeping bag and wrestled my tight blue jeans off.

The morning sun filled me with hope as I woke. I wished my friend a good day as he got ready to show tourists views of the sea lions lounging on the rocks for a quarter a look. A vulnerability showed through his serious, stiff exterior. Conflicting feelings battled within me. I felt suspicious and mistrustful yet, when he returned to me after a hard day of work and treated me to dinner, my heart softened toward him.

During the day, when he was out at work, panic attacks came suddenly upon me. My mind raced and my heart galloped with terror as I thought about going out and applying for jobs. I wondered if medication would help. Yet I cringed at the thought. I had done well without it since June 1980. My father insisted that I had a chemical imbalance which the medication corrected. However, no one had ever proved that.

Finally, after a few weeks passed by, and the new year, 1982, began, I gathered the courage to venture out. A radiant golden sun warmed my face and body as I walked down the street. The Grand Piano was vibrant with conversation. The aroma of herbal teas pleased me as I ordered a cup of ginger tea. A smiling waiter handed it to me. I sat down at a table and met the eyes of a woman with long, dark hair and big, dark eyes. A comforting, gentle energy emanated from her. Her name was Grace she told me sweetly.

"Would you like to take a walk?", Grace asked, her dark, liquid eyes shining with compassion.

"Yes. I would", I replied.

As we walked down the street toward the Golden Gate Park, peoples' eyes seemed to cut through me with mockery. Suddenly, great sobs of sadness tightened my guts and tears trickled down my face. She took my hand gently and led me to an entryway to a building. The concrete felt hard as I sat down next to her. I had a desperate need for someone, anyone to like me because I was convinced that I was unlovable and undeserving.

"I feel lost. I don't like living with this guy I hardly know but I don't know what else to do. I have no money to get my own place. My parents won't send me the money they owe me. I can't find a job and I can't go on like this." I buried my face in my hands, feeling my hair become wet with tears.

I wanted my mother to have the condo at the beach she had desired for over twenty years. She deserved to be free from my mean father. So I had jumped at the opportunity to help manifest her dream by loaning her three thousand dollars that my grandfather gave me. However, I had not discussed it or gotten anything in writing except a letter from my parents' lawyer stating that they owed me three thousand dollars. Now, I wanted to be important to my mother. It had hurt me when she changed the subject when I asked her about my money.

"You're going to be alright. Don't worry. Things are hard for you now but they will get better. You just need to have a home and some friends and relax. Everything is going to work out. You're a beautiful, loving woman and you can get anything you want."

Sunlight sparkled on the trees and colorful flowers as we walked through the park watching children play. People enjoyed picnics on sumptuously spread blankets under the shady, luxurious trees. She told me that her father had left her family when she was very young and that her mother had supported her, her sister and brother by working as a waitress. After walking for a while, we returned to The Grand Piano and drank cool glasses of iced tea while we listened to a classical pianist play.

"I can't go back there", I said.

"We can get a place together. I get a regular welfare check and you will find a job. We can go in with a friend of mine and get a house together on the beach. We'll have a great time." Her eyes glowed with optimism and kindness.

The sun descended, casting a golden glow and painting the sky with pink streaks. The rumble of passing cars vibrated through my bones as we climbed the hill to my rescuer's place. He was sitting on his thin mat watching the news on his tiny T.V. when we walked in. She greeted him in a friendly way and sat down on the floor next to me. As they chatted about the weather, he lit his marijuana pipe. I watched them both inhale. When Darryl handed me the pipe, I inhaled deeply. The smoke warmed my mouth as the earthy taste seeped into my taste buds. A sudden feeling of euphoria rushed through me as everything around me glowed with a magical quality. Time stood still as I pondered about how precious my life was. Light shimmered beautifully on every object I looked at as love moved like a cosmic wave through my heart. The feeling of bliss continued for some time. But it was broken when, suddenly, a torrent of tears gushed out of me.

"Am I alive? I think I have died. There are holes all through me. Am I alive? Am I alive?" I sobbed uncontrollably, running my hands around my body which seemed to be full of black holes.

"You're alive and well and everything is going to be fine", Grace said. Her face glowed with love as she took my hand and held it between her hands. I gazed into her eyes feeling comfort move through me. The peace of sleep beckoned me. I withdrew into the privacy of my sleeping bag and tried to sleep but, instead, ended up worrying most of the night.

I woke to the sounds of Darryl and my female friend arguing. I combed my hair with my fingers as I listened.

"Are you fucking our little friend?" Grace accused, looking into his eyes with disdain burning on her face. Suddenly, she stormed out of the room as sparks of anger flew around her. I wanted to run after her. I hadn't even thought to write down her name and phone number. My mind was swimming in a fog. A feeling of doom crashed down on me like a ton of bricks. I looked the other way as Darryl dressed.

"Well, I'm gonna go out and hassle with the asshole tourists. I swear I don't think I can take these phony yuppies any more. All they ever think about is their BMW or their Gucci clothes. They look at me like I'm something that crawled out from under a rock. Their materialistic values are so sickening. I think one of these days I'm going to punch one of them out."

He lifted his telescope and walked out of the room, closing the door solidly behind him. As his footsteps pounded down the stairs and faded into silence, I longed for my motherly friend. It would be heaven to live with her in a house by the ocean.

I passed the days reading and listening to music. Sometimes, I went and looked for Grace in The Grand Piano yet never saw her. I felt hurt that she would abandon me after her heartfelt suggestion that we could live together. Living with Darryl was frightening yet I acted kind when he came home from work and leaned against his pillow, looking exhausted. A pungent aroma filled the air as he inhaled his marijuana. When he passed me the pipe, I told him a doctor had said I should not smoke it.

"Oh, that's ridiculous. Marijuana is wonderful. It's my teacher. I've learned incredible things from it. It gives you insight and understanding and opens you up to new levels of awareness. All the great mystics and artists throughout history have used it to expand their minds. Edgar Allen Poe wrote his famous poem "The Raven" while he was stoned", he said persuasively.

"Okay. Just a little." I held it to my lips and inhaled a small amount. "Authority figures are always trying to convince creative people that drugs are bad. But the Native Americans understood the importance of them. They used peyote and mushrooms to experience heightened states of consciousness. They knew that nature has an innate wisdom that can be tapped into. They thanked the earth for giving them substances that brought them closer to God. But this society is repressive and it doesn't want people to be free thinkers. I was put into prison for a year because I was caught with drugs", he said resentfully.

My muscles tensed into tight knots of anxiety as I wondered if he was telling me the whole truth. He could have murdered someone. I had turned down Brian's offer of help because he was a drug dealer. Yet, he was a much better choice than Darryl because he was warm and soft hearted. Maybe I was afraid of love and maybe Darryl's lack of warmth felt familiar because it reminded me of the emotional distance of my father. I tried to forgive myself for my bad decision. I had been afraid someone might murder me as I slept in my car.

"Let's go take a walk through the Golden Gate Park", he said, stretching his arms over his head and standing up, yawning.

I followed him down the stairs, down the steep hill and through the Haight Ashbury. Characters of every size and shape careened by me, smiling and beckoning like clowns in a circus sideshow. They contracted and expanded as though they were being magnified by a fun house mirror. My feet rippled with sensual pleasure as I walked over vibrating ridges that massaged them benevolently. I swayed dizzily, like I was falling through the sky on a huge Ferris Wheel. The sound of rackets hitting speeding tennis balls buzzed through my ears as we passed a large, green tennis court filled with white-clad players. People walking by looked like cartoon characters with funny clothes and faces. My body began to heave convulsively in uncontrollable laughter.

"Oh my God. I don't believe it. You mean everyone is a cartoon character", I said with amazed laughter as though I had realized a profound, philosophical truth.

"Yeah. It's true", Darryl responded, smiling with amusement.

I watched intently as a short, thin man walked by in skimpy tennis shorts looking like a cartoon character. I walked over to him and stared deeply into his eyes, rubbing my elbows together frantically.

"Do you have any peanut oil?" I asked, obsessed with the strong desire to oil my elbows. Time froze as I stared into his face and watched his expression change from kindness to fear and, then, to utter revulsion. He hurried away like he was escaping from a leper. Suddenly, an intense feeling of paranoia froze me into place. I felt my illness gripping me. I looked around for Darryl who had walked ahead of me. My breathing stopped when I realized he was gone. My heart pounded as though it might jump out of my chest as a wave of terror rolled through me. Suddenly, I felt all alone in a strange world with no idea where I was or how to find my way back to any safety. The urge to empty my bladder overcame me and I began to look around for a public bathroom. On the far side of the large baseball field, I saw a small, green building. I walked quickly toward it, watching the golden-red, glowing sun descend through the pink streaked sky.

Luckily, there was a restroom inside. I ducked into the building. The earth spun beneath me, rushing at unprecedented speed through the vast cosmos, a tiny speck in the grand celestial orchestration. I rocked back and forth like a person on a ferris wheel as I staggered into the toilet stall, hanging onto the door. I fumbled nervously with my pants and managed to pull them down and sit on the toilet seat before I wet myself. A trickling sound vibrated in my eardrums as I sat staring at the filthy floor, too frightened to move. Each moment seemed like eternity as I sat there frozen in time, zooming like a comet on an eternal flight through the galaxies. It would soon be dark. I pulled my pants on and stood up to hurry home. A sudden panic immobilized me as I walked out of the stall. I dropped to the floor, and brought my legs up to my chest in a fetal position. I hugged my legs with my arms as I rocked back and forth in a terrified stupor. Images of the earth being blown apart by nuclear bombs splintered my mind. Suddenly, I felt the presence of a man sitting in front of me.

"What are you doing here? Are you alright?" He looked deeply into my eyes and touched my chin protectively. I tried to respond but couldn't make a sound come out of my mouth.

"Where do you live? Let me see your identification." He spoke urgently with a look of concern on his face. I stared at him, still too terrified to respond or move.

"I'm trying to help you. You need to get out of here", he said slapping my cheek several times.

I watched him rummage through my handbag, emptying all the contents onto the dirty floor. He pulled me by the arm and led me outside, then walked quickly into the distance, disappearing like a transparent character on a movie screen. My legs wobbled weakly underneath me as I walked across the endless field of green grass, watching the fiery red sun dropping like a ball, getting smaller and smaller by the second. I walked faster and faster determined to get home.

Suddenly, a threatening presence appeared in front of me. I held my breath in terror as I looked up into the cruel, narrowed eyes of a tall man wearing a wool hat. He dangled my car keys in front of my face.

"Here are your car keys. You'll have to get them from me. You can't do it, can you?", he badgered in a mocking tone. I followed him as he walked backward into a wooded area which was thick with tall trees. Darkness fell as I grabbed for my keys.

"See this?" He put a knife in front of my eyes and, as I stared at the razor sharp edge gleaming in the moonlight, he unzipped his pants.

"Suck my dick", he demanded in a voice that curdled my blood.

I lowered my head to his penis as he held the sharp knife against the back of my neck. Taking the firm, warm flesh inside my mouth, I moved my tongue rapidly over its tip and sides. As I went through the motions, a sensation of unreality came over me as though I was floating outside of myself.

"Do it right or I'll kill you", he threatened repeatedly, jabbing the knife against my neck.

Any moment, his knife might plunge deep into my flesh and I would be left to bleed to death. I moved my tongue around his penis, conjuring all the skill I could. I would do anything to get through this alive. I concentrated on giving him maximum pleasure while my overwhelmed mind raced with visions of blood pouring down my body. My heart galloped like a wild horse out of control. Time stood still as I prayed to God to please keep me alive. Suddenly, he pushed me back against the hard ground.

"Please don't get me pregnant", I pleaded helplessly.

He looked at me like I was a venomous snake with no right to live as he pulled my blue jeans off. Then, with a quick, forceful movement, he ripped the front of my shirt in half.

"That's what you get bitch", he snarled, curling his lip in contempt. He forced his knife between my breasts and sliced my bra in half. Then, he shot off into the darkness.

Trembling like a rubber band, I stood up and pulled my pants on. I ran with every drop of energy I had through the dark night as tears streamed down my face. When I arrived at the bright, colored lights shining in the Haight Ashbury, my isolation became intensified by the sound of happy people talking and laughing in the cafes. Like a block of ice, I shuffled into a crowded café. Suddenly, I recognized Dan, the tall, dark man from England who had come to my small gathering at Taylor's apartment before he threw me out. I trembled as I sat down beside him.

"What's wrong?", he asked, his eyes widening with concern as he tightened his grip around his tea cup.

"I got held at knife point", I replied in a zombie like voice.

"That's horrible. Why don't you come and stay with Tim and I tonight. I've been camping out on his floor and he's got an extra sleeping bag you can use." He turned to look at his friend, Tim, who sat beside him. He nodded in agreement, looking at me protectively.

"Yeah. Come stay with us. We'll take care of you." Tim put his arm on my shoulder in a brotherly, compassionate way. I hesitated, hoping Darryl was worrying and waiting for me to come home. But I didn't trust him. I needed to make some new friends so I wasn't totally dependent on him. Besides, I was too afraid to walk to his place in the dark. And I felt my illness taking me over. Feelings of helplessness and hopelessness consumed me. My mind raced with chaos as I pinched my thighs to be sure I was still there. My only desire was to just stay alive through one more night.

The three of us piled into the cab that Tim drove to make a living. He drove us to his small apartment as I sat in silence, hugging my waist. Lost in amazement that I was still alive, I followed my two friends up the long stairs into the small apartment. Tim handed me a sleeping bag and I slid into it gratefully. Images of my attacker threatening me with his knife flashed through my mind as I tossed and turned all night.

Dan left for work early in the morning. I wished he was there as I sat tensely at the kitchen table watching Tim cook breakfast for me. Everything felt like a dream, as though I had died and was observing my life from the spirit world. I admired his intelligence as I listened to him talk about astrology. My curiosity burned eagerly as he pulled his ephemera off of the shelf and looked up my birth chart.

"Your Aries nature makes you very impulsive. I'm sure you must notice yourself doing things on the spur of the moment and taking risks a lot. This side of your nature makes you interesting and fun but it can also get you into a lot of trouble."

He put a plate of warm, steaming pancakes in front of me. I slathered them with butter and maple syrup and put a forkful into my mouth, swooning over the delicious, sweet taste. He sat down at the table and began eating his pancakes, glancing at his ephemera in between bites.

"Your Moon in Leo makes you passionate and dramatic and good at projecting an image to the public. It makes you a good performer", he said.

His attention made me feel special. Though I'd never taken astrology seriously, I was fascinated by it. I told him about my desire to experience the energy of individual planets as we finished eating. I helped him clean up, thanked him for the delicious meal and then went into the bathroom. As I brushed my teeth and washed my face, I saw the silver, flashing steel of the knife and blood pouring down my body in the moonlight. I walked like a sleepwalker into the main area.

Tim was sitting on his small mattress on the floor stark naked, looking intently at me. I averted my eyes in disbelief as he rolled a pink condom over his erect penis. When he commanded me to come over to him I obeyed fearfully. I wanted to run yet, as he pulled me toward him, I became limp like a noodle. As easily as a pancake falling out of a well greased pan, I plopped down onto his lusty lap. His large, warm hands caressed my back as he guided his hard penis into my vagina. I closed my eyes in shame, unable to accept the wanton woman I had become, feeling desperate to be free of my crippling illness forever.

"Hey. You're good", he said, stroking my back. He must have had some compassion because, in about thirty seconds he pulled out of me. I felt grateful that he had not fucked me roughly and repeatedly. He hadn't beaten me so it wasn't that bad I rationalized. Still, I felt humiliated to the core

I retreated to the kitchen table and read his ephemera. He told me goodbye and headed out to drive his cab. I stared at the wall and pondered all day, wondering how I was going to put together the pieces of my shattered life. When he came home from work later, I sat at the kitchen table listening to him talk about astrology.

"I don't understand how the planets could really influence a person's personality", I said in bemused curiosity.

"Because you're ignorant", he replied in a condescending tone that stabbed me like a knife.

Unable to speak up for myself, I watched him cook dinner for me. Then, I ate tacos with him, listening politely. As I helped him clean up, I longed for some real friends. Finally, sweet sleep released me from my misery.

CHAPTER 11 ——————————— MARCH, APRIL 1982
I'm Not a Nut. I'm <u>Not</u> a Nut

SUN STREAMED THROUGH THE WINDOWS the next morning. Tim told me that he had seen Darryl, who rescued me from sleeping in my car, in the Haight Ashbury. They had both decided that it would be good for me to go into the local university clinic where I could talk with a psychiatrist. He said that Darryl had gotten a doctor to agree to admit me. I remembered the kind doctor who had given me therapy three times a week when I was seventeen and looked forward to someone caring for me again. I had no money to pay for it and I made the assumption that they gave free services to the indigent.

I gathered some clothes and my lucky elephant. Tory, the mother of a man I had gone on a date with in college had given it to me. She had been supportive to me when I went to live with my "corrective" family after I spent ten weeks on the psychiatric ward after my horrendous study abroad summer. I followed him outside to his cab and sat down in the front seat. I bit my lip with anxiety as he turned the key in the ignition. The motor began to roar. Images of being drugged up and sitting around all day staring into space, wearing slovenly clothes, moved through my mind. I had already wasted enough of my life that way. However, I was powerless and incapable of getting a job and supporting myself in the dog eat dog world. My illness had me trapped with my back against the wall once again.

"Don't worry. You'll be with a select group of fine people. You'll be well taken care of and you'll come out a lot stronger than you were when you went in. You're a great person and everything is going to get better for you,"

Tim said as he drove through the roaring traffic. He pulled the cab over to the curb, looked directly into my eyes and wished me the best of luck. I wondered if he would call me in a few days and ask me to marry him. Retreating into a world of fantasy was a facet of my illness and it triggered memories of earlier imaginary thinking. As I walked up the long flight of stairs to the hospital I clutched my lucky elephant. It was a few days before the beginning of April, 1982 and I was about to turn twenty five.

My mind ran wild with disjointed, racing, kaleidoscope thoughts as I tried to get the receptionist's attention. Finally, she looked at me. I told her I needed to be admitted. She replied curtly that she couldn't let me in without a note from a doctor. I envisioned another sleepless night on a park bench. My attacker may have stolen my car since he had the keys.

I held my arms out in front of me and started screaming frantically, "My veins are collapsing. My veins are collapsing." As my illness squeezed the life out of me, she looked down at her desk in disinterest.

"Help me please. I got raped last night. I have nowhere to go", I wailed, searching her heartless eyes for sympathy.

"You have to go to the Rape Crisis Center", she said coldly.

"I don't know how to get there", I replied in confusion.

"You can catch the bus in front of the hospital and it will take you most of the way. You'll have to transfer to another bus which will stop right in front of the center. Just ask the driver and he'll tell you where to transfer", she said, handing me a yellow pamphlet which described the center.

The revolving glass door spun around. I walked down the stairs to the sidewalk clutching my lucky elephant like it was my only hope. The smell of carbon monoxide entered my nose as the bus heaved to a stop. The driver smiled as I climbed on. In a whisper, I asked him to tell me where to transfer. He patiently told me where to get off and which bus to transfer to, handing me a transfer.

Hovering above my body, I climbed the steep stairs of the Rape Crisis Center. I'd never heard of such a place. A brunette lady with shoulder length hair asked me to sign in. I sat down in a soft chair and waited until a Jamaican woman with gentle eyes walked toward me. I followed her into a small room and sat down on the sofa. As she held my hand gently and looked sympathetically into my eyes, I mumbled my story, staring at the floor in shame. She wrote on a pad of paper while she listened. Then she instructed me to relax while she called the police.

After a while, they arrived. Avoiding their eyes, I told them I had been held at knife point. I could not muster the nerve to tell them about Tim because I assumed they would treat me like a whore. They asked me many questions, and, after filling out a report, they drove me to the YMCA where I could stay for free for three nights.

A black clerk handed me a room key. A shiver ran up and down my spine as I walked to the elevator, meeting the eyes of fat, slovenly men who reeked of cigarette smoke and alcohol. As I let myself into my tiny room on the fifteenth floor I imagined that I was letting myself into my own prison cell, the one I had lived in all my life because of my illness which kept me powerless and dependent. I turned the light off and reclined back on the bed, pulling the covers over me. Hugging myself in desperation, I wondered what I should do next. Finally, sleep carried me away.

A deep torpor weighed me down the next morning as thoughts of suicide flitted through my mind. I had no pills to overdose on because I had not taken them regularly since June 1980. Suddenly, the idea of walking in front of a moving bus occurred to me. My stomach made hungry noises as I pulled on my clothes and brushed my hair. I opened the door and walked out to the hallway. The heavy, steel elevator doors opened for me and I rode down to the first floor.

The doors parted with an ominous sound. I walked out into a wasteland of red nosed, disheveled winos. Their lecherous eyes explored my body and their stench disgusted me as I walked across the grimy, marble floor and escaped into a tiny room full of vending machines. My coins clinked as I pushed them in and an orange package of peanut butter crackers dropped down. Restless energy coiled in my guts and I felt like a caged dog ready to run.

Pulling open the front door impatiently, I began walking rapidly down the sidewalk, munching on my crackers. I walked all day, except for an hour that I spent sitting in the library reading. The pain of isolation froze my veins like ice and I thought about calling my parents or sister but I felt too ashamed to tell them the condition I was in. My father had refused to send me money when I was penniless and at the mercy of a rapist in Europe. I didn't want the added pain of reaching out to him and getting rebuffed again.

I had felt sure people would think I was a whore if I told them what happened with the man I traveled with years ago, when I was studying abroad in college. He had seemed nice so I had trusted him. I was penniless and still had three weeks before my flight took me back to the United States. I had been taking an anti-depressant called Tofranil for depression and feeling no positive results—only brain fog and excessive sleep. After he had abused me I had felt numb. I had not been sure myself whether or not I had been raped because I had felt too frightened to kick him or scream at the top of my lungs.

I came back to the present moment and returned the warm "Hellos" of some Native American men on the library stairs. They invited me to go see a Cheech and Chong movie. They got me to drink some MD 20—very strong alcohol. After the movie, I jumped up and down in a drunken craze and fell on the sidewalk, twisting my knee out of joint. An ambulance took me to the emergency room, where a doctor stabilized my knee with a wrap around cast and gave me some crutches.

A kind man took me back to the YMCA when I told him I was lost. The elevator rose rapidly as I stared at the green, flashing floor numbers. Bitterness flowed through me like bile. It was a constant fight to just survive one day in this city. The land of milk and honey—what bullshit.

The sun woke me the next morning. I got dressed and rode the elevator down to the lobby. As I limped along on my crutches, I observed the people around me. Sitting on a sofa, I picked up a paper to scan the job listings. I gazed up and met the eyes of a man with thick, brown hair sitting on the sofa across from me.

"Hi. How are you?", he asked in a friendly manner.

"Oh, I could be better. I twisted my knee out of joint and it's really hurting", I responded, looking down at my wrap around Velcro cast.

"Hi. I'm Joe. I'm going over to Saint Anthony's to get breakfast. Would you like to go with me?", he asked, his tall body rising to standing position.

I imagined sweet Saint Anthony preparing breakfast for people. I followed him out of the large glass and steel door, then hobbled quickly on my crutches to keep up with him as he took long, brisk strides down the sidewalk. His thoughtlessness rattled my already overloaded nerves. We traversed up and down several steep hills until we arrived at a Gothic church. Haggard, dirty looking people lined the sidewalk for five or six blocks. They cussed, complained and argued with each other. A drunk woman with a red, swollen nose, wrinkled face and wiry, messy hair rambled a montage of meaningless, confusing sentences. Rough looking men with tattoos and dirty, torn jeans blew smoke everywhere.

Finally, we were led into the dining hall. Long rows of tables lined the room. People in white aprons scurried around carrying dishes and making preparations. A tall, graying man handed us each a round, white token. I held it tightly in my hand as I sat down at a table across from my friend. A chubby, blond woman sat down beside him. When she made eye contact with me I smiled at her.

"Hi. I'm Tar Baby", she said.

"Hi. I'm Brer Rabbit", I replied.

I laughed feebly at my own sense of humor and felt hurt when no one else did. An overweight, black woman sat beside me. When I turned to her and greeted her she glared at me with threatening eyes. A chill ran down my spine

"Watch out. She'll hurt you if you say anything she doesn't like", a heavy, black woman who sat across from me said.

A depressed, pot bellied man handed me my plate. I began to eat, ignoring the bland tastelessness of the unattractive food. As my male friend talked with his blond, female friend, I observed that she seemed to trust and like him.

After the meal, I followed him up and down the hills. I felt complimented when he asked me to visit him. I held onto my crutches tightly as I hobbled up a stairway into a dusty hallway. As we entered his room, I looked through the huge window at a panoramic view of the skyline. As he sat down on his rumpled, double bed, I sat down in a tattered arm chair, making sure to not bend my knee, so it wouldn't hurt. He watched me intently as I looked down at my cast.

"I can hardly wait to get this thing off", I said, confiding in him like he was a trusted friend.

"Can I look at it?", he asked.

In my typically agreeable way, I pulled myself up to standing position. As I balanced myself on one crutch, I pulled my pant's leg up to show it to him. Suddenly, he pushed me down on the bed with an overpowering force. In the blink of an eye, he pulled my pants down and lay down on top of me like a large bag of concrete. I floated out of my body as he pushed his stiff penis into my vagina. Like an insect pinned on a board, I became frozen and motionless, as he thrust in and out. The curtain of insanity closed over me with a sad finality. I prayed he would not get me pregnant or kill me. If I could just get him to stop. A light bulb flashed in my mind. I would stroke his ego.

"Wow. How do you keep from getting women pregnant when you do this? You must be an expert at the withdrawal method", I said in a flattering voice.

Suddenly, he withdrew. My heart beat rapidly like a bass drum as I stood up and pulled on my pants. I hobbled out the door and down the dirty carpet like a fragile, blown glass figurine, balancing precariously on my crutches. My head swam as I maneuvered my way frantically down the long stairway and out of the entrance. Newspapers blew along haphazardly and traffic rushed by deafeningly as I crossed the street to go inside an inviting coffee shop. A small, black and white dog walked up to me wagging his tail. He nuzzled my knee affectionately.

I sat down on a black, vinyl seat at a gray and white table and scanned the room. A thin, old man on the other side of the room was watching me. He walked over and gently handed me two dollars, smiling and wishing me a good day. Warm comfort rolled through me in waves as I drank a delicious cup of hot chocolate topped with a mound of whipped cream. There were men in the world who gave without expecting something in return.

I headed out to the sidewalk to try to find my way back to the university clinic where Tim had dropped me off so callously. Forlorn looking people panhandled for money, a holy roller preached the words of Jesus and a man played an electric violin. I accidentally put my weight on my knee and a sharp pain shot through it.

Suddenly, I saw the black man, David, who had been taken to jail with me, walking toward me.

"Hi. How are you doing?", he asked, his eyes shining with friendly compassion.

"Oh, I'm hanging in there. I'm having pain because I twisted my knee out of joint", I said.

"Would you like to go to a restaurant and have a cup of tea?", he asked.

"Okay", I replied.

We crossed the street and walked into a restaurant. A friendly waitress took our order. I avoided mentioning our hellish experience with the police, wanting to forget it completely.

"I have a friend who likes to help people who have no place to stay. You can stay at his house until you find a place", he said, with desire to help me glowing in his eyes.

After we talked and drank tea for a while, I followed him outside. Like a rudderless boat, I sailed along in a lost fog. A bus squealed to a stop spewing carbon monoxide. Following him onto it, I sat in the seat in front of him and placed my crutches beside me. Buildings flashed by in a dizzying blur as the bus flew up and down the hills. Like a sleepwalker, I followed my friend into the lobby of a large, white building which reached high into the sky. Everything felt unreal as a tall, black man walked toward him and shook his hand with a big smile. I followed them onto the elevator and, soon, we arrived on the eighteenth floor. My illness had me lost in a childlike world of fantasy where everything flowed like an endless, summer day. Discernment, judgement and all abilities to respond had been washed away. The steel doors opened and I followed them down a classy, immaculate corridor.

The tall man turned a key in a door and led us into a clean, white room with a twin bed. I admired the simplicity, thinking how kind it had been of my friend to get me a place to stay. As I sat down on the bed I smiled at my friends. They smiled back. I watched the tall man reach into his pocket and pull out a fat marijuana joint. The sound of a striking match crackled through the air as he lit it. He took a long, slow drag.

"We're going to show you how to be cool", he said, handing the joint to me.

I took a tiny puff reluctantly. Soon, I floated out of my body and began to fly through the cosmos. With a sudden violent movement, the tallest man pushed me back on the bed and tore my pants off. Images of being beaten and killed flooded my mind as he lay his excessively heavy, steel muscled body on top of me. I floated far above the earth as he shoved his long, stiff penis into my vagina. Pain bit through me as I pretended it was not happening. When he withdrew a minute later I tried to stand up but he pushed me down, grinding my face into the pillow.

Feelings of helplessness paralyzed me as his friend climbed onto my back, pressing his weight down on me. I held back a cry as he pushed his penis into my rectum. After a few minutes, he withdrew and turned his back to me. Burying my face in the pillow, I longed for death.

Adrenaline surged through me as I stood up and ran to the door, pulling my pants on as I went. Rage rushed through me like a volcano and if I had had a pistol, I would have shot them.

"You creeps are going to get your just desserts", I yelled as I hurried out.

Reeling with numb dizziness, I staggered down the corridor to a bathroom. An old woman was down on her hands and knees scrubbing the floor. Her careworn eyes met mine with concern for a moment and, then, she left. I stripped off my clothes. A rushing sound filled my ears and steam floated up as I turned the faucet in the bath tub. I stepped into the warm water and pulled the shower curtain closed. Sitting down in the rising water, I tried to forget the attacks. I spread my legs and positioned my genitals under the stream of rushing water, praying that I had not gotten syphilis. I washed and lathered myself with a bar of soap again and again. Then, I dried off with paper towels and put my clothes on.

As I walked down the hall on my crutches, I trembled. The elevator door opened, revealing well-groomed, handsome business men in fine suits and beautiful, elegantly dressed women. I worried that they must think I was a prostitute as I hobbled in to join them, leaning on my crutches. As the elevator descended, hopelessness froze me into silent stillness.

Like a lamb lost in a jungle full of boa constrictors, I made my way out through the lobby and onto the bustling street. Pain shot through my injured knee as I climbed the steep incline, putting most of the weight on my crutches. When I found a bench, I sat down. I spent the afternoon watching people. The day passed slowly and, when the sun began setting, I started walking fearfully. I watched flags flutter frantically in front of a huge, opulent hotel. I scanned the scenery with darting eyes as the black night descended upon me like a predator. A small, elderly man with thin, gray hair was sweeping off the sidewalk in a humble manner. Two drunk, boisterous men talked to him briefly. As they walked away, he turned toward me and smiled sweetly.

"Hello. It's a cold night to be out." His gentle, sparkling eyes softened the hardness in my heart.

"I know. I wish I wasn't out but I have no place to stay", I responded, grateful for his kind attention.

"Where do you live?", he asked, holding his broom as he looked into my eyes with compassion.

"I don't have an apartment. I'm new to San Francisco and I don't have enough money to get a place." I looked down at the sidewalk in shame.

"Would you like to come in and have something to eat and some tea?", he asked.

He stood extremely still, eagerly waiting for my answer. I hesitated, thinking of all the people I had trusted who had turned on me like jackals. After a long pause, I accepted and followed him up the dingy stairway into his apartment. As I looked around his tiny, cluttered room, he disappeared into the kitchen. I settled down into the soft cushions on his sofa.

The shrill whistle of a tea kettle vibrated through my ears and he came walking into the room, his bulging tummy jiggling. In a charming, childlike way he handed me a slice of cake in a small, plastic bowl. Then he handed me a steaming cup of tea. As I ate and drank, the apples and sweet cinnamon flavor lifted my mood.

"How long have you been living in San Francisco?", he asked, his face beaming with interest.

"Not long at all. I'm just getting used to it, learning my way around. I love the beautiful views of the bay with the sailboats sailing."

"I moved here from France six years ago. I love it here. You can do anything you want in America. What is your profession?"

"Well, I majored in Art History in college but I don't know what I'm going to do with it."

"Art. That must have been interesting. I love art. There are many beautiful museums in France. I used to visit them when I was a boy." His eyes shone with fond nostalgia.

His grandfatherly kindness calmed my splintered psyche. I listened to him talk in silent gratitude until I started to yawn.

"Stay here tonight. You can share the bed with me."

I watched him walk into his tiny bathroom. Soon, he emerged wearing a red, flannel nightshirt. He looked as benevolent as a character from a childrens' book as he pulled off his slippers and crawled into his double bed which stood next to his entryway. I watched him prop himself up on his King size, white pillow. I crawled into bed beside him. We both turned onto our sides for sleep and he pulled the sheet over us.

Eight hours later, I woke up hanging off of the edge of the bed, gripping it tightly. He gave me a bowl of cereal and a cup of tea. His kind eyes calmed me as we sat and talked. As I bade him goodbye he wished me the best of luck. I drank in his warmth gratefully, dreading leaving him.

The fog and cold ripped through me and traffic roared caustically as I waited for the bus. I clamored onto the first one that arrived and sat down, putting my crutches beside me. Soon, I arrived in the Haight Ashbury. The feminine man with long, blond hair who had offered to share his place in Berkeley with me walked by. I wished I had taken his offer as I filled my shattered inner being with his warmth. I told him I had torn some ligaments in my knee. His sparkling, soft eyes calmed me and I wanted to ask him to let me move in with him. However, I didn't want to impose my now psychotic self on him. He represented life and love to me. Sadness flooded me as I told him goodbye.

My knee throbbed as I hobbled up the hill to Darryl's place, stopping to lean on my crutches now and then. Climbing the long staircase was difficult but, finally, I reached the door to his building. There was a white envelope taped to it. I sat on the stairs and read it feeling calmed by the words.

"I've been worried about you. I've had the police out looking for you ever since I found out they did not admit you at the clinic. I hope you are alright. Please come in and relax. I will be home at six o'clock." Extreme gratitude that I was still alive and that one person in this jungle of a city cared flowed through me. I folded the page and tucked it into my blue jeans pocket. Leaning on my crutches, I walked up the stairs and into his room. I reclined on his mat and drifted off into a deep sleep.

When Darryl walked in I wanted to collapse in his arms and wail out my sorrow but I swallowed my emotions stoically. He put his hands on my shoulders and looked into my eyes with concern.

"I've been worried about you. Are you alright? I've been putting up notices about a missing person. I was afraid you had been picked up by a pimp. I called up the university clinic to see of you were alright and they told me you hadn't even been admitted. I'm really angry at Tim for just letting you out on the curb the way he did. He was supposed to take you in and make sure you got situated. I went over there and cussed them out.

I've also talked with your parents and they were thinking about flying out here to get you", he said.

"The lady at the desk said I had to go to the Rape Crisis center. I took the bus there and talked to a counselor and the police gave me a room in the YMCA for three nights. I can't even remember how long I was there. When I left there I got raped by three different men." I slumped over in a defeated heap of sorrow and stared at the rug, too numb to cry.

"You're lucky you didn't get your pussy all torn up. You have a choice. You can either let it ruin your life or you can learn from it. Listen. I've been talking to a doctor over at the university clinic. I've told him you've been having some problems. He wants to meet you and talk with you about what he can do to help. I set up an appointment for tomorrow morning. I'll go over there with you so you'll get in this time."

"I don't want to be locked up again."

"Believe me, I don't want to see anyone get locked up but you need to see a professional."

CHAPTER 12———————————APRIL, MAY, JUNE 1982
The Cuckoo Finds A Nest

RAINBOWS DANCED ON THE WHITE walls as golden sun beamed through the window the next morning. Singing birds sounded cheerful as they blessed me with love. I had slept in my clothes and I needed to free myself of their uncomfortable tightness. Deep depression and anxiety smothered me and my head swam as I fumbled through my suitcase for something clean to wear. I hated to think about how awful I must look. Walking listlessly to the bathroom, I tried to forget the violence I had suffered through over the past five days.

I took off my clothes and stepped into the shower. Shivering under the cold water, I rubbed shampoo over my head and body. My hair still felt dirty after I washed it in the hard water. The tattered towel felt rough against my skin as I dried off. A strong dose of anesthesia ran through me, deadening me to the world, as I pulled my clean clothes on.

Darryl sat on his mat waiting as I put on my five dollar coat I had bought at a garage sale. He picked up my paper bag of clothes and followed me down the stairs. A car honked as we walked across the street to the bus stop. The bus lumbered up to the curb, and we climbed on. People in colorful clothes sat quietly or chatted. I wondered where they were all going.

Darryl's hand squeezed mine reassuringly as we walked up the long stairs and through the entrance to the clinic. My stomach felt queasy as we rode the elevator up to the second floor. An Oriental doctor shook my hand and introduced himself as Dr. Chen, then led us down a long corridor into a small room. His slanted, Oriental eyes and serious expression calmed me as he asked me question after question and wrote notes on his clipboard.

Concern filled Darryl's face as he told me goodbye. The doctor spoke reassuringly to me as he led me to the ward. Several nurses and counselors greeted me. They showed me a large collection of records and a snack station where the patients could make tea, coffee, hot chocolate and sandwiches. My stomach became pleasantly full as I munched on a peanut butter and jelly sandwich. No one ever asked me how I was going to pay for my time there and I assumed they were treating me for free. I felt grateful and immensely relieved to have a safe home.

After a while, I walked down the hallway looking around in curiosity. I saw a door with only one small peephole. Gazing through it, I saw a white room with a padded floor and walls. I imagined going in there and yelling my rage out and beating on the walls some day.

Continuing down the hall, I looked into the rooms. They all had two twin beds covered with fresh, clean sheets and attractive bedspreads. Happiness over having a comfortable place to sleep rose within me. Ping pong balls flew back and forth making a whapping sound as I entered the room at the end of the hall. I watched two patients playing ping pong as I sat down on the soft sofa, remembering the fun I had had playing ping pong on my parents' porch. I watched the color T.V. until a friendly, overweight woman asked me to play ping pong with her. My mood lifted as we hit the ball back and forth.

Staring down at the floor, I shuffled back to the main room. Sitting on the sofa in my silk, purple dress I had bought in a fancy shop, I listened with nostalgic longing to old hits from my childhood. I sipped on a cup of hot chocolate topped with whipped cream. A beautiful, slender nurse with long, auburn hair handed me a blue pill, Stelazine. I relived the very first time I took it, when I was admitted to the hospital when I was seventeen. Her kind face comforted me as I swallowed it and handed the cup back to her.

My eyelids became heavy as my muscles melted, becoming soft like jello. Just as I was about to drift into sleep, dinner was brought in on trays. Conversation hummed around me as I ate salad, vegetables and rice, observing the other patients and getting used to my new home. After I finished eating, the nurse with auburn hair showed me to my room. With a long, wide yawn, I put on my hospital gown.

My room mate walked with me to the bathroom, chatting cheerfully. We watched each other in the large mirror as we stood side by side brushing our teeth. With her large, dark eyes, wavy hair and tall, slender body she was exquisite. She had worked as a professional fashion model and she encouraged me to come to her make-up class in a few days.

The scent of the clean sheets and my soft, comfortable pillow soothed me to sleep. For a while, I floated peacefully far above the troubles of the doomed planet.

Hours later, I woke in the grips of extreme panic. My back arched back as I screamed a silent, desperate scream. A feeling of overwhelming terror coiled every fiber of my being into knots. I climbed out of bed, walked out to the hall and paced back and forth for the next hour or so. Finally, I fell into the bed in exhaustion.

I woke up eight hours later. As I ate breakfast with various patients, I listened to them converse with one another. Later, I was led down the hall to speak with my Oriental, male psychiatrist, Dr. Chen. His gentle face and slowly blinking eyes exuded compassion as he listened to me tell part of my story. I could not mention the rapes because I was ashamed and he was a man.

"I've decided to add some Lithium to your Stelazine. Lithium is used for bi-polar illness where someone moves from one extreme to another. Sometimes they are manic and excited and may stay up all night or talk non-stop. Other times, they are low and depressed. You have uni-polar illness where you get very depressed. Lithium will help you stabilize." After my session, I wished him a good day and returned to the ward.

Rummaging through my purse, I tried to find the phone numbers of Tom and Becky. I had not called them earlier because they had been living in their van with no phone. However, I wished I had somehow stayed in closer contact with them so they could have prevented me from getting trapped with Darryl. Hope rose within me when I found the numbers for Tom, Becky and Brian, the married man.

I called Brian and he responded with a shocked tone when I told him where I was. That afternoon he visited. His concerned eyes and warm hand on mine comforted me as I told him I had been raped. I did not want to overwhelm him so I did not tell him it had happened several times.

A week later, the nurses granted me an outing with him. His peaceful, stable vibrations calmed me as we walked along the beach together. He pulled his toddler out of the water when he ran with foolhardy daring into the rolling waves. The sun shone radiantly as the salty spray from the ocean revived my spirit. Surfers rode the waves and seagulls flew gracefully, calling to me.

I longed to be the same hopeful person I was when we hiked up the mountain that beautiful day. I felt changed, damaged, like less of a person. It was as though part of me had been stolen. Overwhelming shame pulsated through my veins as I stared at the white sand in silence. I worried that my depressed condition must be hard for him to handle. I felt grateful when he told me I could call any time and talk.

The long hours on the ward were relaxing. I started doing Hatha Yoga stretches every morning with the kind counselor with auburn hair, Anne. Her soft smile and gentle ways opened my heart. Drawing and painting in art therapy took my thoughts away from the attacks I had survived. I called my parents and talked with them for the first time in five months. Their voices soothed me and I longed for the simplicity of home. I could not tell them that I had survived multiple rapes. I simply did not want to saddle them with that burden. A week later, I received a thousand dollars of the three thousand they owed me. A kind note from my father said that he would be sending me five hundred dollars a month until it was all paid back.

Tom and Becky came and helped me get my car out of a lot it had been towed to. I had to find a locksmith and get new keys made. I parked it on a street near Darryl's place.

A few days later, Darryl came to visit me. Boiling water on the stove and making hot chocolate, I tried to avoid his domineering presence. I didn't like his dagger-like eyes penetrating me like deadly radar. Coldly, I started playing checkers with a fellow patient. I had an abode apart from him now and he did not own me. Yet, I looked up guiltily from my checker game now and then, remembering how he had saved me from sleeping in my car. Finally, I broke down and spoke to him.

"I didn't mean to be standoffish", I said apologetically.

"Yeah. It wasn't much fun watching you play checkers with your friend the first half hour I was here", he said

"Thank you for getting me admitted. I'm feeling a lot more stable", I said, smiling at him with gratitude.

"Yeah. I knew it would be good for you. You'll make a great recovery", he said. Yet I couldn't stop reacting to a lack of warmth he projected, as though his heart was hardened with bitterness. He was a mystery. I wondered if he had been jailed because he possessed drugs or because of something else. As much as my gut tightened and recoiled when I was with him, I could not help but feel flattered because he cared about me. I also felt obligated because he was kind to me. I was all alone in a huge, cold city and having his company seemed to be better than being alone. Yet, things are not what they seem often, and I could sense that my illness was controlling me.

I enjoyed talking with the other patients. A woman with a beautiful face and thick, shoulder length, dark hair had burned wounds into her arms with cigarettes. Another woman was anorexic. Like a concentration camp survivor, her bones protruded from her thin skin. She looked as though a strong wind could blow her away in an instant.

Becky and Tom came to visit me and I came to life as I hugged them. They cheered me up greatly, talking about their jobs. Becky was cashiering in a doughnut shop and Tom was painting houses. They really liked their housemates they said and they were extremely happy to not have to live in the van any more. I never called Brian because I did not want to impose my depression on him and I did not want him to get in trouble with his wife.

I also felt very shy and inadequate, like damaged goods. A nagging voice inside told me I did not deserve his friendship.

My brother flew up to visit me from southern California. He treated me to dinner in a fancy Chinese restaurant. I felt my depression disappearing as he talked about newspaper reporting and said funny things. I laughed for the first time in what seemed like ages.

When my ten weeks stay at the hospital came to an end, it was June 1982. I felt more grounded and stable. Dr. Chen informed me that I would move to a halfway house and continue therapy with him. After a sad goodbye to my friends and counselors, I drove up and down the roller coaster hills to a splendid mansion in Pacific Heights, the wealthiest neighborhood in the city. I assumed it would cost more than the other halfway house and felt relieved my parents had sent me some of my money. I wondered how long I would stay.

Ornately carved wood framed the arcaded entryway of the pastel blue and yellow Victorian mansion. I dragged my suitcase up the long stairs and knocked on the door, admiring the exquisite, stained glass window. A counselor with shoulder length, dark hair opened it and welcomed me in. A lustrous, gold mirror covered with swirling shapes shimmered on the wall in the dark hallway. Dark wood floors, a long, curving, mahogany staircase and very high ceilings gave the place an air of elegance. A pretty, brunette counselor looked at me with motherly protectiveness as she led me into a room with elegant embroidered chairs. I sat and answered various questions. Then she led me up the stairs and showed me the room I would share with another woman.

My room mate's friendly smile put me at ease. We sat on our beds basking in the sunlight pouring through the window. I told her a little about myself. She said she had been there for a month and that it wasn't too bad. I ran my hand along the mahogany, carved banister as I followed her down the stairs to dinner. Everyone was gathering in the kitchen. I listened to conversation buzz around me as I ate spaghetti and salad.

There was a house meeting later on. I learned that I would have to pay five hundred dollars a month for rent. The counselors and patients discussed the schedule for outings. They decided to plan three nights out per week. We would vote on whether to go bowling or to a movie. I sat up late drinking hot chocolate, eating popcorn and watching a movie with the other patients.

The sun streamed through my window the next morning, sending a surge of hope through me. My room mate's face glowed as she brushed her shiny hair. We chatted lightly as I sat on the edge of my bed. Her calm, kind nature soothed my ragged heart.

I pulled on my bathrobe and walked down the mahogany stairway into the kitchen. The big box of cornflakes rustled as I poured them into a bowl. I was starting to feel human again. The Lithium did stabilize me and, though I dreaded getting a needle stuck into my arm to check my blood level, it felt like it was worth it. For a while, at least.

When my stomach was full, I walked into the elegant living area and sat on a carved, beautifully upholstered chair. A female counselor with shoulder length, dark hair listened to me talk about the trials I had been through since arriving in the city. Her eyes filled with tears.

That evening, everyone rode the bus to see a movie called Chan Is Missing. It was about a Chinese man who got lost in China Town. Lightness filled the air as my housemates and I laughed with abandon.

The next day, I talked with the kind, brunette counselor about my desire to be free of Darryl. She listened with deep understanding and sympathy. But, later on, as I sat watching T.V. with the other patients, the pay phone began to ring. I picked it up and, in no time, Darryl had talked me into going to a movie with him.

After the movie, we walked around the rich neighborhood. I listened tensely as he rambled on and on about the evil government in his depressed monotone. Shadow silhouettes of us danced in the sunlight on the sidewalk. I longed to go back to the enchanted world of childhood.

"We are like identical twins. Other people can't understand us the way we understand one another because we're on a different level from them. I know that you've been hurt by your family and you've felt lonely. I've felt the same way. It's because we're different. We're serious, deep thinkers. It scares people and they can't relate to it."

"Yeah. I know I'm different. That's why my parents don't want to talk to me."

"Well, your father would be difficult for anyone to deal with. When I tried to get him to send you your money he was downright nasty. I got forceful with him but I found out that that only makes him withdraw further. Even when I threatened to call his office and ruin his reputation he still refused to send your money. He's a tough nut to crack."

"Yeah. He's not easily influenced."

"I want you to be happy. You have a lot of potential."

The street lamps glowed as we walked back to the halfway house. As we climbed the front stairs darkness descended, swallowing us like a boa constrictor. A persistent feeling within urged me to tell him I didn't want him to come in. Yet, we walked in and sat on the mahogany bench in the hallway. Our reflections shone in the huge mirror which was bordered with an ornate, gold frame. I stared at the floor trying to gather the courage to tell him our relationship was over.

"I need to talk with you about something. I think it would be best for us to not see each other any more. I appreciate all you've done for me and I wish you the best but I need to be on my own."

"Oh, you can't mean that. It would hurt me deeply to not see you any more. You'll never find anyone who loves you as much as I do."

"I need to be alone now."

He wouldn't budge. He stared at me with sorrowful eyes as I opened the front door as a signal for him to go.

"I'm going to bed now. I have to get up very early in the morning."

"It would be foolish of you to throw away everything we have. You'll regret it some day."

"I have to be alone now. Goodbye," I said, closing the door as he walked out. Freedom felt glorious. Now, I could get my old self back. I looked for my favorite counselor, Cathy, so I could tell her triumphantly about my new found assertiveness but I couldn't find her. Running my hand along the mahogany banister, I hopped up the stairs happily to my room. My room mate, Susan, was sleeping. Her angelic face shone in the moonlight beaming through the window. Like waves lapping on a distant shore, sleep pulled me magnetically into a magical, fantasy land. Peace washed every fiber of my being and, soon, I was gone.

Darkness covered me as I sat up, suddenly, in the middle of the night. Sweat moistened my body as anxiety raged like a typhoon inside me. I had dreamed I was running through the woods and had seen my car with a big sign stuck on it that said, "Which way are you going to go now?" I had seen my attacker laughing at me. His humiliating laughter echoed through the woods, getting louder and louder until my knees wobbled. I hurried into my car and turned the key again and again but it would not start. I stared into the darkness, feeling utterly helpless. I wished that my therapy and medication could help me more.

I ate breakfast in silence as I listened to my fellow housemates chat. A frozen, numb feeling pervaded me as I rode the bus to the hospital and had a therapy session with Dr. Chen. As I talked about the things I did not like about myself, the compassion on his face and his slowly blinking, attentive eyes comforted me. I was very grateful to him for seeing me for free. However, I kept getting a nagging feeling that something was missing in his therapeutic method.

Soon, it was over and I hurried hopefully down the front stairs of the psychiatric institute. I walked quickly, looking around eagerly, hoping to see a friend. After about six blocks, I felt invigorated by the energy and blood flowing through me. A shop full of psychedelic posters and comic books called out to me. When I found a comic book called Zippy the Pinhead, I read it with amused absorption. I could not put it down as I identified with the funny main character who moved through life like an oddball having one strange experience after another. He dressed in a polyester, polka dot outfit and wore huge white shoes. His space alien head narrowed to a point at the top where a lock of wispy hair was tied into a bow. Like Zippy, I lived on the edge, a lonely outcast. I heard my father's cruel voice echoing through me saying, 'You stick out like a sore thumb'.

The kind, gentle faces of Tom, Becky and Brian danced in my mind as I walked toward the Grand Piano. Eccentric characters passed me on the street and I refused the requests of a few beggars. Soon, I arrived and the pleasing aroma of garlic and fresh bread rose through my nostrils as the drone of a myriad conversations buzzed through my ears. A surge of grateful happiness flowed through me as Tom and Becky walked toward me smiling warmly. So much had happened since that frightening night they had saved me from my nasty ex.

"How are you? We've been wondering how you were and hoping we would bump into you. We've been too busy working to do much. Tom's been busy painting houses and I've been working at the doughnut shop down the street."

"It's so great to see you. I left the hospital and I'm living in a halfway house now. It's in a beautiful area full of mansions."

My blood went cold when, suddenly, I saw the black man who had raped me, David, walk by. I told Becky he had raped me, pointing to him as he disappeared onto a bus.

"He raped you?"

"Yes. He bought me hot chocolate in the doughnut shop you work in and gave me a place to stay. I thought he was my friend. But, then, the next time he gave me a place to stay, he raped me. Back in March it happened, I think it was March. I still can't believe it happened."

"I think he should be subjected to public ridicule. How dare him do such a thing to you", she said, raising her voice in angry indignation.

"Yeah. Let's string him up in the middle of the street", Tom said with protective vengeance.

"Why don't you come over and visit a while", Becky asked, like an angel of love.

"OK", I replied, feeling my tense muscles relax.

"I've got to go paint houses. See you later", Tom said, walking away suddenly.

I followed Becky down the street to her place. She unlocked a black, foreboding looking gate and we walked up a long staircase. Then she opened a bright blue door and led me into a cozy, clean apartment she and Tom shared with four women.

"Would you like a cup of tea?"

"Yes."

In a few minutes, I heard the shrill whistle of a kettle. She walked toward me and handed me a cup of tea, like a flower child beaming with love. She was saving my life now, in the middle of the violence and hate infested Haight Ashbury, ten years after all the flower children had left.

"I'm really enjoying living here. I've been doing some sewing and arts and crafts. I've always liked making things", she said, settling down into the sofa beside me.

"That's great."

"Yeah. I get along great with my room-mates. I'm really glad I found this place. It's so different from living in Boston. Now that Tom has found work we're more relaxed. It's nice not having to sleep in the van. We'll stay here as long as things continue to go well."

"Do you think you'll ever go back to Boston to live?"

"We might. It's not a priority though."

"Boy. I've been through some rough times with men ever since I've been in this city. I never thought I would get raped. I still can't believe it happened. But I'm glad I'm alive", I said, feeling my muscles tense as memories of my traumas flashed in my mind. I left her thinking it had happened only once because I did not want to scare her away with my shattered condition.

"I'm really sorry that happened to you. You sure are handling it well. You've got a lot of strength. You should be really proud of yourself, you know. You got yourself through a good college and you're making your way alone in a tough world. You're a wonderful person and you deserve better than you've been getting."

"Thanks. I'm sure things can only get better."

"Men can be really pushy. I've had men try things with me and had to escape from them. It's really difficult being a woman. I called my father to help me once when I was trying to get away from a guy who took me to a hotel room. He was really mean and critical toward me. It hurt my feelings so much I cried for days. My father had no right to blame me for something that was not my fault. But we've never been close."

"I've never been close to my father either", I replied, looking down sadly.

As we talked for the next few hours, her gentle presence softened my hardened heart. The afternoon glowed like a priceless pearl that had been miraculously recovered from a shipwreck. Love and laughter lifted me, reminding me that life is a gift to be enjoyed. I would get by with a little help from my friends as the Beatles had told me in their famous song.

CHAPTER 13 —————— SEPTEMBER, OCTOBER 1982

A New Home and Family

I WANTED TO STAY WITH HER forever but I had to get back to the halfway house in time for dinner. Her hug soothed me as she told me goodbye. Rain fell down in gray, sad drizzles as I shivered in the cold, foggy air waiting for the bus.

A clatter of plates and silverware resounded through the kitchen as my favorite counselor, Cathy, greeted me warmly in the halfway house kitchen. I sat down and poured myself a tall glass of grape juice as the aroma of spaghetti, garlic bread and parmesan cheese wafted into my nose, comforting me. The hum of conversation lulled me into relaxation as I twirled spaghetti on my fork, reflecting on my afternoon with Becky.

"We're going out bowling tonight. Anyone who wants to can join us", a tall patient with reddish, curly hair said loudly. His pale face was sensitive and his hand shook slightly as he served himself from the large noodle bowl. Bowling had bored me in the past but I needed company so I decided to go. My new family of patients cheered for me as I knocked down the pins and my spirits rose like a helium balloon.

The cool September breeze woke me and I sat up suddenly in bed the next morning. I knew beyond a shadow of a doubt that I needed a new therapist. All the Oriental psychiatrist at the hospital could do was nod his head and blink his slanted eyes as I poured my guts out to him. I fumbled through my purse and looked for the phone number of a therapist that Randy, the homeless guitar player, who had disappeared after I got evicted by Taylor, had given me. Hope rushed through me when I found it. I hurried to the hall pay phone, remembering that Randy had said he was a very good therapist. I needed a miracle worker to put me back together again.

"Kundalini Clinic" the wise voice of an older man said.

I set up an appointment for the following Friday at two p.m. The rest of the afternoon passed slowly as I talked with a counselor, mentioning that I wanted to get a well paying job. I told her I had applied for dozens of low-paying jobs with no success. She replied that a volunteer job would be better for me. When I told her I had a degree in Art History from a respected university, she suggested that I volunteer at the Museum of Modern Art. The sights of the city fascinated me as I rode the bus to the Museum of Modern Art the next day. A kind woman interviewed me and had me fill out several forms.

Friday arrived quickly. A bright, glorious sun shone down as I rode the bus watching people jog, walk dogs and gaze dreamily into the store windows. The driver let me off in front of the clinic. I admired the Spanish style building with a salmon colored roof. Shaped hedges and vivid, colorful flowers lined the path as I walked to the main entrance. I reached for the ornate, gold handled door and let myself into the large foyer. I had no idea how I would pay for my therapy.

When I saw a large directory on the wall, I scanned it for the Kundalini Clinic. It was on the fourth floor. The elevator rose rapidly and I watched the green numbers flash. The thick, white carpet padded my feet as I walked down the hall to a waiting area. Sun streamed through the window as I sat on a cushiony, comfortable sofa leafing through magazines. Suddenly, a door opened and a young man walked quickly toward the elevator. A tall, grandfatherly, white haired man looked out of the office door.

"Hello. It's nice to meet you. I'm Dr. Stanfield.", he said, a gentle smile gracing his face as he shook my hand. I followed him into his office and my first session began.

My mind raced as I tried to piece together the fragments of my shattered inner self.

"I moved here to San Francisco a year ago and I've had some traumatic experiences since I've been here. I was in the university clinic for ten weeks of medication and therapy and, now, I'm living in a halfway house."

"Oh, you were in a hospital for ten weeks? That's a long time. What caused you to go into the hospital?"

"Yeah. I was having to sleep in my car because I didn't have enough money to rent an apartment and someone let me stay with him and, then, I got held at knife point in the Golden Gate park. Then I stayed in the YMCA downtown and got raped by three men."

"I'm shocked by all you have been through and I'm amazed that you are handling it so well", he said kindly. He listened with a look of great compassion for the rest of the session. I felt glad I had found him. He gave me a warm hug as I told him goodbye.

At the next session, I dug down into my childhood, searching for the key that would unlock the cage that I was in.

"I can remember sitting through dinners with my parents and being completely ignored by my father the whole time. I used to ask people if I was invisible. He never wanted to listen to me and was always telling me to shut up. I was always afraid that he was going to punish me for something. When I was in grammar school, I used to go to a friend's house after school. We would hit a ball up against a wall. When it started to get dark I would be overcome with anxiety about going home. I never knew when my father was going to beat me again with his leather belt. I prayed that my best friend's family would take me in and let me live with them permanently. There was no one I could talk to about how much my father was hurting me. He strapped me a lot when I was under ten. My mother never said a word to protect me. She would just act like nothing had happened. He didn't do it as much when I was in high school but there were still a few times when I had purple, blue and yellow bruises all over my bottom. And my mother was very cold to me. Sometimes, she chased me out of the house with a broom when I was in high school". My muscles tensed as I remembered how hurt I had been.

"That must have been horribly traumatic. Your father took advantage of you. And your mother did too. Parents often pick the most docile child to be the scapegoat. I think that the trauma of going through that abuse was so overwhelming that you cut your feelings off. I want to work with you to get your feelings flowing again. Your true self just could not come out in that environment", he said, reaching to a shelf behind his chair and handing me a book. I looked through it with curiosity. It was called Bioenergetics. It contained photographs of people doing various movements that were designed to release blocked emotions.

"You need to release your anger. I want you to beat this tennis racket against the bed and yell, 'Leave me alone'".

Endless rage boiled inside me as I began hitting the bed with the tennis racket yelling, 'leave me alone'. I imagined my rapists and my parents underneath the racket as I pounded and pounded.

After a while, I leaned over and rested on the floor in exhaustion. We sat and talked and I didn't want to leave when the session was over. I set up my next appointment and told him goodbye, feeling grateful when he hugged me.

Outside, the city looked cold and threatening. Loneliness crept over me as I climbed onto the bus. I decided to ride it to the Grand Piano and look for my friends. Another afternoon with Becky would do wonders for me. She made me feel good about myself.

People hurried by on the street, carrying bags of groceries, walking dogs or pushing strollers. Envy rushed through me as I imagined them walking into beautifully decorated, cozy homes where their loving mates waited for them. The bus groaned up in a trail of carbon monoxide. I sat down close to a window and wrapped my arms around my body for protection as I watched a kaleidoscope of colors flash by outside.

The bus came to a stop. I wandered around the Haight Ashbury and Grand Piano for a while looking for my friends. Panic rushed through me as I became overwhelmed by a sea of strangers. A dizzy, numb, confused sensation overcame me as I breathed shallowly, my muscles tensed with fear. I wondered if Dr. Stanfield knew how to treat my illness. I had not told him that I had been diagnosed as schizophrenic at the age of seventeen. I headed back to the bus stop to wait in silent loneliness. I missed my parents and home town as I watched the scenery flash by. The bus moved up and down the hills and the chaos of the city streets rattled me.

Patients and counselors chatted in the kitchen as I walked into the halfway house. Picking up forks and knives, I helped set the table. Conversation hummed around me as I ate slowly, gazing at my mashed potatoes and sculpting them into various shapes with my fork.

Later on, we went out bowling. Aiming the ball carefully, I watched it roll down the aisle and knock over the pins, imagining they were the men who had abused me. It gave me a sense of power, like I could knock over anyone who ever tried to give me a hard time again.

At my next session with Dr. Stanfield, I wrung my hands as I talked about my inability to break up with Darryl.

"He keeps calling me and we have these long conversations on the telephone. I do most of the listening and, then, he says he is coming to visit me. Something about him makes me feel nervous but I don't know what it is. I feel like I should be nice to him because he saved me from sleeping in my car and really cares about me. I don't want to hurt his feelings after all he has done for me but I really want to get rid of him."

"Well, just hang up on him when he calls. You're too nice. It doesn't work to be nice to people like that. You don't owe him anything because he helped you. Let's do some work on the mat."

"Can I ask you something first. I was put in a hospital when I was seventeen and they diagnosed me as schizophrenic. Is that what is wrong with me?"

"You were psychotic when you came in here. I think that you did not move through your illness fully back when you were a teenager."

My feelings surged as I lay on the mat and kicked my legs yelling, "Leave me alone". The suppressed rage of a lifetime erupted within me like a volcano as I continued for about fifteen minutes. Then, Dr. Stanfield shone a little pocket light, moving it back and forth asking me to follow it with my eyes.

"Your breathing is very shallow. We've got to get your feelings unfrozen."

After continuing this for a while, we sat in our chairs and talked. I didn't want to leave at the end of the session. His warm, gentle hug comforted me as I said goodbye.

When Darryl called me that night, I weakened and agreed to go see a movie with him. It was long and boring and I bounced my crossed leg restlessly. Afterwards, we sat on a bench and drank red wine. Feeling suffocated, I listened to Darryl.

"When I was in prison there was this guy who needed to have an exorcism done on him. He was possessed by a demon. The dark forces in the universe are very satanic. There is definitely a war going on between good and evil. A friend of mine and I did the exorcism. We had to string him up on a pole. We had him hanging by his hands. We were both working together, chanting and praying and sprinkling him with Holy Water. A part of him wanted to be freed of his demons but another part of him was fighting it like crazy. His demon kept coming out and talking in a really strange voice. Then, suddenly, it would put on this friendly voice and say, 'Come on. Let's go to McDonald's and get a cheeseburger.' Even though it appeared friendly it was really very sinister. It was doing everything it could to prevent him from going through his exorcism successfully. Dark spirits thrive on suffering. Seeing someone suffer is like food for them. They will do anything to prevent someone from breaking free." His morbid tone sent shivers through me.

"Well, did he get free of the evil spirit in the end?" I looked at him with wide eyes full of curiosity.

"Yeah. We kept working with him and fighting his demon and, after a while, it gave up and left. He was a totally different person afterwards." He took a long swig from the wine bottle.

"Sometimes I feel like I am possessed by a demon", I said.

"You do have a very strong demon. It is trying to keep you serious all the time."

Feeling controlled and bewildered, I rode the bus with him back to the halfway house. I admired the mansions as we walked down the street in my wealthy neighborhood. He hugged me goodbye on the front steps. Then, with polite shyness, I escaped into the safe, tranquil sanctuary like a prisoner who had been set free.

Hopeful anticipation bubbled inside me as I pulled on a T-shirt and some jeans early the next morning. I remembered my brother with affection as I walked downstairs to the kitchen. I told the counselors that I was going to ask him if I could visit him. I had not called him before because I did not want to impose on him. He lived in the southern part of the state.

I called him from the pay phone. His warm voice soothed me as he agreeably told me to come on down. I ran cheerfully up the stairs to celebrate with my room mate. She perched like an adorable china doll on the edge of her bed as we talked.

A few days later, the bus driver wished me a good day as he let me out at the station. Strange looking characters walked around mumbling to themselves. Loud voices announced arrivals and departures over the intercom and people sat in tiny chairs watching little T.V. sets. Children jumped up and down and ran around restlessly as their harried parents tried to calm them down.

I climbed up the stairs of the bus headed for San Diego. A friendly driver greeted me. I sat next to a window and put my bag on the floor. The bus pulled out of the station like a whale swimming toward fresher water. When the freeway gave way to breathtaking sights of mountains and the ocean I breathed deeply, feeling the euphoria of freedom. I looked at the radiant blue sky with its mounds of vanilla ice cream and whipped cream clouds. After a couple of hours, the driver pulled off of the road for a rest stop.

Walking inside a small, red brick building, I observed eccentric, strangely dressed characters playing pinball and Pac Man in the tile floored lobby. Cigarette smoke billowed from the mouths of various travelers as they talked back and forth and walked around restlessly. I surveyed the junk food hanging and listened to canned drink machines hum eerily. Phosphorescent lights glared harshly from the ceiling fixtures as I found my way to the bathroom. Dirt was caked on the floor and graffiti covered the walls. I grabbed a handful of paper towels and wiped urine off of the toilet seat. Then, I emptied my bowels while pinching my nostrils shut.

Worried looking mothers held their crying childrens' hands and long-haired teenagers wandered aimlessly in the lobby when I walked out. A clinking of coins vibrated in my ears as I bought a bag of chips and a coke. As I munched hungrily, I dreamed of spaghetti with parmesan cheese and cheesecake.

Happy excitement filled me when the bus arrived in San Diego. As I stepped off of the bus into the crowded lobby, frenetic energy bombarded my senses. I watched people play pinball, talk on telephones, rummage through bags and chase wild children around. A gentle breeze caressed my skin as I walked down the stairs. An incredibly bright, blue sky shone brilliantly above the asphalt street which was lined with parking meters and cars. Tall palm trees towered up above the inviting, tropical landscape.

My brother drove up waving and smiling warmly. After depositing my back pack in the back seat, I climbed into the front. He talked with enthusiasm about stories he was writing for the newspaper as he drove through the palm tree lined streets. Old-fashioned shops and charming restaurants flashed by. He parked his car in an asphalt lot facing a swimming pool. I followed him to the front entrance of his apartment building. The elevator groaned strangely as it rose rapidly. An aroma of steaming cabbage wafted through the hallway as we walked to his efficiency apartment. He turned the key in his door and let us in. Piles and piles of books were stacked everywhere.

He asked me if I would like to go swimming and I said I would love to. A cheerful, golden sun beamed down on us as we walked to the pool side. I reclined on a lounge chair and watched my brother sling his towel down and run and dive energetically into the water. I watched him swim a few minutes. Then, like an eagle in flight, I dove into the blue, shimmering depths feeling the coolness invigorate me. I moved my arms energetically through the water, feeling the sun revive my spirit. I floated on my back, staring up at the robin's egg blue sky and watching clouds twist and turn, joining one another and then breaking apart like swabs of cotton candy in a playful, cosmic dance. I sunk down to the bottom of the pool and then launched myself like a rocket with a powerful push of my legs. As I burst through the surface, I spread my arms sending great splashes of shimmering water through the air. I swam like an enchanted dolphin until I was tired out.

My brother joked playfully as we walked back to his apartment. He showed me to his bathroom. I dried off and put on my nicest clothes. When I came out, my brother looked at me and said he wanted to treat me to a great restaurant. His keys clattered as he locked the door behind us. Warm breeze rippled through my hair and I observed the scenery curiously as my brother drove.

My eyes widened as we walked into a restaurant. China and silverware clinked like magical chimes as mirrors shone, reflecting colorful bouquets of flowers and light filled, crystal chandeliers.

"You know, I'm feeling really contented for the first time in my life. I love my job and I have some great friends. I'm writing an article about Alzheimer's disease. It is a very strange disease. Researchers are trying to figure out what causes it. Elderly people who get it have a hard time focusing on anything because it breaks down the chemical messengers that relay information to the brain. Experiments are being done in which they get the patient to take medicine that replaces the chemical they are short of. But they haven't been able to find the right chemical yet."

I sat in silent shame, wondering if the chemical imbalance my father said I had was similar. Later on, the ocean waves lapped along the shore as we walked along a pier underneath the pearly, white full moon. His easy going sense of humor and interesting conversation was uplifting. I wished I could walk with him every night.

Golden sunlight swaddled me like a baby the next morning. Rustling sounds tickled my ears as my brother dressed for work. The door clicked as he stepped out and closed it behind him. I yawned and stretched, feeling safe and secure in a cozy womb of familiarity. He had left me many brochures about various places of interest. As I studied the brochure about the zoo I listened to my rice crispies cheerfully say snap, crackle, pop.

The welcoming zoo lifted my spirits. Beautiful, multi-colored flowers surrounded me. Contented, peaceful animals munched on leaves and wandered around their lush, tropical surroundings. I rode the bus home, staring with curiosity at the pedestrians on the sidewalks.

I read a book called "Centuries of the Expert's Best Advice to Women". After a while my brother walked in. I felt the breeze blow through my hair and watched the orange sun descend over the friendly town as he drove us to a restaurant. A smiling Chinese waiter took our orders.

"I've been writing about a new planet that has been discovered. It is fascinating learning about the new discoveries scientists make every day with their advanced telescopes. Galileo would be ecstatic over the way we keep exploring further and further in this endless universe. Stars are constantly forming and new planets and galaxies are being discovered. Black holes really fascinate me. They are so extremely magnetic that they suck all light and energy inside them and it never escapes."

"I'll never forget seeing the Aurora Borealis when we traveled when we were kids", I replied.

After we ate, we went to see a wonderful movie. As we laughed and munched on popcorn, I began to love California. I ended up staying for two weeks and didn't even bother to call the halfway house or Dr. Stanfield. Unfortunately, the time came when my brother had to get on with his responsibilities. I clasped my hands together nervously as he drove me to the bus station. With a warm goodbye hug, he wished me the best of luck back in San Francisco.

CHAPTER 14————————————OCTOBER, 1982
Return to Hades

WHEN I ARRIVED IN THE city, the carefree lightness I had experienced was replaced by a gnawing dread in the pit of my stomach. Tension tied me into knots as I rode the bus through the dangerous, corrupt city.

I began to relax when I arrived in my wealthy neighborhood. Elegant mansions stood serenely, enjoying the shade of ancient, tall trees. The halfway house shone in opulent splendor as I walked along the sidewalk in the mystical glow of dusk. I jiggled my key in the front door until it opened with a friendly creak.

Warm greetings and hugs from friends and counselors warmed my heart. My favorite counselor, Cathy, commented on how well I was doing. After a delicious dinner of salad, casserole and bread, I helped everyone clean up. Then, I sat and watched T.V. with some of my house mates. Soon after medication time, I drifted into a deep sleep that lasted twelve hours.

Dr. Stanfield greeted me warmly when I arrived for my session the next day. I told him about the wonderful time I had had visiting my brother. He listened attentively for a while and then moved to a new subject.

"I talked with your father on the phone. He wants to make sure that you take your medicine. He is very adamant about it. He's really difficult to talk with", he said with caring eyes.

"Yeah. I know. He's always right about everything and he orders people around. I can't relax for a minute when I'm with him."

"Well, I've just been telling him a white lie and saying that you are taking it. My true feeling about the medication is that it cuts off your feelings. Your father can only look at it one narrow way because he's a medical doctor and they put so much emphasis on medicine. He's the kind of person who is going to insist he's right no matter what. Come on, let's do some release work."

I pounded the tennis racket on the bed, yelling my rage out until I collapsed. Then I sat and talked, soaking in the comfort of his grandfatherly, gentle encouragement. When I got back to the halfway house I talked with a counselor. She said that I would have to move to another halfway house in the next couple of months.

I decided, on my own, to start looking for a house to share with "normal" people. In the mornings, before I went to my volunteer job, I searched bulletin boards, copying down numbers. Everyone had a long list of requirements I must meet. Their renter must not smoke, must be quiet, must like cats, must be vegetarian, liberal-minded, must be employed full-time, must be politically active and on and on.

As I went on interview after interview, I worried that my schizophrenia would show and frighten people away. Riding buses and getting lost for several weeks, I talked with various people who asked me unnerving questions about myself. My last interview was in a big, yellow Victorian house down the street from where I had stayed with John, the alcoholic, and Ron and Mark, when I first arrived in the city.

As I walked nervously up the front steps of the yellow Victorian, I admired the ornate designs and cone-shaped tower on the roof. I knocked on the door and, soon, a beautiful woman with long, blond hair let me in telling me her name was Barbara. I followed her up the narrow stairway and sat beside her on a sofa facing a fireplace.

"We have one room for rent. It costs two hundred dollars a month. You'll also have to pay your share of the utilities. Five people live here now and I'll divide it up six ways whenever we get the bill from the electric and gas companies", she said in a calm, stable manner.

I looked at my tiny room, the smallest in the house, after she gave me a tour of the upstairs and downstairs. Then, she introduced me to a tall, red headed guy named Jeffrey who rented one of the three rooms upstairs. He studied art at a renowned Institute. His friendly warmth put me at ease. Barbara said she would call me in a few days to let me know if they chose me. That night at the halfway house I stayed silent about my plans.

October arrived, filling the air with an invigorating chill, and Barbara called and said they wanted me to move in. With deep sadness, I told all the patients and counselors that I would miss them.

I looked forward to being normal as I drove across town. After lugging my few boxes up to the tiny room in the yellow Victorian, I reclined back on the small, hard bed. I called Darryl and gave him my new address and phone number. The night came and went while I lay there in a numb stupor.

Rushing, obnoxious traffic rumbled through my ears as bright sunlight streamed into my room the next morning. Restless energy rushed through me as I pulled on a pair of shorts and a cotton shirt. I walked down the stairs and closed the door behind me. A friendly bus driver told me how to get to the beach. I settled into the seat behind him and soon, I arrived. Endless energy surged inside me as I ran barefoot along the wet sand, filling my lungs with fresh oxygen. The moist, refreshing ocean breeze blew through my hair. Waves rolled in hypnotically, sending white foam onto the shore as they peaked and crested, breaking rhythmically, one after another. Screeching seagulls flew effortlessly through the sky. Bright sun beams warmed and exhilarated me. I sensed that the Lithium had stabilized me enough to live with normal people. However, it was a painful hassle to go to the downtown lab and get stuck with a needle to check my blood level. I decided to stop taking it.

When I got back to the house, Connie, the Oriental woman who lived upstairs, came to visit me.

"How long have you been living in San Francisco?", she asked with curiosity, looking like a mischievous elf with her short, dark hair and large, dark eyes. A childlike innocence graced her face.

"About a year. It is really a beautiful city. I moved here from Georgia."

"Yeah. It is pretty. And there's always something interesting to do. I grew up here. My parents came here from China. We all get along well here. Bob and Jeffrey live upstairs with me. Barbara and Nick live down with you. Jeffrey goes to the Art Institute and Bob works in a photography lab. I'm working at three different jobs now. I take care of elderly people. I go to their houses and steam vegetables and run errands for them."

"I've got to get a job soon. I've been looking through the paper but nothing sounds right for me."

"Just keep looking. You'll find one. I'm going to my parents' house on Friday to do some laundry. Would you like to go with me?"

"Yeah. That sounds like fun."

"Excuse me if I talk too fast. I take uppers sometimes and they make me really hyper."

After talking with Connie for a while, I excused myself to go out on a job search. Traffic roared past me as I walked to a bakery a few blocks away. A cup of herbal tea and a croissant with butter and strawberry jam relaxed me as I scanned the want adds. Every job listed required computer knowledge. I knew nothing about how to work a computer. My muscles tensed with fear.

Hope rose in me as my eye fell on a possibility that might work---Massage Therapist Needed. I had always enjoyed giving my brother massages and had thought about going to massage school. The waitress smiled sweetly as I paid her for my breakfast. The coins clinked and the cash register made a thudding sound as she shut it. I wished her a good day and walked out onto the noisy sidewalk. When I arrived at home, I went to the wall phone in the kitchen and called the number listed in the add. A woman set an appointment for the next day.

I spent a lonely night in my room, worrying and reading. The sound of roaring traffic woke me up. My room at the halfway house had been so wonderfully silent and I missed it with every cell in my body. I wished I could go back there. I was sure someone had taken my place though. A detached, numb feeling pervaded me as I walked down the hall to the refrigerator. I had one egg and a tiny square of cheese. I had to pay rent and utilities and, after that, I wouldn't have enough money to go grocery shopping with.

Grease sputtered in the frying pan and the yellow egg bubbled as I cooked a cheese omelet. Sitting at the cluttered living room table, I scanned job listings while I ate. All of them mentioned sales. I was no good at sales. I recalled how I couldn't even sell chocolate bars for my high school chorus. Retreating to my room, I sorted through my clothes and found my best dress. I pulled it on, admiring its prettiness. Pulling on a pair of panty hose, I admired my legs. Then, I stepped into a pair of pumps. Gazing into a small mirror, I painted my eyebrows and lids with kohl. Then I put blush on my cheeks and lipstick on my lips. I wondered where my housemates were as I walked down the stairs.

A black child bouncing a ball walked past me as I headed toward the bus stop. A fellow passenger told me where to transfer to the train to Berkeley. Soon, I arrived at the station and I walked down the long flight of stairs into the underground station.

The train arrived in Berkeley. I stepped out onto the crowded, noisy platform and moved quickly, with the current of the crowd, up the long stairs to the sunny sidewalk. My hands shook as I pulled my directions out of my pocket and read them over and over. Looking around at the street signs, I tried to orient myself.

My eyes darted back and forth nervously as I hurried down the sidewalk avoiding the glances of weird strangers. The sounds of gunning motors and obnoxious rap music boomed through my ears. Strange, boarded up buildings full of scrawled, black graffiti sent a shudder through me as I arrived at an ugly, concrete building. When I found a door that was marked with a small number I pushed it open. A beautiful woman with dark hair sat behind a reception desk.

"I'm here to interview for the job."

"Oh yes. You must be the person I talked with on the telephone."

"Yes. I am."

"The job here requires that you do full body massage. The girls here keep all their clothes on and the men are not allowed to touch them."

"Do I have to bring them to orgasm?"

"Yes", she replied in an impatient tone, rolling her eyes as though I had asked a stupid question. I looked at her in silence with flaming cheeks, too stunned to say more.

"If you think what I do is immoral then you need to look for a job elsewhere. I make over four thousand dollars a month. I live in a beautiful, big apartment and drive a fancy sports car. I'm not about to give up my lifestyle because someone somewhere might think what I do is wrong. It doesn't matter what anyone thinks."

"Well let me think about it and I'll call you back." I slithered out of the door in awe over the incredible amount of money she made. However, I wanted a higher purpose in life than to spend my days massaging strange men's penises.

I ducked into a Chinese café where I picked up a pamphlet about the local Psychic studies school. Bright sun blinded me as I headed out onto the sunny sidewalk. A pretty, brunette woman looked at me with concern as I stood and stared, feeling confused. When I told her I was trying to find the psychic school she told me it was only a couple of blocks away. Smiling kindly, she pointed her finger toward it. I walked quickly in eager anticipation. Ever since I was a child I had been fascinated by E.S.P.

When I arrived at the school, a short man with dark hair led me into his office. He asked me the purpose of my visit and I told him that I wanted to develop my psychic ability. He told me a beginning class would be starting in forty five minutes. The regular price was twenty five dollars but he would let me attend for ten dollars he said, looking into my face with gentle mercy.

Curiosity flowed through me as I walked through the halls. I looked inside a small room where two women and a man sat talking. One woman had blond, fluffy hair. The other woman was black and had curly, thick hair. The man was short and pudgy with dark, short hair.

"Would you like to get a reading?", the woman with blond hair and blue eyes asked.

"Yes", I replied, walking into the room and sitting down in a large, comfortable armchair.

The woman with blond hair told me to relax. Then they all took a deep breath and closed their eyes as they went into deep concentration.

"Your aura has a lot of green and orange in it. The green is healing energy. You have the ability to heal yourself and others. Have you ever noticed that people get over colds very quickly when they're with you?" the blond woman asked.

"No. I haven't noticed that", I replied.

I looked at them in fascination as they all sat in deep concentration.

"Do you see what I see?", the man suddenly asked the others.

"The one with the fangs you mean?", the black lady replied.

"Yeah, that one. You have the spirit of an old Chinese man in your aura. He is very stern and authoritarian. He is trying to keep you serious all the time. Let's just clear him out of your aura. You don't need him there keeping you from having any fun."

I watched in fascination as they walked over to me and started moving their hands around me in gentle pulling, scrubbing motions. I felt like I was being massaged even though they never touched my body.

I looked at my watch and saw that my class was about to start so I told them thank you and goodbye. A tall, thin woman, named Lynn, started to lead the class. First, she instructed everyone to put a bubble of protection around themselves. I imagined I was inside a circle of bubble gum. Next, she had us imagine we were holding an imaginary, magic sponge. She instructed us to clean the inside of our bubble. As I scrubbed away in my mind I began to feel lighter until, suddenly, the teacher looked at me critically.

"I want you to leave the class. You are disturbing the atmosphere."

"Hey, wait a minute. I paid to go to this class. You can't just kick me out."

"Oh, yes I can."

"Janet is not always at home so different spirits come in and use her body."

My face burned with shame as I looked down at the floor.

"I want you to leave the class right now", she repeated in an authoritarian tone, cutting through me with disapproving eyes.

I slithered out of the building, staring in humiliation at the dusty wooden floor. The thought of turning back and reporting the rude teacher to the president of the school occurred to me. Then, I changed my mind. A deep depression came over me and I felt as though I had sunk into the underworld as I rode the bus home.

When Connie, my Oriental house mate, asked me to go to a club downtown with her and a friend I quickly agreed. Anticipation hummed through me as I put on the pretty dress Laura, my older sister, had kindly sent me when I told her my clothes had been stolen out of my car.

The cool night air refreshed me as we stepped onto the downtown sidewalk. Tall skyscrapers loomed ominously like dark forces of destruction. Sensing a predator approaching me, I turned my head and looked back nervously repeatedly.

Loud music scraped my nerves raw as we walked into a large, crowded room in a strange, boarded-up warehouse. A maze of pipes ran underneath the wooden rafters in the high ceiling. A tall man with bright pink, spiked hair and a safety pin sticking through his nose walked past. People with multi-colored, wild hair and razor blades and chains hanging around their necks talked with one another. Large, pointed metal spikes stuck out treacherously from their black, leather outfits. A heavy set, black woman wailed out emotionally charged music on a stage which glimmered with multi-colored lights. Connie chatted with a friend as I strained to hear them. I looked up into the face of a tall, Jamaican man wearing a brightly colored, flowered shirt. His white teeth shone as he smiled and shook my hand. A large, colorful button with LOVE written in bold letters protruded from his collar.

"Don't talk to that Jamaican guy. He ripped me and a friend off. He

SOPHIA MOON

refuses to pay back money he owes us. He's a total creep," Connie told me protectively.

She introduced me to a friend and they began talking. I couldn't get a word in so I began to amble restlessly around the room. Like a lost soul, I meandered through the maze of characters with their green, pink and purple hair standing in dramatic spikes on the tops of their heads. Their macabre razor blade and safety pin jewelry protruded in grisly malevolence from their eyebrows, ears, noses, lips and tongues. The loud, dissonant, pounding noise rattled my nerves and the floor spun beneath me as I listened to bits and pieces of conversations and groped my trembling way through the crowd to the bar. Climbing up onto a stool, I rested my arm on a wooden counter. A tall man with green hair and a razor blade hanging around his neck asked me what I would like to drink. I ordered a Black Russian and began gulping it nervously.

My head ached and swayed with dizziness. I saw morbid scenes in my mind of myself laying dead in my casket while family members tossed pennies with disgust, blaming me for always asking for money. I had been off of my Lithium and Stelazine for a few days and I felt my illness crawling over me like a lethal spider. I paid for my drink and began to search through the crowd for Connie and her friend. Suddenly, the Jamaican man she had told me to not talk to was standing in front of me, smiling widely. His white teeth contrasted his dark skin.

"Are you enjoying the party?", he asked.

"Yeah. That singer is really great", I replied nervously. I looked around the room for Connie but couldn't see her anywhere.

"Let's take a walk outside. There's a great café down the street where we can have a quiet cup of tea", he said in a voice that was so kind it took my breath away.

Like a sleepwalker, I followed him down the street to a glimmering, opulent café filled with marble counter tops and shining gold railings. Laughter and conversation bubbled energetically through the air as I sat down beside him, surveying the crowd with curiosity. He bought me a cup of cappuccino, the kind I had enjoyed with my Art History professors and friends in Italy. I spooned up the frothy topping dreamily as I listened to him talk about how he designed and painted T-shirts for a living. I was impressed and I wondered if he could teach me to do the same so I could avoid being a waitress for the rest of my life.

"I'd like to show you my T-shirts", he said, smiling kindly as he put the money for our drinks onto the glowing marble and gold counter. I didn't understand why I said "yes" so quickly, why I trusted him so instantly. Some force seemed to pull me along like I was under a spell. To say "no" to him just simply did not occur to me. Or if it did, I instantly erased it as a possibility for me. I simply did not say "no". Maybe because I made all men my father, in my mind, and I was not allowed to say no to him. My safety with my father had always come from saying "yes" so maybe I presumed that it would be the same with this man. My head swam and my reflexes felt numb, as though my brain had been turned off.

A bright, Yellow Cab shone in the moonlight as we walked out onto the sidewalk. I sat down beside him in the back seat, observing the metal grilling that separated us from our driver. The night was black like a tomb as we rode in lonely silence, listening to the scream of sirens. I narrowed my eyes to protect them from the harshness of the phosphorescent, searing street lights.

He paid the driver and we stepped out onto the hard concrete in front of his home. Heavy, black burglar bars stood bleakly on the windows of the several stories high row house. His key clicked as he turned it in the door. I followed him up a long, graffiti lined, dark stairwell. He turned his key with a click in his door and led me to his kitchen with a white and black checkered floor. I pulled up a chair and sat down at the small table.

"Would you like some tea?" He put several boxes of tea in front of me. I was touched by his brotherly friendliness.

"Yes. Thank you. I'd like the Mandarin Orange Spice", I replied.

Soon, his kettle whistled shrilly and he placed the steaming cup in front of me. I sipped it gratefully, looking into his kind Jamaican face.

"I would like to make my living painting shirts like you do. How do you do it?", I asked in eager curiosity.

"I paint them and then I take them around to street fairs. I sell a lot of them that way. I also show them to friends and they buy them. I've got a huge trunk of them to sell. Come with me and I'll show them to you."

I followed him into the next room and watched him pull shirt after shirt from his trunk. As I observed the intricate, multi-colored designs I admired his great talent. Feeling tired, I sat down in a fold-out canvas chair. He stacked the shirts back into the trunk and then sat down on the edge of his bed—a queen sized mattress covered with a blue comforter which lay on the dark, wooden floor with no box spring or frame for support.

"Come over here and sit beside me", he said, his eyes penetrating to the core of my inner self.

"No. That's alright. I feel more comfortable sitting here", I replied.

"Come sit beside me", he repeated, raising his voice impatiently.

I resisted passively, smiling at him sweetly. He stood up suddenly and grabbed me forcefully by the arm. The room spun as I flew out of the chair and down onto the bed. His weight pinned me into immobility as he sat on top of my legs and pulled my flowered skirt up. Grabbing my stretchy leotard and underwear, he pulled them to the side, exposing my genitals. Then, with the violence of an animal, he forced his stiff, long penis inside my vagina.

"Oh pussy, I love pussy", he crooned in a voice devoid of humanity, thrusting inside me again and again. I considered pounding him with my fists or gouging out his eyes with my fingernails. But images of him beating and killing me froze me into cadaver-like stillness. Suddenly, he pulled his penis out of me. I jumped up and fumbled to the door.

I hurried out and down the long, dark corridor. Street lights glowed eerily as I ran down the sidewalk, too numb to cry. I had no idea how to get home.

When I saw a bus, I motioned to the driver to stop. The door creaked as he let me in, smiling with a gentleness that soothed my massacred heart. I told him where I needed to go in a stuttering voice. The bus made struggling noises as it climbed the impossibly steep hill. I prayed that I would not soon be pregnant. The driver told me where to get off and wished me a good night.

The yellow Victorian stood like a lighthouse in a storm. I fumbled my way up the long stairway and unlocked the door. I wished I had not left the halfway house as I pulled my clothes off and dumped them onto the floor. With a listless desire to die, I put a nightshirt on and crawled into bed. Darkness smothered me as I pulled the covers over me. I curled into a fetal position and hugged myself tightly.

CHAPTER 15 ———————— OCTOBER, NOVEMBER 1982

I Want To Go Home

"DON'T YOU REMEMBER? I TOLD you to not talk to him.", Connie said, perching on the end of my bed the next day.

"I forgot. He seemed so nice that I trusted him."

"Well, just because someone seems nice doesn't mean they are. Are you going to make a police report?"

"Yeah. But I'm not sure where to call to report it."

"Call City Hall downtown. Their number is listed in the phone book."

I stepped into my elegant, white bathrobe and pulled the sash tightly around my waist, then walked down the hall to the phone on the kitchen wall. My hand trembled as I dialed the number of City Hall. A woman's voice came through the receiver.

"I want to report a rape", I said, stammering with shame.

"You'll have to come to City Hall and fill out a case form. You have to come between the hours of eight a.m. and five p.m. Monday through Saturday. Bring the clothes you were wearing when it happened with you."

I floated far above my body as I rode the bus to City Hall the next morning, carrying a plastic bag containing the flowered skirt and crimson leotard I had been wearing that tragic night. Climbing the long stairs of the stately marble and gold building, I imagined the millions of dollars I should be awarded by the Criminal Justice System. But I couldn't afford a lawyer. An overweight, tough looking, black woman ran her metal detection device up and down my body. I asked several people in the hallway which floor I should go to. Then, I watched the green floor numbers flash on the wall of the rapidly rising elevator.

Waiting in a hard chair, surrounded by strangers, I fidgeted and worried until a police officer handed me a form to fill out. I wrote the necessary information, gritting my teeth with anger as a feeling of nausea churned in my guts. Then, I handed it to him, along with my bag of clothes, telling him I had been raped. With no words of condolence, he tersely told me that someone would call me. Loneliness ate a hole through me as I rode the bus back home.

Later that afternoon a police officer arrived. I answered some questions as Connie and her friend listened. I climbed into the back seat of his police car with Connie's friend. Connie directed the officer to the rapist's apartment.

"We'll keep watch on his place for a few days. We ought to be able to catch him", the officer said confidently.

"Good. We can get back the money he owes us", Connie said in a hopeful voice.

As the officer drove us home, I stared out the window feeling completely disconnected from my body. The officer told me he would keep an eye on my rapist and then gave me his card with a look of empathy. I followed Connie up the stairs into her room. As I sat on the edge of her bed I looked around at her trinkets and posters.

"In this city, when you go to a man's apartment it automatically means that you want to have sex", she explained. My heart sank that I had not been told that earlier. I would have known to say "no" to all men and spared myself all my horrible suffering.

The next morning I couldn't wait to get to my session with Dr. Stanfield. I just assumed that my father was paying for it, though he never told me that directly. He was so kind, he would probably see me for free. Looking at my Mickey Mouse watch I sped up my pace. My keys jingled as I put them into my handbag with my wallet. As I drove through the city I yelled at the top of my lungs.

I seemed to be floating far above my body as I walked up the stairs and into the Kundalini Clinic. Dr. Stanfield smiled gently as he opened the door. I sat down in my chair staring at the floor in shame.

"How are you?", he asked.

"I'm devastated. I got raped. I went out with my housemate and her friend and a Jamaican guy asked me to go to his apartment. He served me tea and then, all of a sudden, he raped me. I can't believe it."

"You're kidding. Oh, no…after all you've been through. I'm sorry to hear that. What did he look like?"

"Well, he was Jamaican and he had a gold cap on his front tooth."

"Let's do some work on the mat", he said, standing up and walking over to the mattress. I reclined back on the bed and stared up at the ceiling as he gave me instructions.

"We're going to go through the scene as though it is happening. We won't do it in detail of course. I want you to pretend that I'm the rapist. I'm going to push down on you and I want you to push against me and yell, 'Get off of me.' Put all of your emotion into it and let all of the anger out."

His heavy weight pushed against my chest and I began to yell, "Get off of me."

"See him bearing down on you, that's right. See his ugly, gold tooth. You know what he's going to do."

As I pushed back with every ounce of strength I had, I envisioned stabbing my rapist's heart out. After yelling and pushing for a while, I collapsed in exhaustion. As I hugged Dr. Stanfield goodbye I wanted to stay with him.

The most bitter loneliness I had ever felt weighed me down as I sat in a stupor on my bed that night. The sounds of my housemates playing cards and laughing in the living room irritated me. When I walked to the kitchen to get something to drink, I noticed that they were snorting cocaine and smoking marijuana. I wondered if I needed to start taking my Lithium and Stelazine again. Maybe Dr. Stanfield was not the expert he thought he was.

The next morning, I could barely move a muscle. I lay on my bed like a corpse staring at the ceiling. Thoughts of going to the Golden Gate bridge and jumping off ran through my mind. I could tie a boulder around my ankle and I would drown quickly. Not such a bad way to go.

Deep depression weighed me down as I pulled on my clothes. Slowly, like a zombie, I walked into the kitchen. The burner on the stove became red as I turned it on, poured some oil into the frying pan and took my last two eggs out of the refrigerator. The orange yolks plopped into a bowl and I stirred them quickly with a fork. The eggs began to sputter as I poured them into the hot frying pan and sliced my tiny cube of cheese on top.

After breakfast, I called the city hall to talk with the manager of my rape report. He asked me to come see him that afternoon. I screamed at the top of my lungs as I drove down the confusing streets toward City Hall. Praying that I wouldn't get a parking ticket, I parked at a meter in front of the huge building. I had no change but there was time left on it, luckily.

I ran up the long stairs into the fancy marble and gold building. A tough looking, black woman ran her metal detection device over my body. Tension tied my muscles in tight knots as the elevator rose to the fifth floor. I waited for what seemed like eternity, flipping through magazines nervously. Finally, a tall, slender, white man with graying hair called me into his office.

"The police caught him and brought him in here and we locked him up for about two hours. We couldn't arrest him though because there was no semen on the clothes you gave us. But I really reprimanded him", he said matter of factly.

I screamed at the top of my lungs in a hysterical rage as I drove home. This land of freedom allowed men to get away with murder. He had ruined my life and all he got was a scolding. As I drifted off to sleep, I realized that I had made a fatal mistake when I gave Darryl my new phone number. I simply was not in love with him. His coldness felt like salt in my festering wounds.

He called me a few days later and asked me to go downtown with him to a celebration for gay people. Refusing at first, I felt proud of myself. However, when he persisted, telling me it was an occasion I didn't want to miss, I backed down. His vulnerability moved me when I opened the front door and let him in. He told me he loved me and that he was afraid I would leave him. Big, crocodile tears rolled down his face as he heaved out gut wrenching sobs.

"Please don't leave me. I can't live without you", he cried as I held him in my arms tightly. After releasing his emotions, he looked up gratefully.

"I bought a really great video camera. I'll show you how to use it and you can interview and film people. It's going to be really wild. All the gay men will be dressed up in outlandish costumes. They really go all out. You'll meet some real characters." His face shone with enthusiasm.

We left the house and caught the bus downtown. After a winding, interesting ride, we walked down a hill. My eyes widened in disbelief as men in bouffant wigs and flouncy, ruffled chiffon dresses teetered by on high heels. Brightly colored rouge and lipstick shone on their faces in the glowing streetlights. Eyeliner and beautiful false eyelashes made their feminine, fluttering eyes irresistible. Lively conversation buzzed around us as the spirit of celebration vibrated like electricity through the air. It was nearing Halloween and I reminisced on how that was my favorite night when I was a child.

"Go up to that man and ask him how he's enjoying the festivities", Darryl urged in an enthusiastic tone.

I was shy about approaching strangers and I resisted at first. However, as I held the camera up, I looked through the peephole with intrigue. A friendly man described his experience of the event with gushing praise as he fluttered his long, black eyelashes. His neon, pink lipstick shone as he moved his mouth expressively. Gold hoop earrings hung from his ears. Rings and bracelets adorned his hands which moved gracefully as he talked. His off-white, chiffon dress cascaded down to his knees and bloomed into feminine ruffles. A diving bust line revealed huge, voluptuous breasts. He breathed sexily, heaving them in and out with a sensual, mischievous look. His small waist was tightened with a shiny, satin sash which was tied in a pretty bow.

After I finished my brief filming, Darryl and I meandered through the crowd enjoying the festivities. The cool, night air refreshed me as we walked to a corner liquor store. Darryl bought a bottle of red wine. Birds chirped cheerfully in the trees as we sat on a bench and drank it. Soon, we had consumed the entire bottle.

"I've got to get a good night's sleep so I'll feel refreshed for my therapy session with Dr. Stanfield", I said.

"You don't need him. He doesn't understand your problems. He's just a quack", Darryl replied.

I realized how controlling he was. He didn't want me talking to anyone but him. It was ironic that he had earlier said I needed therapy and taken me to the clinic and, now, he wanted to convince me that my therapist was not good for me. I needed a break from him and felt relieved when he left me at my front door.

Loud traffic and bright sun woke me. Like a sleepwalker, I walked into the kitchen. I sat down at the table and scanned through the job listings. Their unappealing requirements hammered on my ransacked brain. Barbara walked into the room as I read in silent agony.

"Boy, there sure are a lot of sales jobs listed in the paper", I commented to her, looking at her and smiling.

"I avoid any adds that say sales. I don't like doing sales. You have to be pushy and obnoxious and that is just not me", she said, looking at me with affection. I longed for my volunteer job at the art museum and wished that I had not quit it when I moved. Her kind attention calmed me when she invited me to go with her to a great café that evening. I told her I would love to and that I would meet her at five thirty. Wishing her a good day, I left for my appointment.

Dr. Stanfield greeted me warmly and told me that my father had called and sent his love and my mother's. I told him that I wanted to visit them. He responded that it was not a good idea and that it might impede the great progress I had made in my therapy. Still, my mind was made up.

I talked with him for a while and then pounded on the mattress with a tennis racket. Rage poured out of me like hot lava flying from a volcano. I wanted my end of the session hug to last forever, as I drank in unconditional love thirstily.

Later on, Barbara's kind company comforted me as I walked to a café with her. As I sat at the outdoor, umbrella table eating a cheeseburger, I absorbed her caring presence. The spicy taste of mustard, ketchup, tomato and onions satisfied my taste buds. I'd grown tired of eating oatmeal for a week. She listened with compassion as I revealed my desire to get rid of Darryl. I doubted myself when she commented that he really cared about me. I wondered if she had talked with him and become his friend.

After our walk home, I got on the phone and bought a plane ticket home, which I paid for. Even though my father was sometimes harsh and my mother could be cold, I needed them. No one else loved me like they did.

After laying in bed reading for about a week, I decided to get out into the world and try again for a job. A tall man with dark hair started talking with me as I stood at a bus stop. He told me that he worked for an organization that was making efforts to bring about a freeze of the production of Nuclear Weapons in Russia and the United States. In an urgent tone, he told me he needed volunteers and gave me a pamphlet which I read, with interest, as the bus struggled up and down the crazy hills. I filled out applications in some stores downtown.

Three nights later, I rode the bus downtown. A new feeling of purpose lifted me out of my despair as I rode the elevator to the tenth floor of a tall skyscraper. With hopeful anticipation I walked down the hall and into a room. People greeted me with friendly smiles and handed me literature about the nuclear disarmament movement.

The enthusiastic, idealistic leader briefed us for an hour. Then, everyone went out in twos to different areas of the city. Invigorated, determined energy surged in me as I walked up and down long, hilly blocks, knocking on peoples' doors and getting them to sign petitions. Every now and then someone would donate some money. A volunteer had a get together at her house later on. I met a stunningly handsome man named Carl who asked me to give him a ride home. As I drove and he talked, I fell in love with him.

I asked Darryl to keep an eye on my car while I was gone visiting my parents so it wouldn't get plastered with expensive parking tickets. The brutality of the parking police sent my stress level to the clouds.

November 20th, 1982 arrived and I took a plane East to visit my parents. Dr. Stanfield had worried about me going back into the fire. He said that I had made such progress in my therapy that he would hate to have me relapse into old patterns. Yet, I missed them terribly. I longed desperately for love and I remembered the times they had given me that. I felt the need to return to that secure place under their wings, protected from the cruel world. They only abused me because they were frustrated and it did not mean they didn't love me. They were the only people in the world who sat up at night worrying about me.

My visit with my parents turned out to be painful just as Dr. Stanfield had predicted. They talked on and on about their trip to New Zealand or Australia and completely ignored me as we sat eating in various restaurants. I longed for someone to make eye contact with me as they talked about themselves, as remote as ice sculptures.

One afternoon, as I sat with them in a restaurant, I broke down in tears. A waitress asked if she could refill my glass, looking at me with concern. Her acknowledgement helped. My isolation felt unbearable as I realized that my father had barely made eye contact with me since I'd arrived. Not that that was unusual. My mother did say a few things to me now and then. But, I needed someone to touch me, to look into my eyes. The misery of my isolation had frozen me into a sub human, voiceless sideshow freak. I needed them to speak to the real me. I sat in anxious, lonely silence, listening to them talk about themselves.

"Being ignored by the person who is paying the bill makes me feel like a little dog who is being fed", I blurted out suddenly.

A torrent of tears streamed down my face. My father continued to eat, avoiding eye contact with me. My younger sister, Judy, rolled her eyes as though I was being completely unreasonable.

"Well, don't cause a scene in our favorite restaurant", my mother said in a scolding tone, cutting through me critically with her eyes.

Like a lost soul, I teetered precariously at the top of a dangerous cliff. I wanted to cause a scene, to knock the glasses off of the table with an angry sweep and yell at the top of my lungs. My father could have wired me money when I was a naive college student, at the mercy of a rapist in a foreign country. I longed to tell them that I had been at the brink of death again and again. But I couldn't.

I swallowed my rage. Tension filled the air as I did my best to engage in chit chat with them for the remainder of my visit. I tiptoed and spoke quietly, trying hard to not say anything the slightest bit confrontational. I was not taking any medication and I worried that my father would grill me about it but he never asked, luckily. My teeth clenched with anxiety as I said goodbye to them at the airport. I analyzed my parents, myself and my problems as I sat through the three hour flight. The sweet smiles of stewardesses comforted me as they brought me drinks and snacks.

The plane landed with a loud jolt and the high pitched squealing of brakes screamed through my ears. A sea of baggage laden people surrounded me as I disembarked and walked through the bustling corridors of the airport. I dug for quarters in my bag and stopped at the first pay phone I found. My hand shook as I dialed but my emotional hurricane calmed down when Dr. Stanfield's compassionate voice came through the receiver. I told him I was at the airport.

"You need to have a session right away. Come to my house and I will see you", he said with a tone of urgency.

"Okay. I'll take a cab", I said.

"No. Don't take a cab. A cab will be too expensive. Take the bus. Just ask the driver for directions."

I got on a bus. A profound sense of anxiety rushed through me and I couldn't concentrate as I tried to read the various bus schedules. Getting off at the next stop, hoping I was at the right transfer point, I realized I wasn't. I was traveling away from my destination and not toward it. Noticing a Yellow Cab, I waved my arms frantically. The driver pulled up to the curb next to me and I climbed in with great relief. I would make up for the reckless splurge by not eating for the next two weeks. I needed to lose weight.

Finally, the driver pulled up to the curb in front of Dr. Stanfield's house.

Neatly manicured grass surrounded the concrete path that led to the door. My knuckles hurt as I knocked on the hard, wooden door several times. The door opened slowly with a creaking sound.

"How did your visit go?" His eyes calmed me as he gave me his complete attention.

"It was very difficult. I felt really tense the whole time. They never listened to me and they were cold and distant. My father hardly ever made eye contact with me. It was like we were light years apart. I finally broke down crying in the middle of a restaurant."

"I was trying to get you to not go. I didn't think it was a good idea when you had made so much progress in your therapy. They are just not sensitive like you are."

"Well, I keep hoping it's going to be different."

"They're not going to change. You just have to accept their limitations and get on with your life. You can go to the Raja Yoga center where I go and learn to meditate. You will find a whole new family there. You're not going to find such loving people anywhere. So concentrate on the doughnut and not the hole."

"Yeah. I need to get on with my life. It's hard adjusting to the new place I'm in. I wish I had stayed in the halfway house. It must be too late now though. I've been looking for a job but I can't find anything."

"Look. Everything is being computerized." He held a magazine up. It had a bold cover which announced the shift to the computer age.

"I'll take you by the Community College and you can enroll in a computer class. Then you'll qualify for a lot more jobs", he said. I nodded in agreement, even though I knew I didn't have the money for it.

Connie knocked on my door the next morning. She greeted me enthusiastically as I opened the door and then she sat on my bed, looking affectionately into my eyes.

"We all took acid and ran around the house nude while you were gone. We had a blast. You should have been here. You would have had a great time."

Sunlight surrounded us in a golden glow as we sat and talked. She talked about her work and various guys that she had been seeing. I longed to be vivacious and talkative like her. I felt dead in comparison—like I had had every ounce of happiness pounded out of me.

Carl called me the next day and asked me to go to a street fair and collect signatures for the Nuclear Freeze with him in a few days. With great elation, I told him I would love to.

Like a fool, I went to Darryl's place and slept on his mat with him the night before I met Carl. As darkness swallowed me up, I relaxed into the comfort of his warm body.

My arm was twisted into an uncomfortable position, pressed against the hard wall, as the sound of rushing traffic woke me up. Sun streamed through the window as I looked at my watch and realized I only had fifteen minutes to get to Carl's place.

"I've got to go", I said, jumping up in a panic of disappointment.

"Where are you going?" Darryl asked in a suspicious tone.

"I've got to go collect signatures for the Nuclear Freeze", I replied.

"I'll go with you", he said in an authoritarian tone.

I had no strength to speak up to him. Feeling too afraid to face a confrontation, I turned and hurried out. Running down the stairs and out onto the sidewalk, I bristled with determination to be free of him forever. I ran and ran until I reached a street corner. Waiting for the light to change, I relished my freedom.

My blood froze when, suddenly, he appeared beside me. He grabbed my hand and stared threateningly into my eyes. Feeling like a trapped animal, I pulled my hand away. A bus pulled up to the corner and the door opened with a thud. I stepped up the stairs and he followed me. As he sat beside me, I stared straight ahead, recoiling from his domineering energy reeling through me like deadly radar.

Soon, the bus arrived at the corner near my Yellow Victorian. I stepped out onto the street and began running toward Carl's place. Wedding scenes flashed through my mind as I ran up his stairs and banged loudly on his door. I wanted to collapse in his arms and pour out my distress to him. He opened the door holding a card table under his arm. His sea blue eyes and sun streaked, blonde hair graced his perfect gentle face. Trying to appear unruffled, I followed him down his narrow stairway and out onto the street.

Darryl stood with his back leaned up against a car, beckoning me with his hand. Every muscle in my body tightened with dread as he glared at me with cold, controlling eyes as though he owned me.

"Come here. I want to talk to you". His demanding tone cut through me, killing my spirit. I walked over to him submissively and looked into his eyes.

"I don't want you going with him", he said, pulling me toward him to hug me. My body went rigid with disgust.

"Why don't you like Carl?", I asked.

"He's much too good looking to like." His eyes sliced through me like steel knives.

I turned and walked back to Carl who looked uneasy standing there holding the card table under his arm. We began walking toward the bus stop as I looked down at the ground. I worried that he probably thought Darryl was my boyfriend. I longed to tell him the truth-- that I was his prisoner.

We sat side by side on the bus in awkward silence. I worried that Darryl had ruined my chances with him. He spoke with gentle warmth as I fidgeted nervously. We worked at separate tables, passing out Nuclear Freeze literature and then chatted casually as we rode the bus home together. I never got the nerve to pour my heart out to him. I longed for more as I got off of the bus and told him goodbye.

CHAPTER 16 —————————————— DECEMBER, 1982
I Need An Angel To Help Me

BRIGHT SUNLIGHT AND ROARING TRAFFIC woke me the next morning as I longed for someone to talk to. I sat on my bed staring at the wall in a state of complete overwhelm. Darryl came to visit me that afternoon. Like a hateful vulture, he fanned the flames of my misery, beating me with his ugly, frayed wings. I shriveled and died inside as he yelled at me callously.

"Your car is on Stanyan Street. I took care of it while you were visiting your parents. I thought you would come visit me when you got back but you obviously think so little of me it didn't occur to you. You're a very selfish person", he said, narrowing his eyes with contempt. His jaw was rigid with rage.

"I've had a lot of things to do and I was too tired to walk over there", I replied, raising my voice in self-defense. I had been afraid to go into his neighborhood and to see him.

"If you had wanted to see me you would have crawled over", he yelled.

I began to relive all the times in my childhood when my parents had told me that I was rotten to the core. I stood and listened as he continued to accuse and blame, thinking that he must be right about me and feeling my illness, once again, wreaking havoc. After he had raged for a while and watched me shrink in fear he left.

I walked to the telephone in the hall and called my brother. I would buy myself a roundtrip flight and visit him. I would just not buy groceries for a while. It was worth it to get some love. He had not paid for my flight on the first visit and I did not want to ask him to. The five hundred dollars a month my father sent me miraculously stretched a long way. Joy rose inside me when my brother invited me to spend Christmas with him.

After a few days, I went over to Darryl's neighborhood and got my car, avoiding walking by his apartment. I worried that he might suddenly appear. I wished I had never met him.

Time passed quickly and, soon, it was time to visit my brother. Jeffrey, my housemate, offered to drive me to the airport. Darryl insisted on going with me. We climbed into the back of Jeffrey's van. I sat timidly in a fetal position on the floor as Jeffrey drove through the streets, his kind face comforting me as I caught glimpses of it in the mirror.

Jeffrey smiled warmly and wished me a good Christmas as he let me out at the front of the airport. I walked quickly, trying to escape Darryl but he followed me all the way to the gate. He sat next to me, watching me like a prison warden, until a pleasant voice announced that it was time for me to board. I told him goodbye and walked down the ramp with my fellow travelers. A sweet stewardess greeted me as I stepped onto the plane.

My brother, Paul, picked me up at the airport. His relaxed, calm demeanor soothed me and his playful sense of humor made me laugh for the first time in eternity. He took me out to eat in an exquisite, flower filled restaurant. Ice clinked in glasses and chandeliers shimmered.

"I've been feeling really great. I took a trip with a friend to Catalina Island last weekend. It is a gorgeous place with lots of tropical flowers and white sand beaches. We had a great time exploring around."

I listened gratefully, enjoying a delicious plate of shrimp, rice and vegetables. I told him I had been taking art classes and making new friends in San Francisco.

The days passed in a golden glow of lighthearted cheerfulness as I settled into the tranquility of his tiny efficiency apartment. It was a soft cocoon—a sacred haven from the cold city. My heart was thawing as I reveled in his attentive generosity. He had encouraged me to pursue my interests and sided with me when my parents were cruel. I had not called him to tell him the details of all my traumas because I did not want to burden him.

He was not a therapist and would not know how to respond. He took me to good restaurants and movies and we strolled along the ocean under a softly shimmering moon every night. His funny stories and silly behavior made me laugh and I felt myself coming alive again.

Everything was perfect until we drove to L.A. to see Sophie's Choice, the new movie which had been getting rave reviews. The crowd was talkative as we pushed our way into the theatre and found some seats. My head swam with dizziness, like I was flashing back to marijuana trips I had taken with Darryl. The movie told the tragic story of a Holocaust survivor.

When the movie was over, my brother stormed out of the theater. He gritted his teeth and glared at me as he got into the driver's seat, slamming the door in frustration. Too stunned to speak, I looked at him wondering what had precipitated his anger.

"You know, I've finally figured out why you don't have any friends. I was really enjoying the movie but, when you started acting up, you just ruined it for me. In the most dramatic scene I said, 'Isn't this wonderful?' and do you know what you said? You said, 'Needs cutting'. I can't stand your behavior any more. I'm taking you somewhere where you can be alone and think", he said, his voice crackling with anger.

A bolt of pain shot through my heart. I had not deliberately done anything to upset him. I had been trying to impress him with my knowledge about the editing process in film making.

I sat in silence and watched helplessly as he pulled into the parking lot of a Ramada Inn. I followed him into the lobby and watched him book a room with a tall, brunette clerk. Images of our idyllic time together filled my heart with bittersweet happiness as I followed him onto the elevator. Like a bad child being punished by her father, I hung my head in shame. Soon, the elevator reached the tenth floor.

He strode down the hall in fast, furious strides as I followed him meekly, too afraid to say anything. The door clicked as he turned the key and opened it. I followed him into the room and sat down on one of the double beds. He sat down and looked at me with a serious expression.

"I'm doing this because I love you very much. I'm going to leave you here. Your behavior has been really grating on my nerves and I just can't take it any more. I was afraid I might hit you earlier and I didn't want to do that. Here's eighty dollars. You can find your own way back to San Francisco."

I wasn't aware of my behavior yet I guessed that it must be pretty bizarre. Maybe stopping my Lithium had been a mistake.

He put four twenty dollar bills on the bedside table. I racked my brain for some solution to my predicament as he walked out the door. Suddenly, it dawned on me that I had the phone number of my father's cousin. I dialed his number with a trembling hand.

"My brother left me stranded in a hotel room in Los Angeles and I don't have enough money to pay my room bill and pay for a plane back to San Francisco. I don't know what to do", I said in a mouse like voice.

"You can call traveler's aid", he replied.

I recalled his kind manner and his face framed with white hair. I had enjoyed a wonderful visit with him. His spectacles had perched precariously at the tip of his nose as he sat next to his small, quiet wife in their farm house in Northern California. His daughter had been a close friend of mine and had sewn me a stunning, royal blue cape. He was famous for his scientific discoveries.

I hung up the phone and called Traveler's Aid. A worker told me that there was a bus that went up and down the coast called The Green Tortoise. I imagined friendly hippies swinging in hammocks, munching natural goodies, smoking joints and reading as it wound around mountainous roads with exquisite ocean views.

I grabbed my bag and walked out of the door, locking it behind me. My pants legs rubbed together making swishing noises as I took quick, long strides down the hall. I stepped onto the elevator and watched the green numbers change as it made its rapid descent. Looking around nervously, I walked through the lobby. Clerks worked efficiently, looking clean and neat in their uniforms. Sunlight hit my eyes as I walked to the large, glass door and pushed it open with an angry thrust. I hadn't remembered to pay for the room I suddenly realized with a gasp.

Tall, sterile skyscrapers loomed in grisly gloominess along the smog splotched skyline. Gunning car motors pierced my eardrums as I hurried across the street. Waitresses hurried back and forth as I sat down at a table in a diner. A tired looking, wrinkled waitress took my order—a bowl of prunes. I felt completely lost, hopeless and desperately alienated. No one loved me in the whole world except Harold. My eyes darted around the room, nervously scanning for predators.

My mind raced and my muscles tensed when I walked outside. A huge truck barreled along the smelly asphalt, almost blowing me off the ground. I hurried along, observing the endless sprawl of concrete high rises and clutching my shoulder bag tightly as my mind raced with images of criminals. When I arrived at the grimy parking lot of a fast food place, I looked with disgust at the garbage which was strewn haphazardly around on the ground. I sat down on the curb. Suddenly, I saw a white station wagon stop near me. A man with light, brown hair leaned his head out of the window.

"Can I give you a ride somewhere? Where are you staying?", he asked with a concerned expression and gentle voice.

I narrowed my eyes at him suspiciously, then began looking down at the ground and wishing he would go away.

"You need to get out of here. It's not safe to sit out here", he urged me compassionately.

I scowled at him, then walked away, ignoring him as he tried his best to convince me he wanted to help me. As I pulled open the door to the hamburger joint, I gagged as I inhaled the stench of sweat and bloody meat. My mind raced with chaotic fragments of dramas, moving in a continuous kaleidoscope, pulling me into a swirling, frenzied whirlpool. I sat down in a hard booth and looked out of the grease and dirt smeared windows. Outside, the street screamed hideously with the clamor of barreling trucks and speeding cars. Exhausted looking drivers clutched the steering wheels tightly, their eyes glued vacantly on the road ahead. Poisonous, smelly carbon monoxide spewed through the air. If hell existed, this was most definitely it.

Knots of anxiety hardened inside my body as I walked back to the hotel, sweating profusely. I pushed my way through the revolving door and looked around the fancy lobby. My mind raced with worries that a convention had been planned and people were traveling from all over the world to humiliate me. Their voices blared through me —"Whore, loser, failure, schizophrenic, fat, crazy, stupid, lazy, unnatural child, bitch, incorrigible." They scraped my nerves raw until an endless scream welled up inside me. I rode the elevator to the tenth floor and walked down the empty corridor to my room. The door made a death like sound of finality as it slammed shut behind me. My miserable fate seemed sealed. I would have to hobble through life as an emotional cripple, unable to function. Tears streamed down my face as I collapsed on the bed feeling conquered. I wanted to give up. Life was just too hard.

I jumped when I heard a knock on my door. I opened it fearfully and two desk clerks told me I would need to pay my bill. I told them I did not have enough cash to pay the whole bill. They suggested that I call someone and ask for help. I didn't know who to call. It seemed like I had driven everyone away.

I didn't even know how many days had passed and time was a blur. I reflected on how inspired and alive I had felt when I studied Art History in Europe. It had been an enchanted summer. I missed my friend Sandra who I had formed a special bond with. She was the only person who I had told about the rape I experienced that summer. I had not seen her since August, 1981, when I had left her house she shared with my German travel companion to drive across the country. Rummaging through my bag for her number, I groped madly, hungering to feel like a human being again. Hope rose within me as I found her number. I picked up the receiver and dialed it. The warm feeling of familiarity rolled through me as her voice came through the phone. I asked her how she was doing.

"I'm fine. I've been really busy working. I'm planning to go back to school. I like living in Washington D.C. There are a lot of interesting things to do and I enjoy going to the museums. I've been dating a lot of different men. How are you?", she asked.

"Not very good. My brother left me stranded in a hotel room in Los Angeles. I'm here all alone and I'm really worried about how I'm going to find my way back to San Francisco. I moved there about a year ago."

"Why did he do that?"

"I said something in the middle of a movie that he didn't like but I didn't do anything intentional to upset him."

"Boy, that was really lousy of him."

"Some men came into my room about fifteen minutes ago and told me I would have to pay my bill. I owe two hundred and seventy six dollars. My brother only left me eighty dollars. That's all the money I have in the world. I don't know what to do."

"Well, just tell them you have every intention of paying the bill but you didn't expect it to be so high. They'll understand", she said in a sweet tone which calmed me down.

Fifteen minutes later I heard a knock on my door. The two brunette, heavy set men looked at me as I opened the door.

"Do you have someone to help you pay your bill?" I dreaded calling my father, remembering how even asking him for lunch money in high school had terrified me.

"Here is my brother's phone number", I replied, writing it down and handing it to him. Then, I called my father and told him where I was and that my brother had left me in a strange hotel room in Los Angeles.

I whiled away the evening, sitting in the fancy hotel restaurant. Chandeliers shimmered in the mirrors and moonlight glowed on the blue water of the outside pool. Artichokes, spinach, tomatoes, olives, lettuce and blue cheese dressing soothed my emotions and my stomach. The days blurred together as I watched T.V., listened to my inner voices and watched myriad images flash on the movie screen of my mind.

A knock on my door brought me back to reality just when I couldn't bear another minute of isolation.

"Your brother is here to take you to the airport," the clerk said sweetly one morning. He smiled, feeling happy to see me delivered from my dilemma. I shuffled into the bathroom. Combing my fingers through my hair, I looked at my haggard face in the bathroom mirror. Puffy bags stood out hideously under my eyes. The sound of trickling water calmed me as I washed my face with the small bar of soap. I dried it with a clean, white towel. The taste of mint refreshed my sour mouth as I brushed my teeth.

Riding the elevator down to the lobby, I dreaded going back to San Francisco. The elevator doors whooshed open. I saw my brother standing at the check in desk talking with a clerk. I looked sheepishly up into his blue eyes.

He sighed with impatience and looked disapprovingly at me. I followed him to his car. The motor chortled and he began driving. I sat in silence, clasping my hands nervously, terrified of saying something that might set him off again. He gave me the silent treatment as he drove down the crowded, frenetic freeway. When he dropped me off in front of the airport I told him goodbye. Then, I thanked him for paying for my return flight.

I pushed the steel and glass door open and began walking down the airport corridor. As people hurried this way and that, I searched their faces like a lonely scavenger looking for love. After a brisk walk full of chattering voices and colorfully clothed people, I arrived at my gate. I flipped restlessly through a stack of magazines until a voice came over the loudspeaker and told us it was time to board. I read quietly and, soon, the plane raced down the runway and rose into the sky.

As I watched clouds hover below me, like fluffy mounds of cotton, a dreadful suspicion that I was pregnant festered inside me. Remembering Barbara's sad tale about how her boyfriend had gotten her pregnant and then dumped her, I wondered if Darryl had gotten me pregnant a week or so ago. He had promised that he would never get me pregnant so I had not worried about buying birth control. I never had the money to pay for it and

I had trusted him. However, I wasn't aware of my naivety or the danger I put myself in by not protecting myself. Pleasing others was what kept me going. All the therapy sessions I had participated in had not cured me. I was still an emotional cripple, incapable of taking care of myself. Time passed quickly and, soon, the plane began to descend. I watched checkerboard squares becoming larger by the second as though they were being seen through a magnifying glass. My ears popped and the ground moved closer until the trees were just beneath us. With surging sounds, the plane hit the runway and began coasting toward the gate.

I followed the line of passengers down the ramp and out into the gate. Walking quickly, I found the information desk. A clerk told me that the Airporter was the cheapest way to get into the city. My jaws tightened with angry frustration as I climbed onto the huge vehicle. Staring out of the window, I looked at the foggy sky and the tall, depressing skyscrapers. The city sprawled like an endless evil trap, running its greed machine and inflicting wounds on its population. Satanic beings walked its filthy streets and preyed on trusting strangers. Murders, rapes, robberies---everything that was evil existed in this deceptive, concrete hell.

I got off of the bus downtown. My hair became wet as rain drizzled down. Flailing my arms, I signaled for a cab. Soon, a man drove toward me and I climbed inside a Yellow cab. After a long ride, he let me out in front of my house. Weariness overcame me as I climbed the stairs and unlocked the door. I walked into my room and pulled a cave of blankets around me for protection.

The next morning, I was woken by a knock on my door. I opened it and looked into Barbara's beautiful eyes. She looked gorgeous in a purple, velvet pantsuit and beaded earrings.

"We're going to have a house meeting this afternoon. Everyone needs to be there", she said in a serious yet gentle tone.

"Okay. I'll be there", I replied.

As I pulled on a cotton T-shirt and a pair of shorts, I looked forward to a walk by the ocean. Yawning widely, I combed my fingers through my hair. Putting a couple of dollars in one pocket and my keys in the other, I tiptoed down the stairs and out the front door. Playful children ran along the graffiti-filled street as I walked to the bus stop. I leaned against a white post and, soon, my sweet chariot to freedom arrived.

I ran along the beach, listening to the crashing of waves. Refreshing spray moistened my face as the cool breeze rippled through my hair. Seagulls flew gracefully, circling and crying poignantly. Pelicans swooped down, flapping their huge wings and landing with a splash on the water. They looked comical as they caught fish in their huge beaks. The hypnotic rolling and cresting of the waves in the vast, blue ocean relaxed me. I walked barefoot, dipping my feet into the cool water which foamed with white bubbles.

I didn't want to leave but, when I looked at my Mickey Mouse watch, I realized I needed to hurry. When I got back to the house everyone was gathered in the living area. As I walked in and sat down in an armchair, I felt everyone scrutinizing me.

"We're having this meeting because we have all noticed that you are very unstable. We think that you need to be in a place where you can get the help you need. This is a really high stress environment with all of us going different ways with busy schedules. You would do better in a place where you had less stress to deal with and where you could get regular counseling. We want you to find another place to live", Barbara said, speaking with calm decisiveness.

"Well, you can't just kick me out. I'm doing the best I can and I don't have anywhere else to go."

"Well, we are having trouble living with you. It is just not working for us. We're looking for someone else to move in", Connie said firmly. Her words cut me to the core. Her friendship had meant everything to me.

"Your alarm goes off at three in the morning. You stay in your room all the time and you seem to be afraid all the time", Nick, who lived in the room next to me, said.

"I'm sorry. I'm not good with mechanical things. I couldn't figure out how to set it", I replied in a faltering, self-conscious voice.

"When you came upstairs and screamed, my mother was so concerned about me she was going to find me another place to live", Nick continued.

"I'm sorry. I react badly to pot. I won't ever smoke it again", I replied, staring at the floor in shame.

"Well, we're giving you two weeks. You'll have to be out of here in that time", Bob, the Jewish photographer, said forcefully looking at me with critical eyes.

"We really care about you. We just want to see you get the help you need", Barbara said.

"I've been on the phone all morning trying to get someone at the Haight Ashbury clinic to counsel you", Nick said looking at me with genuine concern.

"We all want to see things get better for you. Ask Larry to help you", Barbara said.

I slunk into my room in a state of profound despair. Larry was a skinny, black guy who hung around the house. He had made it obvious that he wanted to get inside my pants. I needed his "help" like a cup of poison. Crawling into bed, I curled into a fetal position and hugged myself. As I pulled my blanket over me, I longed for death. I looked at my Mickey Mouse watch and realized I had a session with Dr. Stanfield.

CHAPTER 17 ———————JANUARY/FEBRUARY, 1983
Street Urchin Blues

D R. STANFIELD HUGGED ME WARMLY when I arrived for my session. I held back tears as I told him that I no longer had a home. "I'm going to make an appointment for you to see a social worker. You need someone to help you while I'm gone. I'll be gone for three weeks", he said.

I listened to him talk to the social worker on the phone. He wrote down the time and place of my appointment and handed it to me.

"I'm going to India for three weeks. While I'm there I will talk with the Supreme soul. We call him Baba out of affection. He will give you everything. He wants you to be completely happy," he said.

Then, he listened with compassion to my woeful story. I hit the mattress with the tennis racket and yelled for a while. He gave me a long, warm hug at the end of our session.

Without Harold, I could barely make it through a day. As January 1983 arrived, I deteriorated in my bed, contemplating jumping off of the Golden Gate Bridge. Rain poured down and a depressing, gray sky filled with fog chilled me to the bone. My stomach grumbled with hunger as I walked despondently into the kitchen. I had no food, not even a slice of bread. My wallet money had dwindled down to only two dollars. Suddenly, the telephone rang. I jumped nervously.

"This is Darryl. I want to talk to you." His voice cut through me, rattling my nerve endings.

"I've got a lot of things to do."

"Oh, come on. Don't give me that bullshit. I'm coming over there." He slammed down the phone.

I sat on the sofa fidgeting and worrying. I picked up the phone when it rang again.

"I'm across the street in a phone booth. I've got to talk to you." His cold tone sent a shiver down my spine.

I held the phone in my hand, too numb to move, to think, to speak. Dr. Stanfield had gone to India just when I needed him most. I tried to hang up but couldn't. My good girl politeness gripped me mercilessly.

"I don't want to talk to you. I think it is best that we stop seeing each other."

"Oh come on. You can't be that selfish. Not after all I've done for you. I'm getting drenched out here. I might come down with pneumonia. I've walked all the way over here in the pouring rain to talk to you. I'm walking up to your front door now. If you care anything about me at all you'll let me in."

I walked down the stairs to the front door and looked through the peephole. He looked like a drowned rat as he waited, his hair flat and sopping wet. Water trickled down his face as he stared through the peephole with sad eyes. Remembering his words of eternal love, I opened the door for him.

His face turned stone-like as his eyes stabbed through me like swords. Suddenly, his hands were around my throat. He heaved the weight of his body against me. As I fell backwards onto the stairs, a sharp pain shot up my spine. His wet, heavy body crashed down on top of me. A sensation of terror went through me as he gripped my throat tighter and tighter, destroying my ability to breath. I tried to scream but couldn't. I remembered him showing me how he could kill someone by striking a certain organ. Scenes of my life flashed before me as I realized that I might only have a few moments left.

Suddenly, he pulled himself off of me. A deafening sound rushed through me as he left, slamming the door with every drop of strength he had. I walked up the stairs and collapsed on my bed. Hugging my pillow desperately, I remembered seeing a pregnancy center on the first floor of Dr. Stanfield's building. With lonely despondency, I walked to the kitchen phone and called the clinic. A kind woman's voice soothed me as she set up an appointment for a pregnancy test the next day.

I took the test and, three days later, I rode the bus to the clinic to get my results. A gentle woman told me I was pregnant. She touched my hand as she told me I could make my own choice about whether to have the baby and raise her myself, put her up for adoption or have an abortion. Then, she handed me a pamphlet from Planned Parenthood. Part of me was captivated as I thought about rocking an adorable, little infant in my arms. The other part of me recoiled at the thought of becoming a hopelessly insane mother wandering the streets, searching for shelter as I tried to scrounge together enough money to feed myself and my baby.

As I hurried down the street to the bus stop, I realized time was critical. A precious being was growing second after second inside me. Would it be a boy or a girl? Would she love me, be like me, call me Mommy with pure devotion? I prayed to get her yanked from me immediately before I grew to love her.

The ocean called out to me and I decided to take a drive to the beach. I gasped in horror when I looked into my car. A large rope, formed in the shape of a noose, hung forebodingly from the ceiling. Grabbing it fearfully, I pulled it free and, when I saw a trash dumpster, I threw it in. As I drove up and down the hills, clutching my steering wheel tightly, I wondered if Darryl or one of the guys I lived with had put the noose in my car.

The blue sparkle of the ocean cooled my feverish anxieties and the fresh air opened my lungs and heart. Movies of wealthy, fashionable people soaking in the saunas of the Cliff House went through my mind. I saw women wearing short dresses with bobbed hair. Long, shiny beads hung around their necks. They did the Charleston, laughing with delight. Handsome, well-dressed men got drunk and swallowed goldfish. Sadness rolled through me as I remembered my grandmother teaching me how to do the Charleston. I wanted to return to those simple days when she told me I was her favorite. I had lost her a year ago. I had not had the money to fly back East to her funeral.

I walked down a path to a special place that looked out over the ocean. Sea lions sprawled on the cliffs below, calling out in their unique voices. Seagulls flew effortlessly through the air. Pelicans bobbed up and down on the waves or swooped down to scoop up fish in their huge beaks. Now and then, a big boat would go chugging through the water.

The rhythmic rolling of the waves, as they crested and broke with a white froth of foam, lulled me into relaxation. Nature always gave me certainty that a force of divine love existed. As I observed the precision with which she moved through her seasons, her tides synchronized perfectly with the movement of the planets, the sun and the moon, I realized there was a divine being behind it all. I missed Dr. Stanfield with all my heart. At first, I had thought he was just another California nut case. Yet, I wanted to believe that he was, in fact, talking with God. I needed God more than ever.

That night, I sat in the living room reading through the job listings. Suddenly, I heard someone storm into the kitchen. As they walked toward me I reeled in reaction to a heavy, angry vibration. I looked up into the eyes of Bob, the photographer. They cut through me with hostility.

"Have you found a place to move to?"

"No. I haven't"

"Well, you've had plenty of time to find one."

"Well, I've been busy looking for a job but I can't find one."

"You can be a presser in a laundry", he said.

"Oh yeah. Maybe", I replied, looking down at the floor despondently.

"I worked as a presser for five years. It wasn't what I wanted but I stuck with it." He talked down to me as though I was childish and irresponsible.

"Well, I'm doing the best I can but it's hard. You don't have any right to kick me out on the street."

"Oh, poor little thing. What about the stain you got on Barbara's dress and your red neck parents?" His eyes cut through me with disrespect.

"You don't have any right to talk to me like that."

"Oh, you're just pathetic."

Suddenly, he walked angrily toward me. Hate burned in his eyes as he pulled me up and slammed me against the wall with all of his strength. Pain shot through my hand as it hit the wall. I looked at my bleeding fingers with the nails broken below the quick. I had never had any prejudice against Jews but anger rose in me like an erupting volcano as his tall body loomed over me with a haughty, domineering vibration. His huge nose protruded from his arrogant, mean face as he gloated like a blood thirsty vulture feasting on my pain.

On trembling legs, I walked to the phone and called the police. In about ten minutes, two female police officers appeared at the front door. One was short and fat with dark hair and the other was tall and skinny with bleached, blond hair. I led them into the kitchen to explain what had happened.

"He threw me up against the wall. Look. My fingers are bleeding", I said, holding them up for them to see. They looked through me, totally unmoved. Suddenly Connie appeared.

"She is not supposed to be here. She's been evicted", she said. Her face, which had been so sweet was now cold and hard.

"She has been given her notice to leave. Everyone in the house decided together that they didn't want her living here. She is impossible to live with. She's supposed to be gone", Bob said with contempt.

"You can't press charges because you are not even supposed to be here. You've been evicted. You better pack your bags and get out of here now", the police officer said, looking at me with hard, punishing eyes.

Barbara suddenly appeared in my doorway.

"Larry said you can stay at his place for a few nights. He will help you move your belongings. Here's his number", she said, handing me a small scrap of paper.

I didn't want to be totally dependent on another man who wanted to screw the daylights out of me. But I went to the phone and called him. Twenty minutes later, he arrived with a friend. They carried my things down the stairs and put them in the back of a large, blue station wagon. I tried my best to behave in a polite, appreciative way as I sat, stiff with tension, in the front seat, zooming through the meandering city.

Soon, we arrived at their house in a quiet suburb. Larry said I could store my things in his garage until I found a place of my own. Compassion glowed in his eyes as he showed me a bathroom I could use and a room I could sleep in. He listened with silent caring as I told him Bob had thrown me against the wall. Handing me a box of Epsom salts, he suggested that I soak my hands to relieve the pain.

I went into the bathroom and filled the sink with warm water. Soon, my fingers felt better. I dried my hands with a fresh towel. My mind raced and a wave of panic swept through me as I realized that I might not have enough money to pay for an abortion. I better call the only person I knew who might give me some money. Shame gnawed my insides as I went to the phone and called my brother to ask him for money. My friends listened with compassion as I poured out my predicament to him.

"I've got to get an abortion and I don't have enough money to pay for it. I need you to send me some money." I stared at the floor in shame, hoping the news didn't go down the gossip vine in my family.

"There are places where you can get it done free." His detached voice sent a chill through me.

Nightmare images of going to an illegal rat hole at the end of some dark alley and having some callous butcher scrape my insides with dirty knives ran through my mind. I could get a lethal infection or bleed to death.

"I can't do that. I need you to send me some money."

"No. I'm not going to send you a penny."

I couldn't believe it. A hundred and fifty dollars was nothing to him. He could save my life by merely sacrificing a week of eating in restaurants. I looked at my friends with despair.

"Hang up on him. Hang up on him", they urged, echoing one another and moving their arms to signal me.

"Well, I have to go", I said, then put the receiver down. I began to pace back and forth frantically, cursing myself for becoming involved with a sadistic drug addict. I had been better off sleeping in my car. I called Planned Parenthood and a kind woman set an appointment for my abortion. If I had faith, the money would be provided I decided.

Larry and his friend were perfect gentlemen for the three days I stayed with them. I took hot baths, read through job and apartment listings and talked with them. Then, Larry drove me to the YMCA downtown. I walked through the neighborhood and found a bank three blocks away. Using my automatic teller card I checked my balance. It was a hundred and sixty three dollars much to my great surprise. I breathed a deep sigh of relief, feeling the racing in my heart calm down. Now I could pay for my abortion. I would just not spend a penny until the morbid job was done.

Suddenly, I remembered I had an appointment with the social worker Dr. Stanfield had set me up with. I got lost as I rode the bus through the city. Finally, I found the tall, ugly building. With my head down and my heart exploding with grief I walked into the lobby. Scanning the directory on the wall, I found the floor I was supposed to go to. I longed for one of Dr. Stanfield's warm hugs as I rode up to the fourth floor.

Walking into the office, Murdock Social Services, I smiled at the receptionist and signed my name in the appointment book. In a few minutes, a conservatively dressed social worker introduced herself as Sheila Murdock and led me into her office. Her penetrating eyes scanned and judged me as I explained to her how I became homeless. She suggested that I move into a boarding house and said that she could help me locate one. In a condescending tone, she advised that I see a psychiatrist and get some medication. She commented on my disheveled hair and the stains in my clothes. At the end of my appointment, she handed me a card with her name and number on it. Even though I knew I needed her help, I cringed at the thought of going to see her again and of experiencing her demeaning energy.

Numbness moved like ice through my senses as I struggled to find my way back to the YMCA. I walked quickly through the lobby, reeling with dizziness, and worried through the night in the grave-like silence.

Bright sunlight fell on my face the next morning. I opened my eyes slowly, yawning and stretching. Grumbling noises came from my deprived stomach as I dreamed of a delicious meal. I floated far above my body as I rode the elevator down to the main floor. The vacant eyes of old, lecherous men followed me as they sat puffing on big cigars and mumbling with one another. Phosphorescent lights shone caustically into my eyes and a mechanical humming sound moved through me as I walked into the room of snack machines. Eating a good breakfast would bring a little cheer into my misery. Rummaging through my handbag eagerly, I managed to scrape together one dollar and twenty three cents.

I dropped some change into the coke machine. A loud thud vibrated in my ears as the cold can clunked down. My coins clinked as I dropped them into another machine and watched a bag of Cheetos move forward and drop down to the pick-up slot. Grabbing the bag and ripping it open with bestial hunger, I sat down at a round, white table to eat. A thin, small woman with curly, brown hair and a lined face looked at me. She was dressed in an orange and brown polyester outfit.

"Hi. How are you?", she asked energetically, looking at me with curiosity.

"Well, I don't know where I'm going to stay tonight. I just had one night here and I don't have my own place. I got evicted from the last house I lived in", I replied, studying her wrinkled face with its small, dark, eyes, framed with short, brown hair.

"Oh, don't worry dear. You can stay with me. I live in Oakland. I've got a great room with a color T.V. I'll show you around town. We'll have a great time. My name is Mary", she said, holding out her hand. We shook hands with friendly faith.

She was strange, but staying with her seemed better than sleeping on the sidewalk. I felt my heart opening as her acceptance flowed through me. My muscles relaxed. Now, I had a way to avoid the disparaging looks and scrutinizing questions I would have to endure if I went back to the Social Worker.

I followed her out of the revolving door of the YMCA. She held her hand out protectively toward me as her eyes darted back and forth surveying the passing cars. I crossed the street by her side. She chatted enthusiastically as we walked quickly down the sidewalk. It must be about February now I guessed, watching busy looking businessmen hurry by as beggars asked for change. The sound of a rushing bus flooded my ears as we walked down a long stairway into the subway station.

"I know some girls who live in an orphanage. I go and visit them sometimes. They always look forward to seeing me. You'll have to come with me and meet them", she said, looking at me with affection.

Announcements of arrivals and departures came over an intercom. People sat waiting. Suddenly, she raised her arms dramatically and started singing The Star Spangled Banner. Her loud voice echoed through the station as she sang with inspired enthusiasm.

"You have a beautiful voice", I said, patting her on the shoulder.

"I've always loved to sing. I sang in the church choir when I was married. I used to be married to a lawyer. We had a wonderful home and two great children. Then, one day he told me he wanted a divorce", she said, her voice dropping with sadness.

The loud clattering sound of a train speeding down the tracks vibrated through me. The doors opened quickly with a whooshing sound and we stepped on and sat down. I studied her thin, aged hands with their blue veins standing out. She looked frail and vulnerable in her polyester suit which swallowed her up.

"Look at you", she said, studying me with affection as though she was cradling a special baby in her arms.

When we arrived in Oakland, we walked up a long stairway and out onto the street. Cars and buses sped by spewing carbon monoxide as we walked past shop windows displaying elegantly dressed mannequins. Soon, we arrived at a hotel. A desk clerk gave her a friendly greeting. I wondered why she lived in a hotel as the elevator rose rapidly to the fifth floor. Her key made a clicking noise as it turned in the door to her room.

"Come on in and relax. You can take a bath. Then I want to take you out to a great, Chinese restaurant. Have you ever had Won Ton soup? This place makes the best in town", she said with happy anticipation.

She reclined back on the bed. I stretched out on my back beside her, listening to birds chirping outside and feeling blessed that I wasn't wandering the streets. Soon, the sound of peaceful snoring, like the purring of a contented cat, filled my ears. I studied her face, marveling at how the forces of grace had brought this eccentric character into my life at my time of direst need. My eyelids became heavy and I fell into a deep, peaceful slumber. Like an angel floating on a cloud, far above the troubles of the world, I drifted effortlessly in a sea of grace and mercy.

I was roused out of my peaceful reverie when she jumped up suddenly. Running my fingers through my hair and yawning sleepily, I looked at her through half-opened eyes.

"Let's go and eat some Chinese food. Here are some nylon stockings you can wear. Put on your best dress. Do you have some nice, high-heeled shoes?" Her voice radiated happy excitement as she gazed into the mirror, brushing her hair in quick, jerky strokes with a white hairbrush.

She pulled the top of her pantsuit over her head and dropped it onto the floor. Then she sat on the edge of the bed and pulled the pants off. Her bones stuck out from her chest and her breasts hung limply in her bra. The skin all over her body sagged like a loose fitting garment about to slip off of a skeleton. With quick, excited movements, she walked to her closet and pulled out a blue dress. She pulled it over her head and adjusted and smoothed it. Then, she pulled some nylon stockings onto her skinny legs and stepped into a pair of black pumps.

I brushed my hair and put on some mascara, then rummaged through my suitcase. Pulling on a wrinkled, pink dress my older sister had kindly sent to me when my clothes got stolen, I looked into the full length mirror. We exchanged sweet looks like two school girls as we primped. Soon, we were both ready to go.

"You look fantastic", she said, smiling and winking.

I listened with amusement to her effervescent chatter as the elevator descended, flashing floor numbers and making groaning noises. Doorways and windows of office buildings reflected sun splendidly, as well-dressed people walked along, looking forward to the peacefulness of home.

CHAPTER 18 ————————————————FEBRUARY, 1983
An Unusual Friend

AS WE WALKED INTO THE restaurant, a tall, immaculately dressed Chinese man greeted us and led us to a table with a clean, white tablecloth and a vase of pink and white carnations. I remembered Dr. Stanfield telling me they were his favorite flowers. I sat down across from Mary, relaxing into the love shining in her eyes as she looked at me. We both studied our menus for a few moments.

"You've got to get the Won Ton soup", she said, beaming with anticipation.

A polite Chinese waiter took our order. In no time, he set a bowl of steaming soup in front of me. Then, a large, pretty blue and white bowl of rice appeared. I inhaled the satisfying aroma as he placed colorful platters of chicken and vegetables on the table.

"Be sure to eat your Won Ton soup", Mary said, smiling at me with twinkling eyes.

I put a large spoonful of it in my mouth and chewed the soft noodles, savoring the earthy taste.

"Isn't it delicious?" She looked at me, eagerly waiting for my response.

"Yeah. It is", I replied, feeling a warm satisfaction in my stomach. A carefree feeling bubbled within me.

She let out a rapid, non-stop stream of chatter as she gesticulated dramatically. Jumping from subject to subject, she talked with great enthusiasm. Soon, I was full. We laughed and read our fortune cookies out loud to one another. Then she paid the bill. She beamed with joy as I thanked her.

I watched her exceedingly thin body move jerkily as we walked to the bar next door. Sitting down next to her on a stool at the bar, I listened to her chat vivaciously with the bartender and admired the colored lights around a big mirror.

"This one's on the house", he said, smiling warmly and handing me a glass of coke with a cherry and a lime on the side. A jukebox glared from the back of the room. I strained to hear Mary's chatter. After a while, I told Mary I wanted to go back to the hotel.

The sky grew darker by the minute as we walked past department store windows. Mannequins stared vacantly like people frozen in time. When we got home, the desk clerk greeted us with a kind smile and Mary told him about our wonderful evening. The elevator rose rapidly and we walked down the quiet, empty hall. She fumbled with the key and let us in. Looking gratefully at the bed, I got undressed and put on a nightshirt. The soft, clean sheets soothed me as I slipped underneath them and fell into a deep sleep beside my generous companion.

It was getting close to Valentine's Day. Mary sprung energetically out of bed the next morning. Sunlight streamed through the window as I watched her move around restlessly, reading mail and sorting through things.

"Let's go downstairs and have breakfast. I want to introduce you to my friend Fred." She pulled her nightgown over her head and dropped it onto the floor. Then, she pulled on her beige polyester pantsuit.

"They have a great buffet downstairs. There are lots of different things to choose from", she said with excitement.

I pulled myself out of bed and got dressed. She spoke with childlike happiness as we rode the elevator down to the lobby. A line of people stood waiting as servers standing behind steaming containers did chores. A sweet, smiling woman served me toast, grits and fruit. We carried our trays to a table.

"Hi Fred. How are you?" Mary asked as we sat down across from an elderly man.

"I'm doing great. I drove my Cadillac to San Anselmo yesterday", he said, his eyes shining like a teenager bragging about his first car.

"That's great. I know you had fun. Have you been playing bingo lately?", Mary asked. She took a bite of syrup smothered pancakes.

"No. I haven't in a while but I'll probably go back to it some time soon", he replied.

His thinning, white hair lay flat on his shining head. His wrinkled face revealed years of hard earned wisdom. He must have been in his mid-eighties at least. He gazed directly at Mary with wide, deep blue eyes. I listened to them talk like two playful children for about a half hour, enjoying my buttery grits, toast and jelly.

Suddenly, Mary stood up and said she needed to go to the bank. She told Fred goodbye quickly. I jumped up and followed her out to the street. Businessmen in three-piece suits and pretty women in dresses sauntered by. Shop windows sparkled with expensive looking clothes and furniture.

When we arrived at the bank, Mary pulled open the front door with a burst of energy. Suddenly, she made a dramatic, sweeping motion with her arms. A handful of pennies went flying through the air and clattered onto the marble floor. In a loud, exuberant voice she sang Pennies From Heaven. Tellers, who were trying to concentrate, looked up with surprise. A desk worker stared in disbelief. A tall man in a black suit walked toward her with a disgruntled scowl. He took her by the hand and led her out of the bank as I followed behind.

"You've got to be careful. I don't want you to get arrested", I said as we walked down the sunny street.

"Oh, I was just having fun. They loved it. Everyone needs some excitement to brighten up their day. Look, there's a McDonald's. Let's go in and get a milkshake."

Striding quickly across the street, she dodged cars, ignoring the aghast looks of the drivers. I followed her into McDonald's. Rows of plastic tables lined the white, sterile walls and long lines of people waited as harried cashiers rang up orders and counted out change. Mary talked non-stop as we read the large menu on the wall. Finally, I got a vanilla milkshake and she got a strawberry one.

A man observed us as we sat down at a table. While Mary talked quickly, he studied us both.

"She's serious", he said to Mary, looking at me.

"Yeah. I think she's from Russia", Mary said, smiling at him and sipping at her milkshake. She touched my shoulder and searched my eyes as she remained silent for a few moments.

"Let's go visit my son, Jim. He still hasn't recovered from Vietnam. He gets depressed and lonely. He works in the baggage department at Macy's," she said.

We finished our milkshakes and dumped them in the trash. The rush of cars and the bustle of pedestrians rattled my nerves as we ambled through the streets. Soon, we arrived at Macy's. When she recognized her son working behind a cash register, she walked toward him. I watched her approach him, then turned to survey the merchandise. I noticed a section full of yellow, pink, blue and green yarn. I remembered the way I had passed my time, in the institution when I was eighteen, crocheting afghans. I sifted through the beautiful colors for a while.

Suddenly, Mary appeared behind me. Tears streamed down her face which was contorted with pain.

"He wouldn't even talk to me. He told me to go away", she cried, wiping tears from her face. Her chest rose and fell as she heaved out gut-wrenching sobs.

"Well, if that's the way he treats you, you don't need him", I said, putting my arms around her shoulders.

"I can't believe it. I always did everything I could to make my family happy. And now he sends me away like I'm nothing. I can't believe he would be that cruel", she wailed as crocodile tears rolled down her cheeks.

I held my arm around her shoulder as we walked onto the escalator and rode it down. Trees shimmered as we walked out into the bright sunlight. Great, mournful sobs came from her all the way back to the hotel. She collapsed on the bed like a wounded bird. Her thin, bony body looked fragile as she lay there. After a while, she began to snore. The rhythmic sound lulled me into relaxation. I drifted off to sleep beside her, bathing in a golden glow streaming from the window.

We woke up around dinner time. My stomach rumbled as we rode the elevator down to the cafeteria. Fred motioned to Mary to come over and sit with him. I listened to them chatter non-stop, like two excited children, as I enjoyed green beans, potatoes and squash. Sleepily yawning, I told Mary I wanted to head back to our room. Soon, I drifted off to sleep. I dreamed I was back in my parent's house sleeping in my old room with my grandmother in the bed next to me.

Mary bounded out of bed energetically the next morning. I basked in the sensual glow of the bright sun as she talked rapidly with boundless enthusiasm.

"I want to take you to Newberry's. I know all the waitresses there. They have a great breakfast special for only two dollars. You can get grits, eggs, toast and hash browns. The waitresses are really sweet. Let's go!" She pulled her nightgown off and put on a black pair of pants and a blue shirt.

"Okay. That sounds like fun", I said, pulling myself up and sitting on the edge of the bed. I combed my fingers through my hair as I yawned.

"Come on. We've got to go. It's best to get there early."

I pulled on my clothes quickly and brushed my hair. Then, I followed her out the door and watched her lock it behind us. My stomach jumped as the elevator descended.

"Newberry's is a five and ten cent store. They have every sort of thing you can imagine. And it's all really cheap", she said happily, gesturing with her hands.

Birds chirped in the lush trees as we walked energetically down the street. The sun radiated a heavenly, golden glow. Huge, fluffy clouds floated through the intensely blue sky. Brightly colored Valentine's cards and pink and red boxes of candy tied with pretty bows leaped out at us in a splash of colors as we walked through the front door of Newberry's. We walked to an old-fashioned dining counter and sat up on stools. A beautiful waitress with dark hair came over, holding a pad and pencil in her hand.

"Hi. It's so good to see you again. I haven't been here in a while. I wanted to show my friend here what a fun place this is", Mary said, looking with affection at the waitress.

"I'm glad to see you again too. It has been quite a while", the waitress replied.

"Get the special", Mary urged me in a motherly tone.

The waitress smiled sweetly as she took our orders efficiently. Soon, a large plate full of hash browns, toast and grits was sitting in front of me, filling my nostrils with a wonderful aroma. I ate hungrily, letting the waitress bring me more and more freshly baked biscuits which I smothered with butter and strawberry jelly. Drinking cup after cup of coffee, I listened in amusement as Mary wove interesting tales. Just like an Eveready battery, she kept going and going and going.

When I had eaten so much I felt like I might bust the seams out of my clothes, Mary told the waitress goodbye and paid the bill. I followed her out onto the sunny street. We walked around town, looking at displays in store windows and watching people throw bread crumbs for pigeons. Elegantly dressed people sat on park benches while playful children swung on playground swings and slid down slides.

"Hey, let's look in this thrift store. It's full of great clothes and they're all really cheap", Mary said suddenly, looking toward a red, brick building.

I followed her into the discount store, looking at the racks of clothes with total apathy.

"Here. Try this on. It will look great on you", she said, handing me a beige, polyester pantsuit.

"No. It's not my style."

"Oh, come on. Try it on."

Not wanting to disappoint her, I took it and walked into the dressing room. Pulling my clothes off impatiently and tossing them on the floor, I pulled my arms into the jacket and buttoned it up. Then I pulled the pants on. Gazing in the full length mirror, I thought about how awful it looked. Walking out of the dressing room sulkily, I showed it to her.

"That looks great on you. Buy it."

"No. I can't be spending money."

"Oh, come on. You can't find that price anywhere and it looks really snazzy. Go ahead and buy it. You need to treat yourself."

"No. I don't need it."

We walked around for a while longer, basking in the glorious sun. When Mary said she wanted to watch T.V., we began sauntering peacefully back to the hotel. I sat on the bed and watched some of my favorite old T.V. shows until dinner time. Then, I ate fried chicken, a baked potato, corn and green beans, listening to Mary and Fred chatter. Fred's eyes shone and his face radiated light as he talked about driving his Cadillac and looking out at the ocean.

"I want you to be careful and keep a watch on the speed limit Fred. I worry about you getting a ticket some day. It will use up your whole Social Security check if you get caught speeding." She paused and looked at me. "He's a speed demon. We've got to make sure he behaves."

"Now Mary, you know I never speed. I have a good head on my shoulders and I'm a very cautious driver", he replied. His wrinkles and gray hair shone in the light as his hand shook.

"Sure Fred, sure. I know how you rebel against rules", Mary chided him.

"Don't believe anything he says. He just acts innocent", Mary said, turning to look at me. We laughed together like two children.

After a long, playful conversation they wished each other a good night. I breathed deeply, reveling in the serenity and simplicity gracing me. Fred smiled warmly at me and wished me the best. Brimming with gratitude over the fun Mary had given me, I followed her to our room. We drifted off to sleep together, side by side.

A sensation of intense panic moved through me as I awoke the next morning. I jumped out of bed and began pulling on my clothes as fast as I could.

"I've got to go. My appointment at Planned Parenthood is at ten o'clock. I can't be late", I said, combing my hair as I held my breath with tension.

"I'll go with you", Mary replied, jumping out of bed and pulling on her pantsuit.

I slung my bag over my shoulder and opened the door. Mary locked it behind us. She chattered buoyantly as we walked down the red carpeted hall. I kneaded my hands nervously and worried as the elevator descended. Mary said goodbye to her friend, the desk clerk. The morning air was cool as we walked outside and down the sidewalk to the train station. Soon, a train came clattering down the tracks. The automatic doors creaked open and we stepped aboard and sat down next to each other.

The train came to a halt in San Francisco. We walked up a long, crowded stairway onto a busy street. I had forty five minutes to kill before the operation. When I noticed a corner coffee shop, I suggested we go inside to wait.

We sat down on stools at a dark, mahogany bar. Colorful bottles of rum, vodka and whiskey glowed in the sunlight. A friendly waitress asked us what we would like. We both ordered a cup of coffee.

"Planned Parenthood is about five blocks from here. I've got to make sure and get there on time for my abortion", I said, staring morosely into my coffee cup.

"You shouldn't do it. That's a living human being inside you. How would you feel if someone murdered you before you were born?" Mary asked.

"I have to. I can't afford to take care of a baby", I said, making eye contact with the bartender.

She smiled sweetly, then rolled her eyes at the accusing behavior of my friend. My hand shook as I gulped down coffee, checking my watch every minute. The waitress dried a glass and wished me good luck, then said the coffee was on the house. I hurried out onto the street. Mary ran to keep up with me as I started climbing a steep hill with every drop of energy I had. A group of innocent looking Catholic school girls stood on the corner wearing fresh, clean uniforms. Frightful images of the pope chastising me ran through my mind.

The steep, endless hills were grueling. I struggled for oxygen as I pushed myself up them, feeling pain in my muscles. Loud wheezes came from my throat which became tighter and tighter by the second. I opened my mouth wide in desperation, trying to get oxygen into my lungs but, like a fish out of water, I couldn't. Finally, I reached Planned Parenthood and threw open the door desperately. I walked to a glassed in cubicle where a brunette lady told me to sign in.

Suddenly, a high pitched scream vibrated through the air. The receptionist looked stunned. I turned my head and saw Mary standing outside yelling.

"She's a killer. She's a killer." I watched in disbelief as she held a cigarette lighter up to a bush until it burst into orange and yellow flames.

"Who is she?", the receptionist asked me.

"A friend of mine", I replied.

She called the police. In a few minutes, the sound of a screaming siren filled my ears as blue lights flashed. A slick, clean police car appeared and a tall, handsome officer got out and stood proudly, his gold star shining on his chest. Mary looked helpless as he pulled her arms behind her skinny back and locked handcuffs around her thin wrists. She wailed in protest like a child being punished. With stern detachment, he ordered her to get into the back seat. My mouth hung open in shocked sadness as I watched him get into the car and drive away. She had saved my life and I loved her with all my heart.

The receptionist gave me directions to the waiting room. As I sat down in a comfortable chair, I looked at a large poster on the wall. It showed the sorrow filled face of a young girl. The caption read, "Should she bear her rapist's child?" I pondered sadly about all of the abuse women had endured throughout history. Being raped, killed, persecuted for being witches, denied equal rights, neglected in pregnancy, demeaned and treated like second class citizens. We were the nurturers, the life-givers, the healers. We deserved to be venerated, loved and protected.

A nurse in a white dress appeared before me. She led me to a small room where a gentle-faced man dressed in a white coat greeted me. I stared at the floor, blushing in shame over my dirty, torn, wrinkled dress. He instructed me to remove all of my clothes, put on a clean, white hospital gown and then lay on my back on the table. He left the room to let me undress.

I pulled off my clothes and put on the clean, hospital gown. I called him to come back into the room as I climbed onto the table. He instructed me to lay back and put my feet up in some silver holders. Then he covered my legs with a fresh, clean sheet and opened them at the knees, telling me to spread them as wide apart as I could. I stared at the ceiling, holding my breath in frightened silence. A strange sensation of pressure went through me as he inserted a hard tube into my vagina. Closing my eyes in dread, I floated out of my body. Suddenly, a loud sound like a vacuum cleaner roared from a machine against the wall. I gritted my teeth with tension as it continued for the next few minutes. Finally, he pulled the tube out of me.

"It's all over", the doctor said with a kind expression. He held my hand for a moment and then left the room. As I stood up, I saw a counselor at the door, looking at me with empathy. She took my hand and led me into a room. I sat down facing her.

"You're a very strong woman. Now I want to see you tap into some of that strength." She looked gently into my eyes, holding my hand.

"I'm glad it's over. It wasn't painful at all."

"You can go lay down on a cot for a while. Would you like some juice and a snack?"

"Yes. Thank you."

I followed her to a room filled with rows of cots. As I lay down and pulled a blanket over me, I listened to a man comfort the woman laying on the cot next to me. In a few minutes, the counselor handed me a cup of apple juice and a cup of mixed nuts. I decided to tell her my predicament.

"I don't know where I'm going to stay tonight. I was evicted from the house I shared with five people", I said.

"I'll give you a pass to stay in Glide church. They'll let you stay three nights. Then, you can stay in Grace Cathedral for three nights." She left and then returned a few minutes later with a green paper pass.

Bitter loneliness ate holes in my heart as I pulled myself off of the cot after a short rest. Looking like a wretch and feeling ancient, I walked down the stairs and through the front door of Planned Parenthood. My head swam with dizziness as I walked to a corner bus stop. Great gushes of blood soaked my sanitary napkin.

As I climbed onto the bus, I asked the driver to let me out near Glide church. I arrived there soon and, as I stepped down onto the sidewalk, I was dismayed by a line of hungry people waiting for food stretching for two, long blocks. I squeezed in somewhere, trying to ignore the noise of the passing traffic and the rough voices and hardened faces surrounding me. Feeling like a nobody sinking into oblivion, I worried about what would become of me.

After waiting in line for half an hour, I sat down at a table to eat. Strangers looked through me as I ate the bland food. Soon, I had eaten a full plate and I felt my strength coming back. I stood up and walked out into the hallway, where a man who supervised the shelter sat at a desk. He talked to me in a friendly way and handed me a pass for a three night stay. Then, he led me down a stairway and showed me a long line of cots filling the room.

"Here is a vacant one. Keep your belongings with you always. You must leave by eight a.m. to go look for work. You'll have to be back here no later than five p.m. And you cannot go out at night. The first time you break any rule, you will have to leave right away. Breakfast is served at seven, lunch at twelve and dinner at five. The bathroom is over there and you can take a quick shower. I wish you the best", he said.

I spent three miserable nights, tossing and turning on my uncomfortable cot, bleeding like a rushing river. My mind raced with crazy, fragmented thoughts. A paralyzing feeling of helplessness and hopelessness pervaded me. I worried that I might have to start sleeping on a park bench. Luckily, the supervisor gave me a pass to stay three nights in Grace Cathedral. He wished me the best of luck and shook my hand warmly when I departed.

CHAPTER 19————————————————FEBRUARY, 1983
Mercy for The Terrified

I LOOKED OUT OVER THE CITY, with its menacing skyline and cute trolley cars rumbling by. An elderly woman tottered by supporting herself with a cane. Two fat men ambled along talking and laughing. A bus came to a stop and I climbed onto it. I asked the driver how to get to Grace Cathedral. Concern glowed in his eyes as he told me he would let me out a block away.

Soon, I arrived at the magnificent Gothic Cathedral. Exquisite, stained glass windows sparkled in a rainbow of colors. I walked up the stairs and through the ornate front door to the lobby. A woman sitting at a desk asked me for my pass and then told me to walk down the hall and claim my mat. I walked into a gymnasium sized room and looked in awe at the rows and rows of mats on the floor. Light shone through long, narrow windows at the tops of the high walls. People sat on the blue mats and talked. Mothers and fathers with small children cuddled together. Single people sat quietly, looking like they were grateful for the mercy they had been shown. A friendly woman, who sat on the mat next to mine, smiled as I sat down. I enjoyed talking with her until dinnertime.

I followed everyone into a large dining hall. Suddenly, a gush of blood soaked my sanitary napkin. Looking down with shame, I walked to the bathroom. A blond woman smiled at me and asked me if I was alright. Hurrying into a stall, I locked the door. Mounds of toilet paper turned red as I cleaned myself. After securing a pad into a clean pair of underwear and pulling them on, I felt better. I smiled at the woman who was brushing her hair, looking into the mirror.

"How are you?", she asked, her beautiful, blue eyes overflowing with love.

"I'm alright but I don't know where I'm going to stay after my three nights here. I'm homeless", I said forlornly.

"Here. I want you to have this shawl. My name is Starshine."

She looked like an angel as she handed me a beautiful, crocheted shawl made with earthy colors. With a gentle smile, she draped it around my shoulders and pinned it into place. Then she stuck a red, silk flower into it. Squeezing my hand lovingly, she led me out into the lobby. As I sat down in a chair, I listened to her explain my situation to a tall man with dark, curly hair. They seemed to be close friends. After a while, she walked over to me and placed her hands gently on my shoulders. A deep relaxation came over me as she began to brush my hair. The soothing sensations permeated every cell in my body as I drank in her loving attention. Tears rolled down my cheeks.

"It's so nice to have you to talk to. What made you talk to me?", I asked her.

"You moved me. I didn't want you getting raped or beaten living out on the street."

She departed to take care of her duties in the church. I retreated to my mat and read a book the kind lady next to me lent me. The food and company calmed me for a few days.

Sunlight sparkled on the faces of the strangers surrounding me as I awoke one morning, with no idea how many days I had been there. The Grace Cathedral staff served us a nice breakfast of cereal, milk and fruit. I listened to people around me talk. Hope rose within me like a buoyant wave as I saw Starshine walk toward me.

Starshine told me she had found a place for me to stay. I finished breakfast and followed her and her friend to her car. A golden lamp burned incense on her front dashboard, spreading a flowery fragrance. As I listened to her talk with her friend, I wondered where she was taking me. My mind raced frenetically as I watched the buildings, cars and people flash by outside my window.

Starshine parked in front of a tall, white building. We all stepped out of the car. My muscles tensed as I read a sign that said San Francisco State Hospital. I rationalized that, even though it was not the ideal environment, I owed some gratitude to the state for providing for me for free. Large glass doors opened automatically and let us into the front lobby, where white clothed nurses and orderlies bustled through the corridors. Sterile, fluorescent lights glared harshly. Starshine held my hand as we waited. Soon, a pretty nurse arrived. Starshine gave me a goodbye hug, telling me to take good care of myself. I watched her turn and walk away, wishing I had her phone number.

The nurse talked in a kind voice as we rode the elevator up to the psychiatric ward. She introduced me to the head nurse who shook my hand and greeted me sweetly. A medication station stood solidly with imposing, authoritarian energy. I gnashed my teeth in anger as I thought about swallowing those mind numbing drugs. Some disheveled, glassy eyed patients sat in front of a T.V. motionlessly. The nurse led me down a white corridor to my room. I put my bag down next to my bed and sat down. On the other side of the room, an Oriental woman with long, messy hair sat on the edge of her bed, clutching a stuffed animal and babbling to herself

A nurse brought me some Stelazine and a small cup of orange juice. I swallowed it and, in a matter of seconds, my eyelids began drooping. I took my clothes off, pulled the covers over me and curled into a fetal position. Wrapping my arms around my legs and hugging myself, I gave way to the drowsiness overcoming me, looking forward to escaping from the cruel world. Gradually, I began falling down a dark tunnel, like Alice falling down the rabbit hole.

When I looked at the clock the next morning, I realized I had slept twelve hours. Babbling sounds came from my room mate. I looked over at her sitting in a fetal position, clutching her stuffed animal nervously and rocking back and forth. Sunlight streamed into my eyes as I stood up slowly and put on my putrid, green hospital robe. Yawning and combing my fingers through my hair, I shuffled despondently into the living area.

A large, overweight man sat eating breakfast off of a plastic tray. I asked him where to get breakfast and he told me to go to the nurse's station. A smiling nurse handed me a tray. I walked into the living area and sat down on the sofa to eat. The scrambled eggs were tasteless and the toast was like Styrofoam. I longed for a huge glass of orange juice as I drank my tiny one.

I settled into a deadening, boring routine of reading magazines and watching T.V. Taking my medication obediently, I slept twelve hours or more every night and woke up foggy and depressed. The patients were lost in their own worlds and I missed higher functioning patients who could converse intelligently. The atmosphere was barren with no decorations, plants or cushions. With no records to listen to, piano to play or ping pong table I felt extremely bored. I paced the hall restlessly or sat in a stupor missing my friends.

At the end of two weeks, they needed me to move on and make room for another patient. A kind man drove me in a dark, blue station wagon to a halfway house. Fear froze my bones as he let me out in a dangerous run-down section of downtown San Francisco, just around the corner from porno movie houses and streets full of pimps, rapists and killers. A nicely dressed intake counselor with dark, neatly styled hair, big, gold earrings and a pretty face interviewed me. As she asked me what type of medication I took and what my problems were, she wrote my answers on a big, yellow legal pad. Then, she gave me some Stelazine, an anti-psychotic.

I walked into the living area after my interview. Disgust filled me as I observed the tattered furniture full of cigarette burns, newspapers strewn every which way and smelly ashtrays. The ugly, brown carpet was torn and dirty and the walls were grimy and soiled with graffiti. Sinking to the depths of depression, I walked back to my counselor and followed her to my room, carrying my suitcase. I plopped down onto my twin bed and looked glumly at my room mate.

"Hi. How are you?", she asked sincerely. Her shoulder length, blond hair fell onto her shoulders gracefully. Her blue eyes shone beautifully.

"I'm okay. I just moved in", I replied, cringing at the unattractive sadness in my voice.

"You'll get used to being here. It seems really weird at first but the counselors are nice. No one will bother you. I haven't had anything stolen. I've had this room to myself for two weeks, since the last person left. I'm glad I have a room mate now. You seem really nice", she said in cheerful appreciation.

"Yeah. I guess I am nice", I replied laughing.

"How long have you been living in San Francisco?", she asked. Her face glowed with curiosity as she shifted her weight on the bed.

"Over a year. I moved here from Georgia", I replied. I pulled my legs up on the bed and sat in a lotus position.

"Is your family in Georgia?', she asked.

"Yes. My younger sister and parents are. My brother lives in California and my older sister is married and lives in Maryland", I said, thinking they seemed like distant shadows in a dream.

"That takes courage to come here all alone", she said, looking at me with kind respect.

"Yeah. It does. It hasn't been easy", I replied, drumming my fingers on my knees restlessly.

When she asked me if I would like to take a walk across the street I said I would. The dark, dirty hallway smelled foul and dust in my nostrils made me sneeze. We closed the front door and stepped down onto the hard concrete. Drivers sped by, gunning their motors and spewing trails of smelly exhaust. Abandoned buildings with smashed out windows loomed ominously and skyscrapers hovered like monuments to a dying civilization. I imagined what the gang members, pimps, drug dealers and murderers were doing with their evening.

We waited for the traffic light to turn red. Then, we playfully ran across the street. The bold, red sign on a Revco drug store shone. As we walked inside I looked at the magazines and boxes of candy. My friend bought me a candy bar and a coke. I admired her slender, long-legged figure and her shoulder length, blond hair as she pushed open the door. We walked out onto the sidewalk. Her innocent, childlike face shone as she talked about how she was hoping to prove to her parents that she was getting better. They had been disturbed by the fact that she stayed out late with her boyfriend and came home drunk. They had ordered her to see a psychiatrist. I was touched by her vulnerability as she talked about how she wanted her parents to be proud of her. I knew how painful it was to feel not good enough.

When we got back to the dingy room, I collapsed onto my bed and sunk into a blinding depression. I was too tired to move a muscle for the rest of the day. Scenes of all the traumas I had been through ran across the movie screen of my mind again and again. The fact that I was afraid to call my parents and tell them what I had been through magnified my unbearable isolation.

After a while, my room mate's cheerful voice lifted my spirits and roused me out of my miserable stupor.

"Would you like to go down to the dining hall with me?" She looked at me with wide, expressive eyes.

"Yeah, sure. I'm hungry", I said, following her down the stairs, grateful for her company.

In silent curiosity, I looked around the room, observing people scurrying around making preparations. The tables were covered with red and white checkered cloths. Steam floated out of huge, black pots which boiled on top of large, blue-flamed stoves. I plopped huge portions of spaghetti, bread, potatoes and salad onto my plate. Sitting down across the table from my room mate, I began to eat, relishing the sensation of it sliding down my throat.

Refilling my plate again and again, I ate enough for ten people, hoping to fill the emptiness within. My room mate's face was soft with compassion as we talked like old friends. I wondered where the various patients around the room came from as I watched tall, short, fat, skinny, black and white ones eating their simple meals, their one source of solace from the harshness out in the world.

I got up from the table and put my plate on the metal, kitchen counter. The drabness of the walls closed in on me as I climbed the stairs with my room mate. Telling her I would see her in a few minutes, I walked toward the pay phone to call my older sister, Laura.

She had gotten married over two years ago and had seemed to not want to talk to me when I called so I had given up for years. My heart still hurt over the time I had driven a long way through several states to visit her and she had told me I was no fun to be with. Yet, there had been times when we were close and I hoped to revive that. I held my breath with anticipation as I dialed her number. As her voice came on the phone, I did my best to put a cheerful tone into my beaten down, sad voice.

"Hi Laura. I haven't talked with you in a long time. I was wondering how you were doing", I said.

"Oh, hi. How are you?" An insincere, cold chill came through her voice. Pain shot through me.

"Oh, I'm just trying to make the best of this halfway house I'm in", I said timidly, longing for a loving word from her.

"I don't think much of you asking Daddy to send you money. It has been a real strain on him. You should get a job", she said in a stinging tone of contempt.

I told her I was having trouble getting Mom and Dad to talk and that they always hurried off the phone.

"No. I don't buy this," she responded. She obviously still regarded me as a trouble maker.

I wished she would walk a mile in my moccasins. She had no idea what it was like to be raped repeatedly and to wander frightening, chaotic streets with no place to eat, bathe, sleep or call home.

Suddenly, she said she had to go, impatiently. The phone clunked with a dead sound. Grief seeped through every cell in my body as I tried to understand her animosity. Holding my breath in despair, I climbed the stairs and walked into my room. Conversing with my room mate, I soaked up the gentle acceptance in her eyes. She appreciated my good points. Maybe I wasn't such a bad person after all. We talked until midnight, sharing stories and encouraging one another.

The days passed slowly as I sat on my bed or wandered the halls, too drugged up to concentrate on anything. Every morning, a kind, beautiful, brunette counselor taught a class in daily living skills. It explained mundane but important things like how to get a driver's license and how to apply for financial assistance. Three days a week, we all piled into her van and she drove us to a public swimming pool. As I pounded my arms and kicked my legs through the water with every drop of energy I could muster, an endless rage surged through me. Some days we played volleyball instead of swimming. My confidence soared every time I hit the ball over the net. I tried to congratulate myself for every little thing I did well, even if it didn't seem like much compared to what "normal" people were doing.

One day, I talked with a kind, black patient. He offered to fix my car when I told him I was having trouble getting it to start. We walked to the place where it was parked. I watched him work diligently until he fixed it. I was deeply touched that he did not charge me a penny.

After I had lived there about six weeks, my counselor told me I would have to interview at another halfway house. When the evening of my interview arrived, I dressed nicely and put my hair back in a barrette. Stopping in the counselor's office, I told her goodbye. She smiled sweetly and wished me good luck.

Wind whipped around me as I stood at the bus stop, clutching my shoulder bag nervously. A bus pulled up to the curb. I climbed up the steps. Coins clinked as I dropped them into the box. The dangerous streets stretched forever in an endless labyrinth of evil. After a long, hilly ride, I arrived in the Haight Ashbury. I asked the driver to let me out in front of the Grand Piano. As I stepped down onto the sidewalk, I longed to see one of my friends.

Suddenly, I saw John walking toward me. A jolt of emotion knocked me off balance. I watched him approach, feeling a mixture of longing and fear. I remembered the romantic night we had bathed in starlight as we walked by the ocean. Guilt ran through me as I remembered how George had threatened him cruelly.

"I haven't seen you in ages", he said as though he was genuinely glad to see me. I admired his ability to forgive me and didn't feel that I deserved it.

"Yeah. It's been a long time", I replied, looking down at the sidewalk with shame.

"You've really gained weight. You need to get it off. Start exercising and eating only healthy food. If you just let yourself go you're going to look awful", he said, looking at me with concern.

My cheeks turned crimson as I berated myself silently for being a loser. My miserable fate was sealed. I had never been good enough for my father and, now, I wasn't good enough for men I desired. I really did look ugly and couldn't stand to look in the mirror. My mother had been a beauty queen who men sought after when she was my age.

"Well, I've got to go meet my boyfriend", I said, hoping to make him jealous.

"Oh, yeah. The scrawny guy with the balding head. I've seen him", he replied in a disparaging tone, rubbing salt into my festering wound.

I told him goodbye and walked down the side walk and into a brightly lit store. Pistachio nuts, chewing gum and cigarette lighters lined the counter. I asked a convenience store clerk how to get to the halfway house. His thick, brown hair framed his sweet face as he looked at me through his glasses and pointed in the direction to walk. Soon, I arrived in the prosperous looking neighborhood near the Golden Gate Park. Nervousness flowed through me as I walked up the front stairs.

"Come in. You must be from the other halfway house. We've been looking forward to meeting you", a counselor with wavy, brown hair said. I followed her back to the kitchen area where residents were busy preparing dinner. Steam floated out of a big, black pot on the stove. People carried plates and silverware to a round dining table.

Soon, the table was set and everyone sat down to eat. A withdrawn, mousy woman with short, dark hair sat next to me. A tall, young man with dark hair sat across from me. I reached for a bowl of mashed potatoes and put a huge spoonful on my plate. As I blended butter into them, an overweight woman with shoulder length, brown hair asked me when I would be moving in.

"As soon as I get accepted", I replied shyly. I asked how long I would be staying. The counselor replied that the usual stay was three months.

The two counselors introduced me to everyone and their laughing, relaxed demeanor put me at ease. Yet my hand still trembled as I raised my fork to my mouth carefully, hoping I was making a good impression. There was nothing I wanted more than to get out of my downtown hell hole.

Dinner passed too quickly. I dreaded heading out into the treacherous night as the counselors told me goodbye. A suffocating sensation came over me as I watched the night grow darker by the second.

The bus arrived and came to a noisy halt. I climbed up the steps, gripping the handrail nervously. The driver revved the motor forcefully, throwing me off balance as he sped forward. I hung tightly to the handrail and tottered down the aisle, then fell down into a seat with a thud. When the driver let me off, I ran through the dark streets. Thoughts of being raped or murdered raced through my mind.

The kind, brunette counselor let me into my downtown zoo. I felt grateful to the system for keeping me off the streets until I got accepted at the next halfway house. I followed her up the musty, foul smelling stairway into her office. Her dark eyes glowed with affection and light reflected in her gold earrings as I told her about my interview. She listened attentively, smiling and nodding. I kept talking, absorbing her healing energy, until she gave me my evening dose of Stelazine and wished me pleasant dreams.

CHAPTER 20————FEBRUARY, MARCH, APRIL, MAY, JUNE, 1983

A Divine Plan

FEBRUARY, 1983 WAS NEARING ITS end and Dr. Stanfield finally came back from India. I rode the bus to see him with happy anticipation and knocked on his door eagerly. It opened slowly and, as I looked into his gentle, accepting eyes, a feeling of well-being flowed through me. I drank in his love as he gave me a long, strong hug.

"How are you doing?", he asked, settling back into his armchair.

"Well, I have really been through a lot since you left. I got kicked out of the house I was living in. On top of that, I had to have an abortion. I also went to spend Christmas with my brother and he got mad at me and left me stranded in a hotel room in Los Angeles." I looked down and wrung my hands in anguish.

"Why did he do that?", he asked compassionately.

"I don't know. We went to see a movie and something I said while we were watching it made him angry."

"Well, you couldn't have said anything so bad that you deserved to be left stranded in a hotel room in Los Angeles…. of all places. That is a terribly confusing place. Especially for you who are in such a fragile condition. I know that must have been very frightening. Your family members fly off the handle over nothing", he said in a tone of deep concern.

"Yeah. It hurt me deeply. I didn't say anything to intentionally upset him."

"Did the social worker help you?"

"Well, I went to see her. She was going to get me into a boarding house but things happened so fast, one after another. A kind lady I met at the YMCA took care of me for several days. Then, after I had my abortion, I went to stay at a church for several nights. While I was there, I met a lady who brushed my hair and was very sweet to me. When I told her I was homeless, she drove me to San Francisco State Hospital. I stayed there a while and, now, I'm in a halfway house downtown." I didn't tell him I was taking heavy medication because I knew he would not approve of it.

"Well, I'm glad you're in a safe place now. How are things going for you there?"

"I don't like it at all. The neighborhood is frightening and dismal and the streets are full of pimps and drug dealers. I'm afraid to take a walk. I have a room mate who I get along well with but I don't have any other friends there. There is a female counselor who I like and I talk with her a lot."

"I want to encourage you to go to the Raja Yoga center and take the seven day course in spiritual knowledge. It is free. Just give them a call and they will set up a time for you to go in and take the course. When I was in India, I spoke with Baba, the Supreme Soul. When you go to the center they will show you how to develop a relationship with Baba. He is the unlimited ocean of love. He will give you everything. He's the great transformer."

The session went well. When I arrived back at the halfway house, I called the Raja Yoga center and set an appointment for my lesson in spirituality.

A few days later, I stood at the bus stop shivering as a torrential downpour soaked me to the core. Gusts of wind blew my hair and clothes around. I was relieved when, finally, the door of the bus creaked open. Like a drowned dog escaping a monsoon I walked up the steps and found a seat. After a while, it arrived near the Raja Yoga center.

I stepped off of the bus and walked along the sidewalk, observing cafes and shops. Soon, I reached the center. I opened the door and stepped onto a soft carpet, looking at the row of shoes. Looking up a stairway, I saw a woman with long, dark hair in a white, flowing garment that covered her entire body. She instructed me to take my shoes off. I removed them and left them in a pile of shoes at the bottom of the staircase. Then, I walked up the stairs and followed her into a room. The soft cushion comforted me as I sat down on a red, velvet sofa. Incense came from a golden holder, making hypnotic curling and swirling movements through the air. A shaft of golden sunlight illuminated it as it exuded the wonderful fragrance of a garden of flowers.

"The first lesson is about the soul. Everyone is a soul. The body is just the vehicle that the soul uses to go through life. The soul is eternal and it continues to take one body after another. The body is just a temporary costume that the soul uses. The soul is an eternal point of light and it is located in the middle of the forehead."

Her peaceful vibrations comforted me as she showed me colorful pictures which illustrated the knowledge. When she finished explaining, she showed me how to meditate. She instructed me to center my attention on the point of light in the middle of my forehead and let all thoughts subside.

I drew myself inward, like a tortoise. As I concentrated on the middle of my forehead, an incredible stillness calmed my mind. Thoughts ran through me, yet I felt detached from them all, like I was being emptied. A profound peace saturated every cell of my being from the top of my head to the tips of my toes. When she told me the lesson was over I did not want to leave.

At my next session with Dr. Stanfield, I told him I was enjoying taking the course in spiritual knowledge. He lit up like a sunrise.

"I'm so glad you agreed. Keep thinking about the knowledge. It is called churning when you go over the knowledge in your mind. Baba has given us the gems of knowledge because we are special souls. It makes him happy when you delve deeply into the knowledge and it increases your power. The Yogis are the best people you'll find. Be sure to talk with them and get to know them. Baba has given you a whole new family. Being in that loving atmosphere is going to do wonders for you. I can tell that you are less depressed."

We talked for a while and then I beat the bed with the tennis racket and yelled out my anger until I collapsed on the floor, trembling all over.

"Great work. You've made remarkable progress. You're getting better and better. You're getting your feelings back. The Raja Yogis have a rule that you are not supposed to get angry but that doesn't apply to you. You're not hurting anyone doing this therapy." His long hug relaxed me at the end of the session. I told him goodbye and headed home.

The city streets looked strange and threatening. I pulled open the halfway house door and ran up the dirty stairway to my room. My roommate was dressed in a pretty flannel nightgown and white slippers that looked like bunnies.

"Would you like a piece of gum?" she asked, looking at me with kindness.

"Yeah. Thanks", I replied.

I enjoyed the mint flavor as I talked with her for a while. I tried to read a book but the medication gave me the concentration abilities of a worm. Dr. Stanfield was right when he said that stuff was dangerous. However, I was completely confused and didn't know who was right. I decided to keep taking my meds. I would just change the subject if it came up in therapy with Dr. Stanfield I decided. I wished my room mate a good night and drifted off into a deep sleep.

A week passed quickly and the day for my next spiritual lesson arrived. It was hard to believe I had been in the downtown halfway house for a month. I rode the bus across town brimming over with curiosity. The tranquil vibrations calmed me to the core as I removed my shoes and walked up the stairs. Sister Carol greeted me warmly.

"How has your meditation been going?", she asked.

"It's been going well. It really relaxes me", I replied.

"Good. Baba teaches us to meditate in the early morning at four a.m. because that is when the world is most peaceful. It is called Amrit Vela which means the hour of nectar. You've been doing fifteen minutes. After a while, you can increase it to thirty minutes and then to an hour. You will purify yourself quickly this way. Baba showers us with extra blessings at Amrit Vela."

"Let's meditate", she said sweetly.

Feelings of embarrassment flowed through me as she began our meditation. I didn't want her to know I was a nut living in a halfway house. Her voice soothed me as she spoke soft, relaxing words, telling me to focus on the point of light in the center of the Shiva Lingam, an orange red oval on the wall. Tranquility flowed through me as I meditated, feeling my heart open like a lotus blossom. I experienced my eternity, my indestructible pure light body. For a blissful period of time, I floated in the sea of endless love and mercy. There was nothing like God's love.

I didn't want to leave as the session ended. Deep depression overcame me when I arrived back at the dismal downtown halfway house. The Raja Yoga center was the only place where I could relax. I looked forward to my time there with every fiber of my being.

March and April flew by and I was surprised when the last day of my course in spirituality arrived. Sister Carol's warm greeting brought me back to life as I walked into the fragrant, peaceful room for my spiritual lesson.

"There are two rules we must follow in order to purify ourselves so we can become Deities in the Golden Age. We must be vegetarian and we must be celibate", she said.

"Why would God create sex if he thought it was evil?", I asked.

"It is not that he thinks it is evil. He asks us to make this sacrifice at this crisis point in the World Drama because it deepens our connection with him. Having sexual relations interferes with our ability to commune with Baba. There is not much time left and we need to get the most out of this special time with Baba. We are becoming deities. Deities never have lustful thoughts."

"How will deities have babies if they never have lust?", I asked, reeling in confusion.

"When two married deities exchange drishti, a loving gaze, the female becomes pregnant", Sister Carol replied.

"But Jesus ate fish and he was a great master. Why do we have to be vegetarian?", I asked, feeling very puzzled.

"We do it for moral reasons and for health reasons. First of all, it is participating in the killing of innocent animals which brings bad karma to us. We refrain from anything that comes from an animal, including milk, cheese and eggs. Eggs are a chicken embryo. We must not participate in violence against animals. An animal experiences intense fear when it is slaughtered and that fear vibration is stored in the meat. So, we take in that negative vibration when we eat it. We also damage our health when we injest the harmful antibiotics and chemicals that are fed to animals. Our intestines are not designed to digest meat and it putrefies in the colon. That's why we have such a high rate of colon cancer."

I would probably be happier being celibate since men had given me nothing but sorrow. But I sure would miss barbequed chicken.

Sadness seeped through my bones as I told Sister Carol goodbye. I would miss her one on one attention. I churned the fascinating knowledge as I rode the bus through the meandering, city streets which rushed with loud traffic.

That Sunday, I meditated in the early morning with the sisters and brothers at the center. After meditation, Sister Dianne read the Murli—the magic flute that transforms the world.

"Baba has come to change the graveyard into the land of angels. The time of sorrow will soon end. Now is the time to claim your inheritance of happiness from Baba. You have become beggars. There is so much worry and you work so hard for so little. What happened to your pure wealth? The path of Bhakti took you further and further away from your connection with your all loving father. The priests in churches put on pompous acts and convince others that they are enlightened but, in fact, they are stone-headed. Forget all the scriptures you have read and do not listen to the puffed-up religious leaders who claim to know the truth. They are charlatans. Go inside in deep meditation and tell your troubles to Baba. He is the great transformer, the one who showers you with blessings. Give him your stones and he will change them into diamonds. Now is the time to become God-like and claim your unlimited inheritance."

A wonderful peacefulness pervaded me as the murli ended. The sister who read the murli handed a delicious, sweet cookie to everyone. As she gave out the sweets she gave drishti, a loving gaze, to each person. I absorbed her loving gaze thirstily, feeling it heal my ragged heart.

I did not want to leave as I told my sisters and brothers goodbye. As the bus roared up and down the hills, I pondered the knowledge. I wondered if God was really speaking to the world. It might be some deceitful spirit pretending to be God.

Later that evening, I talked with my counselor. She told me that I would be moving to the other halfway house in a few days. My room mate said she would miss me and my heart sank with sadness.

When the day came for me to move, the counselor, who had taught me the daily living skills class, helped me load my belongings into my car. She wished me the best of luck and gave me a warm hug. I got lost as I drove through the chaotic streets to my new home.

I was greeted at the door by Miriam, the brunette counselor who had talked to me the night of my interview. She took my hand sweetly and led me upstairs to my private room. With its twin bed under a window and small, wooden desk it was cozy. I had a view of a cheerful, blue house. The Golden Gate Park was a block away. It was a nice contrast to the boarded-up warehouses and intimidating skyscrapers of downtown. I would pay five hundred a month in rent. I sent my father my new address so he could send a check to the staff at the beginning of every month.

I wrote in my journal until everyone was called for dinner. Soon, the table was set. Twirling spaghetti on my fork, I got lost in thought. I had learned so many new things. It was as though my mind was expanding too fast for me. When I realized that the spaghetti sauce had meat in it, I requested some without meat. Miriam, the counselor, smiled sweetly as she heated some up for me. I told her I had taken a course in spiritual knowledge and had decided to become a vegetarian. She encouraged me kindly when I told her I was going to pound the pavement looking for a job.

A new day came and fresh determination surged within me as I boarded the bus. The June sun shone brightly in the dazzling, blue sky as I descended onto the concrete of Fisherman's Wharf. I saw an open air market in front of a seafood restaurant. Two rows of racks were filled with Mexican shirts. A display case was filled with jewelry. A short man with brown hair was speaking in a French accent with various customers. I observed him from the entryway and, when he was free, I approached him and asked him if he could hire me. He replied, in a French accent, that he could. My mood rose as I filled out the application. His stubborn face scrutinized me as he questioned me, his eyebrows knitted together seriously. He would be busy interviewing for the next two weeks he said, wiping his brow. When he made his decision he would give me a call.

I observed the lively activities on the street as I walked around the area. A woman played guitar and sang on a corner. Another person sold jewelry. Several artists sketched lovely portraits of passing tourists. A man played an upright piano from the back of his truck. I was fascinated by the spirit of freedom and celebration as I walked from place to place filling out applications.

Soon, I'd been living at my new halfway house for a month. I was taking my medication and feeling more grounded than I ever had since I moved from the East Coast. I wondered how Stan, Dot, Tom and Becky were. Now that I lived near the Grand Piano I could meet them there. A warm glow of confidence came over me as the counselors congratulated me for going on my job hunt. I filled my plate with vegetables several times, not even looking at the roast beef. Later, I talked with a fellow patient who liked me.

For the next two weeks, I went to the Grand Piano a couple of times a day to search for Tom, Becky, Stan and Dot. I was pleasantly surprised when, one day, Stan, the funny comedian, appeared in front of me as I drank a cup of chamomile tea. He asked me to meet him and his friends for dinner that night. I liked sitting around the round table at the halfway house and having dinner with my fellow patients and counselors. There was more of a family feeling than there had been at the downtown halfway house. However, I longed to be with my exciting actor friends too. Socializing with my normal friends gave me a shot of self esteem. I took every invitation I got, never telling the counselors.

Looking around for passing counselors, I tiptoed down the stairs and out of the front door before dinner the next night. The cool night air enlivened me as I walked leisurely through the golden glow of dusk. Streaks of orange, pink and lavender painted the sky. A fingernail thin crescent moon was starting to shine ever so faintly in the light sky. Electrical cadences of conversations rippled through me as I walked into the Grand Piano. I looked around the room observing happy, attractive people until I found Stan and Dot sitting at a table in the back room.

They both welcomed me with warm hugs and introduced me to their friend, Donna, a kind woman with dark hair falling below her shoulders. A happy feeling came over me as I sat down with them. Striking several water glasses, Stan smiled and talked in his childlike voice. Then, suddenly, he catapulted a roll across the table with his fork, laughing hysterically.

"Stop it Stan", Dot said in an irritated voice. She slapped him on his head.

A cowed look came over his face and he looked at her as though he was pleading for forgiveness. She looked gorgeous as she fluttered her long, dark eyelashes. Her sun-streaked, golden hair cascaded over her shoulders and her low-cut dress complimented her voluptuous figure.

"Greg wanted me to pinch his balls today", Dot said nonchalantly.

"Yeah. They always want something different and kinky", Stan replied.

I felt my cheeks burn. I'd never heard such talk and my curiosity overflowed.

"Dot works in an S & M parlor", Stan explained to me, looking directly into my puzzled face.

"Jeanine was showing everyone her new tattoo today. She got a rose put on the inside of her thigh. A new girl started today. I don't like her energy. She acts like she just arrived straight from the country", Dot said, exuding worldly sophistication.

I had heard about S & M parlors and had felt they sounded like sinister, dark places. However, I did know that the male sex drive was the most overpowering force I had ever experienced and I could understand how they would be willing to pay for a variety of appetizers to satisfy their sexual appetites. They were insatiable. I enjoyed the wonderful aroma of a freshly baked roll as I slathered it with butter.

"Do you want some butter?", I asked, passing it to Stan.

"We'll use it in intercourse tonight", Stan replied mischievously, looking at his girlfriend, Dot.

We ordered spaghetti. It felt like love as it slid into all my empty spaces, nourishing me. Soon, my stomach was full of enough food for ten people. Donna and I talked about our job searches. Her gentle kindness touched me and my heart began to open. The evening rolled over me in soft, soothing waves, healing my ragged emotions. After a while, Stan said we better head on to the party. I waddled out of the Grand Piano, my oasis of love, and down the noisy street. We all piled into Stan's van and he drove us across town.

People talked loudly and gesticulated wildly, moving around the crowded room. I followed Dot to the refreshment table, feeling knocked off balance by the intense energy. In desperation, I began shoveling large handfuls of potato chips into my mouth. Then I began eating cheese, crackers and fruit, withdrawing into myself and wanting to disappear. My eyes darted around nervously as I observed the long haired, self-absorbed strangers who surrounded me. I worried that they wanted to hurt me.

Loneliness tore through my heart as I meandered with Dot into a room where a group of people were playing jacks in a big circle. They looked connected, relaxed and happy. Suddenly, a frightening sensation came over me. I felt like I was floating alone out in cold, black space. I turned and walked back toward the snack table. Suddenly, Stan appeared beside me. He put his hand on my shoulder and looked into my eyes. I started sobbing convulsively, pouring out the grief of a life time.

"My parents hate me. They refused to send me my money, even after my friend told them I had been raped. My mother is cold to me every time I call and she never calls me or writes me letters. She calls me "treacherous" and "liar". My father yells at me and blames me a lot. All he said was, "I'm not surprised", when my friend told him what happened to me. They don't care about me at all. They call me a hopeless case and failure," I cried.

"Whatever your parents told you about what an awful, worthless person you are you have got to forget it all. You better start believing right now that you're just as good as anyone in this room. In fact, you better believe that you're better than anyone in this room. You are a beautiful, intelligent woman. There is no reason for you to ever feel put down by anyone. You have the power to do whatever you want to do. You're a good person, a caring person. Not everyone is nice like you are. There are a lot of assholes who just don't care about anyone and they'll try to rip you off. I am always here for you if you ever want to talk", he said, looking gently into my eyes.

"If your mother is going to treat you like shit then you don't have to have anything to do with her. My mother used to beat me. She lives here in town and I never speak to her. You don't owe your parents anything", he continued with deep empathy.

"I feel so hurt. I'll always want their love", I sighed.

"You don't need their love. Fuck them if they can't treat you right. The world is full of people who will appreciate you and love you", he said hugging me warmly.

I drank in his love, feeling my anxious loneliness disappear. Then I told him I needed to go to the bathroom. Tears gushed down my face as I looked into the mirror at my swollen, red eyes. Splashing my face with cold water revived me. I opened the door and walked out into the room. Dot touched my shoulder and looked into my eyes.

"Would you like a back rub?", she asked.

"Yeah. That would be great", I replied.

I followed her into the bedroom and lay down on the bed. A wonderful peace filled me as she rubbed the tension out of my shoulder muscles.

When I woke the next morning, a new surge of hope lifted me out of bed. I walked a few blocks to visit Becky in the doughnut shop. Her warm greeting sent waves of happiness through me. She gave me a free doughnut and, as I enjoyed the chocolate crème sweetness, I watched her work.

CHAPTER 21 ————————————JULY, 1983

Stepping Out On The Town

D OT COMMENTED THAT I HAD a beautiful face and Donna nodded in agreement. I ordered a Black Russian and tried to look sophisticated as I drank it nervously, straining to hear my friends above the hum of conversations around the room. I contributed a word or two when I could. Stan started acting silly, asking people if they were wearing clean underwear or if they had applied underarm deodorant. Gales of laughter came from intrigued people. A spirit of celebration danced in the carefree, magical night.

"I'm going out for a while", Dot said, getting up from the plush, red sofa and walking out into the night with a handsome man.

"She's going to do a line", Stan said, looking at me, touching my hand.

Stan's dark eyes gleamed as he told funny stories and talked in a child voice like a court jester. I listened with fascination, drinking kahlua and cream, one after another. Soon, I was out of my mind with inebriation. The room swayed beneath me as I stood up, stepped up onto a table and looked out around the room, observing people laughing and talking. I felt like I was a child again, going on a carnival ride at the annual May Fair. Just when I felt like raising my arms and flying around, the grounding touch of Stan's hand brought me back to earth. I stepped down off of the table and he led me back to my chair.

Donna looked at me with an incredulous expression. Her brows knitted together in protective concern. Stan sat down beside me and squeezed my hand protectively. My head swam dizzily as the loud, buzzing conversation around the room overloaded my senses.

"I'm going to walk home now", I told Stan, slurring my words.

"I'll walk with you", he replied.

Donna gave me a warm hug and said she looked forward to seeing me again soon. Dot hugged me and told me to take good care of myself. Stan opened the heavy brass handled door and we walked out onto the empty sidewalk which shimmered in the light of the full moon.

"I don't like seeing you drunk", Stan said, holding my hand.

"Why won't anyone hire me? I feel like a weird alien from outer space. No one wants to rent to me and I can't make any friends, except for you and Dot", I cried.

"You need confidence. You're a great person. You just don't see it", he replied.

"I am confident in some ways", I replied.

"You're not confident. How do confident people act?"

I thought about that as we walked, drinking in his affection as his firm hand grasp soothed me. All of my life I had prayed for a man who really loved me. The fresh air invigorated me as I watched people engaging in lively conversations in the cafes.

Soon, we arrived at the halfway house. I opened the door and we tip toed up the stairs into my room. He put his arm around me as we sat down on my bed together.

"I've got to figure out what it is about me that makes people want to not deal with me. Can you please tell me what it is?" I asked in a pleading, desperate voice.

"You scare people." There was a long silence as I bitterly tried to digest what he had told me.

"Be careful who you sleep with. You could get Aids. I worry about you because a lot of men will try to take advantage of you. You have to insist that they use a condom."

I enjoyed the warmth of his body next to mine for a few minutes. Then,

I told him he would have to go. I didn't want the counselors to find him there. He held my hand as I led him to the front door. Hugging me sweetly, he said goodbye. I agreed to get together again soon. I imagined he was hugging me as I held my arms around myself and fell asleep.

A hazy depression kept me motionless in bed the next morning. My head pounded as I turned it to the side, adjusting my pillow underneath it. I wanted to do nothing but lay there all day.

Finally, I gathered the strength to stand. A cold shower revived me from my hangover. I pulled on my bathrobe and walked downstairs to the kitchen. A bowl of oatmeal with butter and brown sugar and a glass of orange juice lifted my spirits. I had a conversation with a soft spoken, kind patient. He told me to be careful to not talk to any strangers. When he told me he thought I was a special person my heart overflowed.

That afternoon, I got a call from the man who ran the place that sold Mexican shirts on Fisherman's Wharf. I cringed from the sound of his authoritarian voice as he told me to report for work at nine o'clock the next morning. The counselors congratulated me for getting a job that night at dinner. I basked in the golden glow of their approval.

CHAPTER 21 ——————————————JULY 1983
Work and Music

A NEW FEELING OF DETERMINATION SURGED through me the next morning as I dressed in my nicest outfit, basking in the golden sunlight pouring through my window. Birds sang a cheerful song of hope as I counted out my bus fare and put it into my pants pocket. Miriam wished me good luck at work as I sat at the kitchen table eating a bowl of cornflakes and peaches. The friendly man with dark hair said he knew retail could be hard and he hoped I would be able to have a good day.

The bright sun surrounded me with a golden glow as I walked a couple of blocks to the bus stop. A short, chubby man smiled at me and I smiled back. I told him I was starting a new job and, when I told him I played the guitar, he said that he gave lessons. Shaking my hand warmly, he introduced himself as Mike. Then, he wrote his number down and handed it to me.

The bus carried me up and down the roller coaster hills. I analyzed my life in silence until I arrived at Fisherman's Wharf. As I stepped down onto the sidewalk, the sound of seagulls screeching reverberated through my ears. The smell of salt air and fish wafted into my nostrils and the hard concrete felt solid under my feet. People in dark sunglasses carrying large shoulder bags hurried along. Colorful sidewalk markets overflowed with crab, shrimp and lobsters. I pushed my way through a crowd of people until I arrived at the tiny space in front of the seafood restaurant. Tourists hustled in and out, talking loudly and carrying big bags of souvenirs.

With an air of authoritarian superiority, my boss greeted me. Then, he showed me how to run the charge card machine and cash register.

"You must smile at everyone. Let me see you smile... Good. And tell them to try on the sweaters and jackets and jewelry. And say, 'That looks good on you' so they will buy it."

"Okay. I'll do my best", I responded cheerfully.

"I've got to go run some errands", he said.

My muscles went rigid with anxiety. I battled my shyness as I encouraged browsing people to try on shirts. As I clasped necklaces around their necks, I told them they looked beautiful. Then, I handed them a mirror so they could admire themselves. The credit card machine and cash register were daunting. I needed eight arms to handle the jewelry case, the cash register, the credit card machine, the clothes and the customers.

When my break finally came, I walked around enjoying two freshly baked, warm oatmeal cookies and a container of milk. A feeling of enchantment rose in me as I watched jugglers and street musicians perform. A man dressed as a clown rode a unicycle around a stage as he juggled with flaming pins. A street artist with long hair, wearing a long, flowing dress put the finishing touches on a pastel portrait.

After I'd been working for a week, I called Mike, the friendly man I had met at the bus stop. When he said he would like to teach me guitar for free I knew I had found a genuine friend. I was surprised when he said that he lived only a couple of blocks away. I counted the days excitedly until my lesson day arrived. Mike greeted me warmly.

"Come on in. It's great to see you", he said, motioning for me to sit down on his comfortable sofa.

"Would you like some tea?', he asked.

"Yes. I would", I replied.

"Would you like honey in it?", he asked.

"Yes. Thank you", I replied.

I watched his large stomach jiggle as he walked to the kitchen. Admiring the green plants around his small apartment, I breathed deeply. I looked at various photos and pictures on the walls. Suddenly, the shrill whistle of a kettle tickled my eardrums. With a warm smile, he walked toward me and handed me a brown cup of tea. He settled down into a chair facing me.

"I'm glad to have you over. It makes me feel great to help someone. I'm a recovering alcoholic. I've been sober for a year now. I'm really happy about the progress I've made. I had a really bad drinking problem for years. One night I got so drunk I went completely bananas. I chased down and attacked a bus, trying to tackle it. I kept chasing it, trying to jump up on it. I was acting like a demented fool. I'm glad I've grown beyond that", he said, taking in a deep breath and releasing it with a sigh.

"I admire your inner strength. I've had problems too. I'm living in a halfway house now. I had a difficult childhood and I've been in institutions three times. The counselors at the halfway house are nice. I just hate having to follow their rules and take medication", I said, looking at the floor in shame.

"What do they have you take?", he asked with curiosity.

"Lithium and Stelazine", I replied.

"Lithium and Stelazine?" His voice rose in alarm as his eyes widened. He walked over to his bookshelf and picked up a large, blue book.

"Lithium is metal. Metal is a poison to the body. This physician's desk reference tells about all the pharmaceutical drugs on the market and their negative side effects", he said in a tone of deep concern.

I watched him flip through the pages of the book.

"They both cause liver and kidney damage. You've got to stop taking them", he said.

"They tell me I need them", I replied, in meek confusion.

"The only reason doctors invented them was so they could make a lot of money, the greedy creeps. Making money by damaging bodies. They're more interested in their bank accounts than they are in getting people well. It is really a shame how obsessed this society has become with popping pills. It's total bullshit. The doctors laugh all the way to the bank while all the poor, trusting souls end up with liver damage and another huge medical bill to pay. They're not helping you. They're poisoning you. You might as well be a billy goat eating an aluminum can."

"You don't know how much it means to me for you to be on my side. My father is a doctor and he has yelled at me, saying that I have a chemical imbalance and I will need to take drugs for the rest of my life. I've been on about twenty different tranquilizers and anti-depressants and they all made me feel awful." I stiffened with anxiety as I remembered my father asking me if I'd been taking my medicine in a harsh voice, glaring at me with threatening, mean eyes.

"Don't listen. Doctors think they are Gods but they don't know everything. Let's have our guitar lesson", he said, picking up his guitar and laying it across his thighs.

I leaned over and took my guitar out of the case. Then I set it on my lap and strummed it.

"Let's get in tune with each other. Give me an A", he said, playing his A string loudly.

As I played my A string over and over I watched him turn the peg on his guitar until it came into perfect tune. Then, he tuned all his other strings quickly and efficiently.

"Let's start off with this simple tune, The Holly and The Ivy. Just watch how my fingers move and you can memorize it. You don't need any music. I learn everything by ear", he said.

I watched his fingers move deftly across the fingerboard as he plucked the strings with his right hand. After watching a few times, I began to play along. After doing that for a while, he showed me how to play several scales. I listened with awe as he turned on the radio and played along spontaneously.

A few days later, I walked to the doughnut shop and visited Becky. She was able to sit and talk with me on her lunch break.

"I am really proud of you and you should be proud of yourself. You got yourself through a hard college and you had the courage to move all alone to a strange city where you knew no one. It's terrible that you've gotten hurt by mean people. Tom and I both think the world of you. We are so glad you got out of that university clinic and that you are recovering so well. We knew you were a great person from the first night we met you", she said, with moist glowing eyes full of love. It seemed like ages since I had last seen her. I had not seen her since I moved into the first halfway house after I got out of the university clinic. I had not wanted her to see me in my fractured, pathetic, psychotic state for fear that I would lose her.

"Thanks. That means a lot to me. I'm really glad I can visit with you now. That downtown area I stayed in gave me the creeps. I can't believe what I've been through. Sometimes I pinch myself and realize it's a miracle I'm still alive", I said, longing to return to the person I was the night we first met.

The soft afternoon sun surrounded us in a golden bubble of protection as the calm, loving mood of the moment healed me. I was experiencing the treasures contained within my Buddha nature. Her warm hug filled me with peace as we said goodbye. Her sweet eyes twinkled as she waved. I promised to call soon.

Stan called a few days later and asked me to meet him, Dot and Donna at the bar. Optimism surged through me as I walked down the streets, watching the sun set. Its red, gold and orange beams shone in café windows and on chrome plated cars. Laughter pealed through the doorways of cafes as people celebrated the leisurely, free night. The bar pulsated with exuberant conversation as I pulled the polished brass door handle and let myself in. Stan, Dot and Donna were lined up together on the crimson sofa. I waved and smiled as I walked toward them. Sitting down next to them, I relaxed.

Stan joked around asking people silly questions. It was a fun, carefree evening and my confidence was growing because my friends made it clear that they liked me. My faith in people was coming back. Hours passed as I listened and watched people, saying things here and there.

My eyelids began drooping and drowsiness overcame me so I said that I better go home. Stan said he wanted to walk there with me. I felt deeply touched as I agreed, feeling my cheeks grow warm with a blush. The dark night shimmered with stars and the breeze invigorated me.

"I'm working on Fisherman's Wharf selling Mexican shirts and jewelry. On my lunch break I walk around and watch jugglers and street musicians perform. It is a really fun area", I said.

"I'm so proud of you for getting out and getting a job. You have got a lot of courage and strength", Stan replied, taking my hand gently.

"Yeah. I'm glad I found one", I said, enjoying the calming sensation of his hand squeezing mine. I wanted to have him for myself. I wondered what he would do about his girlfriend if he fell in love with me.

The moon shone playfully on us as we walked down the quiet sidewalk. There was an endless hunger for love within me. I wanted him to hold my hand forever. I felt awkward though like I was just borrowing him from his real love. We arrived at the halfway house. After lingering in the ecstasy of his hug, I told him goodbye. His handsome face and glowing eyes lingered in my mind as I drifted off into a deep, peaceful sleep.

Another work day arrived. The sun streaming through my window cheered me as I dressed. I ran my hand along the banister as I walked downstairs. I talked with Tim, the kind, overweight man with dark hair, as I drank a tall glass of orange juice and ate a bowl of Rice Chex and a banana. Then, I ran a few blocks, waited until the bus roared up and climbed on board. I greeted the driver, paid my fare and sat down next to a window. A haze of buildings, cars, people, trees and billboards flashed by in a foggy blur. I observed the unique outfits and facial expressions that my fellow passengers wore. When I got off at Fisherman's Wharf, the smell of salty ocean air and fresh boiled shrimp floated into my nostrils. Happy tourists in shorts, sandals and sun hats walked by.

The day went smoothly until my boss stormed in. His livid, red face and aggressive posture tore through me as he scolded me in a harsh tone.

"A leather jacket was stolen. I told you that you had to keep a watch on the merchandise. You should not have let this happen. It cost ninety dollars. I've subtracted the cost of it from your paycheck." His brows knitted together seriously as he looked at me with scorn.

My legs trembled underneath me and it was as though a lead block had fallen on my chest. I had been working conscientiously, doing everything to the best of my ability. My reward for an entire week of hard work and aching feet was going to be a paycheck for eleven dollars.

It comforted me greatly to have counselors to talk to that night at dinner. They reassured me as I ate my plate of vegetables. A new feeling of power surged through me when they told me I could report my cruel boss to the Labor Board.

The next morning, fog floated in the cold air giving a Shakespearean aura of mystery to the day. I clenched my teeth with anger as I rode the bus to a large, downtown office building. A person behind a glass window gave me several forms to fill out. I sat on a chair and filled them out in detail. When I handed them back, the person behind the window said I would hear something from them within the next couple of weeks.

I got on a bus and headed toward my work place, feeling proud that I had done my best at this job for two months. Soon, I stepped out onto the sidewalk of Fisherman's Wharf. I settled into my routine of cleaning the jewelry case and straightening the Mexican shirts. Everything went smoothly for the rest of the week and I had a serene weekend at the halfway house.

On Monday morning, my boss came storming in.

"You're fired", he yelled, walking toward me aggressively.

I backed away fearfully, attempting to explain myself and reason with him.

"Get out of here", he yelled, looking at me like I was the lowest slime that ever crawled the face of the earth. My entire body became weak as his raging voice thundered through me, shaking me to the core. I slithered out of the corridor and hurried down the busy sidewalk.

Later, at the house meeting, I told the counselors I had been fired. They reassured me that I had done the best I could and reminded me to constantly tell myself the things that I was doing well. A week later, I got a check for ninety dollars from the Labor Board.

I quickly found another job taking care of an elderly lady. She had fallen and broken her hip and had had to have surgery. She was about to be released from the hospital.

Meeting her in an antiseptic smelling hallway of a large hospital, I walked toward her and extended my hand in greeting. With a friendly smile she shook my hand and told me her name was Martha. Then she sat in her wheel chair quietly as an attendant drove us to her high-rise apartment.

He parked his van and lifted her out. We rode the elevator up to the tenth floor. She talked with childlike enthusiasm as he wheeled her down the hall to her room. Rolling her into her small kitchen, he wished me the best of luck. Then he left, closing the door firmly behind him. I sat at her small, round kitchen table and observed how she looked fragile but resilient.

"I'm glad to have you spend time with me. We'll have a great time. There's a great cafeteria near here. We can go there and have pie and coffee. I like to stay active. My husband died ten years ago. He was a great man. He worked as a director in Hollywood. He worked on a lot of famous movies. He was a lot of fun to be with, always singing and laughing", she said, her eyes sparkling happily behind her wrinkled eyelids.

"I'm glad to be here. I can tell we will get along well together", I replied.

"Do you have a boyfriend?', she asked, her face filling with curiosity.

"No. I don't", I replied.

"Well, why not? You ought to have one. Maybe it's the way you dress. That long skirt and that blouse buttoned up to your neck makes you look matronly", she said.

"Yeah. You're right. I've never been much for keeping up with fashion", I replied, looking down self-consciously.

Picking up a pen and a scrap of paper, she wrote a list of things for me to get for her from the store. As I rode the bus to Kroger, I looked at the strange words--Gefilte Fish and Matzo Balls. I had never shopped for such unusual items but I managed to find them among the thousands of foods on the endless shelves.

She welcomed me back as I walked into her small apartment. As I unloaded the bags on her table, she talked effervescently. I put the tea kettle on to boil. Soon, it whistled shrilly and I poured us each a cup of tea. She looked at me with affection as we talked for an hour or so. When I looked at my watch and told her it was time for me to go, she wished me the best and said she looked forward to seeing me again.

CHAPTER 22————————AUGUST, SEPTEMBER, 1983
Hard, Cruel World

EVERYONE GATHERED AROUND THE DINNER table back at the halfway house. Miriam smiled at me and asked me how my new job went. She and the male counselor listened with proud expressions as I talked about the elderly lady I was taking care of. Maybe I was taking the curative powers of my medications for granted. I had definitely improved after being on them for months. Yet, I still wanted to be free of them.

Soon, the day for my next guitar lesson arrived. A glorious, golden sun shone down on me as I walked past the trees filled with twittering birds. I knocked on the door and, soon, my guitar teacher's warm smile sent a comforting wave of well-being through me.

"Would you like some tea?", he asked as I sat down on the sofa.

"Yes. I would", I replied. I daydreamed until I heard the kettle begin to whistle. Then I came back to focus on the present moment as a steaming cup was placed in front of me.

"How's everything going?', he asked as he sat down in a chair across from me.

"Well, I got fired from my job on Fisherman's Wharf but I got another one part time taking care of an elderly lady", I replied.

"Wow. You really find jobs fast. Don't worry about getting fired. There are a lot of assholes out there. I'm sure you were doing your best", he said, reassuringly.

"Yeah. I really tried. My boss fired me because I reported him to the Labor Board. He took money out of my pay check because a leather jacket got stolen. I got my ninety dollars from the Labor Board. They mailed it to me. I'm glad I reported the creep", I said, in angry triumph.

"I am too. I'm proud of you. No boss should get away with crap like that. You were completely justified in reporting him. He just couldn't stand that you called him on his unethical business practices. He should get his license taken away."

We drank our tea and talked for a few minutes. Then, Rob took his guitar out and set it on his lap.

"Let's have our lesson", he said enthusiastically.

"Sounds great", I replied, taking my guitar out of the case and resting it on my knee. I plucked the strings, tuning each one.

"Give me an A", Rob said.

We both plucked strings and turned pegs until we were in tune with each other. I looked into his kind, gentle face, thinking how lucky I was to have his sincere friendship. He played The Holly and The Ivy and then asked me to play it. I stared at the floor in shame as I played it, fumbling nervously and making mistakes. He gave me some new scales to practice and told me to practice every day. I didn't want to leave him at the end of the lesson.

That night I lay back in bed contemplating my life. Drowsiness washed over me as I looked at the pearly white moon shimmering, blessing and healing me. I had taken both of my pills obediently. They were spreading throughout my system, tranquilizing every cell in my body. Deeper and deeper I descended, until sleep took me far away from planet earth.

I didn't want to move a muscle when the alarm blared through my ears at four a.m. I forced myself to sit up and meditate but my head kept dropping down to my chest. I got back in bed and fell asleep. I woke up at five and pulled on a pair of blue jeans and a baggy shirt quickly, feeling anxious about getting to the Raja Yoga center by six o'clock. I hurried down the stairs, yawning and combing my hair with my fingers.

I sat behind the bus driver and read a book as he drove through the dark streets.

When he let me out a block from the Raja Yoga center, the September air chilled me. I walked down silent streets that were just beginning to be touched by early morning light. The shops and restaurants stood frozen in stillness. A beautiful Indian sister with long, shiny, dark hair and large eyes let me in. Her immaculate, white sari flowed gracefully. She looked like an angel as she led me up the stairs into a peaceful room where a handful of white clad souls sat in silent meditation.

I sat on the floor in lotus position. Then, I began imagining I was in the center of my forehead, experiencing myself as an eternal point of light. I imagined God, the Supreme point of light, showering me with peace, love and happiness. Thoughts darted through my mind and I imagined that I was detached from them, observing them from a distance. After a while, the most sublime, wonderful stillness I had ever experienced came to my mind. The choppy, turbulent sea became a placid, still lake. All the muscles in my body relaxed completely.

When our blissful meditation came to an end, a sister read the murli, the magic flute that transforms the world from hell to heaven. I sat listening, feeling amazed over the fact that God had come to speak to humanity.

"God has come to change the graveyard into the land of angels. Always stay in remembrance of God and know that he brings treasures worth multi-millions to you. Now is the time to purify the entire world and to change the corrupt souls into pure souls. All those with a stone-headed intellect are now being changed to those with divine intellect. The new world will be heaven. The golden palaces which are studded with diamonds and colored gems will shine in the sun. Everyone will be happy and prosperous. You will be able to fly in your golden viman to the other side of the world in less than two hours. Everyone will be loving and gentle. There will be no such thing as sorrow. Now, you fortunate children have the intoxication of receiving love from the father. This love saves you from many other intoxications, doesn't it?"

After the murli, the sister handed sweet toli to everyone, giving loving drishti from her eyes as she placed it gently into their open hands. It was baked in deep remembrance of God so loving vibrations permeated whoever ate it. Hope and optimism filled me for the rest of the day. I loved my new, spiritual family.

Bright sunlight streaming through my window woke me the next morning. I rode the bus to my elderly care job, lost in deep thought. As the driver let me out I wished him a good day. I walked up a hill and into the large lobby of the high rise building. Admiring the gorgeous Grand Piano in the living area, I longed to play it. It had been ages since I had played a piano. The elevator rose rapidly. I walked down the quiet hall and turned my key in Martha's door.

Her frail, skinny body looked like it could break as she pulled herself up slowly from her bed. I helped her rise and walk over to the kitchen table. She winced with pain as she sat down in a chair. Her bony, thin hands rested on the table in front of her. The lines on her face reached everywhere like a weathered road map. Thin wisps of white hair stood haphazardly around her head as she looked at me with tiny, tired, wrinkled eyes. A stubborn pride resonated in her voice as she instructed me to make her a cup of tea.

"I'm in a bad mood today. I'm tired of hearing all the bad news about the terrible things that go on in this city. I read a story in the newspaper about a drug addict who escaped from prison. He was staying with a friend who had a little baby and he raped the baby. There are some really evil people out there. It makes me want to go live on a tropical island somewhere", she said with a helpless, sad look that made me want to cry.

"I know exactly what you mean. It is shocking that there are so many evil people in the world", I replied.

After we had talked for a while, she suggested that we take the bus to her favorite cafeteria and get a piece of pie. She walked confidently, using her cane to support her, as we made our way to the elevator and out of the building. An iridescent, baby blue sky and a glorious, golden sun sent warm, cosmic rays of light through me as we walked to the corner bus stop.

A bus groaned to a halt. I extended my arm to help her up but she refused. I watched with amazed admiration as she stepped up the stairs onto the bus. As I sat beside her on the bus, watching the traffic and pedestrians flash by outside the window, I listened. Raving about the great desserts the cafeteria had, she put her hand on mine.

Soon, the bus came to a halt and I followed her down onto the street. I watched her hobble fearlessly, stepping in front of cars as shocked drivers slammed on their brakes. I put my hand on her shoulder protectively as she stepped up onto the sidewalk. Stabilizing herself with her cane, she walked with firm determination up the steps and into the cafeteria.

We each took a tray and a roll of silver ware. A fabulous assortment of colorful cakes and pies made my mouth water as I pushed my tray down the line. She talked effervescently as we found a table and sat down. Her bright blue eyes sparkled with satisfaction as she watched me eat, swooning over the deliciousness of my carrot cake. After a fun conversation, we walked outside.

We rode the bus back to her apartment. Sitting at her little table, she talked about the boxes and boxes of shoes she never wore. With a nostalgic look in her eyes, she reminisced about her early married life and her brilliant, fun husband. When I looked at my watch and realized my shift was over, I told her goodbye, reassuring her that I looked forward to seeing her soon.

When I arrived back home, the secure atmosphere at the halfway house calmed me. I sat and talked with the male counselor. He congratulated me on doing well at my new elderly care job. Restless energy simmered inside me and I told him I wanted to go for a walk. Swinging my arms and taking long, bold steps, I walked quickly through the Golden Gate Park, looking up at the radiant sun in the dazzling sky full of puffy clouds. Feasting my eyes on the beauty surrounding me, I studied the multi-colored flowers and the many varieties of trees.

When I got back to the halfway house, I stretched back on my bed. Just as I started reading a book, Miriam called up the stairs to tell me I had a phone call. I walked downstairs to the hall phone and answered it. My happiness barometer rose as Stan's voice greeted me warmly. He invited me to join him and Dot at the bar.

I escaped the halfway house without telling anyone. A new feeling of aliveness surged through me as I walked quickly past the cafes and stores.

Stan and Dot greeted me warmly and we laughed and talked as we sipped on Kahlua and Cream. They had opened a whole new world to me. I had even taken an acting lesson from their teacher. I imagined becoming an actress. Time flew quickly and I was shocked when I looked at my watch and realized it was past eleven p.m., I told Stan I needed to go. He told me he would walk me home.

This personal, one on one attention was what I needed to help me become whole again. The moon shone down on us as we walked. Now and then I swayed, feeling the effects of the alcohol combined with meds. I felt comforted by the feeling of Stan's hand as he held mine.

We arrived at the halfway house. The key clicked in the door as I let us both in. Putting my finger over my lips, I signaled for him to be quiet. We tiptoed up the stairs into my bedroom.

He put his arm around my shoulders as we sat down side by side on my bed. Then, he leaned me back on the bed and, suddenly, his wet mouth was on mine. His tongue moved around mine and then began moving down my neck. Pleasure rippled through me as he unzipped my dress and pulled it down to reveal my bare breasts. He ran his tongue along my neck, across my breasts and down to my navel. Emotion flooded me as, suddenly, he pulled my underpants off. With calm command he parted my legs. Moisture flooded my genitals as he moved his wet tongue, sending electrical surges of pleasure throughout my body. An explosive orgasm vibrated through every cell in my body.

I lay there in awe over the mystery and magic of sex as he rested his head on my chest. It didn't seem like such a pleasurable force could really be evil. I questioned the principle of celibacy the Raja Yogis insisted upon. If expressing my sexual being made God not love me, then he couldn't be the unconditionally loving God they said he was.

"I don't want to cause any trouble between you and Dot", I said.

"Oh, she wouldn't care. She fools around with other men all the time. We let each other do whatever we want. We just don't tell each other. Don't worry", he said, rubbing my head gently.

I rested in rapture as he held me gently. The warmth of his arms around me filled me with a sense of security. When he left, his footsteps made hardly a sound as he tiptoed down the stairs. He closed the front door quietly and I drifted off into a deep, peaceful sleep.

The next morning, I moved around restlessly as I waited for the bus. Soon, it arrived. I greeted the driver as I climbed on and asked him to let me off in front of the Grand Piano. As I stepped down onto the hard concrete, I looked around for familiar faces. A man at the counter of the Grand Piano smiled as I ordered a cup of chamomile tea.

I looked with curiosity around the room as I sat and drank it. I overheard some people talking about a man who had been found dead in the Golden Gate Park. His head had been chopped off and some chicken feathers had been put in its place. It had been a ritual murder instigated by some drug deal.

When I arrived back at the halfway house I thanked God for putting me in this protected environment. I was getting settled into a routine, getting my feet on the ground.

Days later, I bumped into my old room mate, Connie, who lived in the yellow Victorian I had been evicted from. She told me that her friend, Pam, wanted to rent me a room for two hundred dollars a month. She explained that she was a devoted Buddhist and very strong person. She encouraged me to move in there, saying she would be very good for me.

I impulsively started packing my things and told the counselors and patients I was going to move out. When the counselors questioned me I responded tersely that I was "well". That was far from the truth. I was in denial about all I had gone through. Maybe my inability to talk about my fears and accept help from the counselors was part of my mental illness. Or maybe my rebellion against authority figures was an automatic habit and ingrained part of my personality. Also, I was a people pleaser and was easily influenced and unable to refuse suggestions. I immediately regretted my decision when I moved into the tiny room in a run down, small place in a bad area of town.

Pam took me to some Buddhist meetings and encouraged me to chant.

Her son and his girlfriend lived in the room next to mine. He had been addicted to heroin and he seemed to be lost in another world. His unfriendly girlfriend had pink, orange and blue hair. She stared into space and never greeted me. I hid in my room, feeling the unbearable pain of isolation. When my job with my elderly companion suddenly ended, two weeks after I moved in with Pam, I felt like there was nothing worth living for any more.

One day the mime, who had modeled for my art class, appeared. He talked in a friendly way with everyone. Pam said she had known him a long time.

He gave me a job painting houses. I worked hard scraping paint from walls and sanding wooden wall borders. The paint and turpentine smelled awful and the dust irritated my eyes, making them red and ugly. When he bought all his workers a huge box of doughnuts, I gorged myself like a lion on a safari. Filling my loneliness with food increased my depression. My hips got larger and larger until I couldn't stand to look at myself in the mirror. Soon, I had gone without meds for a month and I felt a suffocating depression gripping me relentlessly.

I wished I had stayed in the halfway house as I sat in my room alone night after lonely night. I was too far away to walk to the bar to see Stan, to visit Becky at the doughnut shop or to walk to my music lesson. I hated walking out on the sidewalk because the street was always rushing with heavy, noisy traffic. People who looked like criminals hurried along the chaotic sidewalks. I missed the concerned counselors and friendly residents yet I was too afraid to go back there and ask if I could move back in.

The next morning I dragged myself into the kitchen, feeling myself drowning under the weight of a deep depression. I greeted the woman with blue, pink and purple hair. She didn't respond. Alienation crashed through me as I longed for my friends back at the halfway house. My landlord, Pam, came into the kitchen with her son and sat at the table talking with him while I ate a bowl of oatmeal. Standing up nervously, I quickly washed my dish and wished them a good day.

The traffic screamed through my ears as I walked outside and down the street to the bus stop. Soon, I arrived back in the neighborhood of my last halfway house. I walked through it with lonely longing, watching a pretty lady walk her adorable dog. The atmosphere was safe and pleasant, the opposite of the miserable ghetto I had moved to. I knocked on my guitar teacher's door. He let me in with a warm greeting and I sat down on the sofa.

"I've got a job for you. A friend of mine has a lot of pots and pans that she needs to have washed," he said compassionately.

I tried washing the pots and pans in the greasy, smelly, roach infested kitchen. But the sink was piled high with the filthy dishes of my housemates. They ignored me coldly when I requested that they remove them. Finally, I gave up and returned the pots and pans to my guitar teacher apologetically.

I knocked on the front door of my old halfway house and asked Miriam, the counselor, if I could move back in. She said she would like to say "yes" but someone had taken my place. My depression was so deep it was hard to talk as I resigned from my house painting job. My fingers ached from the endless rubbing of woodwork with sandpaper.

At my next session with Dr. Stanfield, I yelled out my rage and pounded the tennis racket on the mattress. I didn't tell him I had suddenly stopped taking the medications that the halfway house counselors gave me. I told him how miserable my new living situation was making me and how I wanted to return to the halfway house. After we talked for a while, he gave me some good news.

"There's going to be a free Raja Yoga retreat at a ranch thirty miles north of San Francisco. It is a beautiful place. All the yogis will make meals together and meditate together. You can hike around the beautiful grounds. You'll love it", he said with enthusiasm.

"That sounds great. I'd like to go", I replied hopefully, looking forward to escaping the noise and chaos of the city.

Dr. Stanfield's warm hug nourished me at the end of my session. I wished him a good week. Riding the bus home, I decided I wanted to sell my car and be free of the expenses of repairs and parking tickets. Stopping at the Grand Piano, I looked around hopefully for my friends. I felt surprised when I suddenly saw John. I hadn't seen him in over a year. He acted very happy to see me and asked me to take a walk around the neighborhood with him. I felt sorry for him, like I should apologize for the time that George threatened him and sent him running in fear out of my bed. He had tried to warn me that George would be too fast for me and I wished I had listened. I wondered if he could forgive me and if we could get back the love we had felt for each other when we walked along the beach hand in hand that enchanted evening. All of his warnings had turned out to be true. I didn't want to tell him about the devastating traumas I had gone through. I wanted to be the trusting, innocent girl who had gone skinny dipping with him that glorious, sunny day soon after I arrived in the city.

"I warned you that people here are mean. Remember? The guy I'm sharing a place with attacked me with a knife last night. I can't stand this town any more. I want to go back to Germany", he said, raking his fingers through his hair.

I admired his muscular, slender, sun bronzed body as we walked past shops and restaurants. Deep affection welled up in my heart as I realized that he had forgiven me. I could have spared myself the damage George had done to me if I had just accepted his protection gratefully.

When I told him I wanted to sell my car, he offered to buy it from me for a dollar. I responded that it was worth a lot more than that. He replied that it might not be and that people often sold vehicles for that amount.

We walked back to The Grand Piano. Much to my surprise, Stan suddenly appeared. He gave me a warm greeting and long hug. Then, he began talking with John. I daydreamed, not following their conversation. Stan seemed to like him at first but, after a while, an irritated angry tone came into his voice.

"Come on. Let's go", he said, pulling me by the hand.

I followed him out onto the street, wondering why he was behaving so strangely.

"He just wants to steal your car. He doesn't care anything about you", Stan said protectively, looking with empathy into my eyes.

"Well, he said that he would buy my car for a dollar", I said, in a daze of conflicted emotions. I still wanted John to fall in love with me.

I stood on the sidewalk talking with Stan for quite some time. Suddenly, out of the corner of my eye, I saw John moving toward me. He smiled lovingly as he moved closer and then handed me four gorgeous white lilies as he looked deeply into my eyes. I felt like Elizabeth Taylor being reunited with Richard Burton. Maybe our love was meant to be, I thought hopefully. He could get counseling to stop drinking and we could live in marital bliss in a cozy cottage in the Black Forest in Germany.

"Come on. He doesn't care about you", Stan said, taking my hand and pulling me toward an approaching bus. I looked back longingly at my handsome first love as Stan led me up the steps onto the bus.

"I'll buy your car from you. You can ride the bus all around town. You'll be a lot happier because you'll be saving a lot of money on tickets, gas and car repairs. You've been through too much struggle. Let me take care of you. That guy is a jerk. He acted arrogant and rude. I don't want him bothering you", Stan said firmly.

I swallowed my pain, remembering how John and I had run like children hand in hand under the breathtakingly beautiful stars. And he had given me the most passionate kiss I had ever experienced.

"He was just giving you those flowers because he wanted to get your car from you. I'll take your car to a mechanic and get them to check it out. Then I can buy it from you. It will be easier for you to get around on the bus", Stan said.

"I get confused sometimes. I need you. I have mental problems. Sometimes I think I just can't handle this crazy world", I said, looking at Stan with sad eyes.

"I know you have problems. That's why I'm your friend. You can come visit us any time. We're always glad to see you", he said, putting his arm around me.

CHAPTER 23 ———————SEPTEMBER, OCTOBER, NOVEMBER, DECEMBER, 1983

A Test Of Faith

A WEEK LATER, STAN GAVE ME two hundred and fifty dollars for my car. With my savings growing, I was getting closer to India and to God. I continued to miss John but I lost his phone number and never saw him again.

Lamenting about my loneliness and desire for intimacy, I sat in Dr. Stanfield's office at my next session. I didn't want to be a nun who never got touched. I wanted a husband I told him in a frustrated tone. Dr. Stanfield told me to concentrate on building relationships with my divine brothers and sisters. Then, he reminded me that the retreat was coming up soon. He suggested that I hitchhike there. He was booked up with meetings and would have to rush to get there so he could not give me a ride. I hid my hurt feelings that were caused by him recommending such a dangerous activity.

Grateful to escape the September cold air, I climbed on board a bus headed for Fairfax. A pretty, tender mother gave snacks to her adorable children. An older man sat alone. I sat observing people and day dreaming. Lovely, rolling hills filled with grazing cows replaced the noisy, traffic jammed streets. The driver wished me a good day as he let me out in Fairfax. I walked around admiring beautiful, purple, snow-capped mountains, feeling invigorated by the brisk air. A small, charming café looked inviting and I ambled in, enjoying the easy going, mellow vibrations. A friendly employee took my order for Peppermint Tea. As I sat down at a table to drink it, a handsome man smiled and greeted me. When I told him I was trying to get to Olema, he told me which bus to take and where to catch it.

I waited and waited for the bus and it never came. A paralyzing fear overtook me as the sun started descending rapidly. Pointing my thumb out toward the road in a hitchhiker's pose, I observed drivers anxiously as one after another passed me. The orange, blazing sun moved rapidly toward its exit behind a huge hill. Thoughts of wandering around in the dark and sleeping under a tree listening to coyotes howl raced through my mind. When a car slowed down, I observed the two men sitting in the front seat suspiciously. Yet, they looked at me with gentle eyes.

"Can you give me a ride to Olema?", I asked, observing their innocent faces. They looked like college students.

"Yeah. We're passing right through there on the way to our parents' vacation home", the driver replied in a friendly tone.

"Thanks. I really appreciate it", I said, pulling open the door and climbing into the back seat.

"I'm going to a meditation retreat at a ranch", I said, watching the driver's eyes in the front mirror.

"That sounds like fun. I'm sure you'll enjoy it", he replied.

"Yeah. I'm looking forward to it. This is beautiful country. All these rolling hills are really incredible. I've never been in this area", I said.

I gazed dreamily out the window at the expansive, rolling hills dotted with cows, horses and farm houses. The dazzling, green foliage was abundant and lush. It shimmered under a brilliant, blue sky which was soft with fluffy, drifting clouds. The serenity of nature filled me with a transcendent, spiritual vibration. It was as though angels were protecting me.

We arrived in Olema and they let me out at an old-fashioned gas station. Pointing toward the direction I should walk in, they wished me good luck. Darkness began to fall as I walked quickly down the dirt road lined with cheerful, yellow wild flowers. When I reached a large, colored sign in front of an expansive estate, I realized I had found the place I was looking for.

As I walked through the entrance gate, I leaned my head back to drink in the luxurious, cool canopy of emerald green leaves. Tall, wide trees, which looked three hundred years old, bowed benevolently over me, enfolding me in their healing arms. The brown dirt road felt nourishing under my feet as I kicked rocks and listened to them skittle along. Soon, I arrived at an ancient, columned plantation house. I walked onto a charming porch and through the door. A group of white-clad yogis was gathered in a cozy room. I exchanged greetings with several of them and then began to peruse the books that climbed to the ceiling. They were all about meditation and spiritual knowledge.

A beautiful Indian woman tapped me on the shoulder and said that she would show me where my room was. I followed her to a clean, nicely furnished, minimal room with two twin beds like a dormitory. My room mate greeted me warmly as I put my suitcase down. With a long, wide yawn, I fell back onto the bed. Soon, a serene slumber carried me away.

A loud knock on the door woke me. It was Sister Dianne, exuding peace in her long, white sari. She said that everyone was gathering for dinner. My room mate and I chatted lightly as we followed her to the house. People were setting a table, stirring big pots and chopping vegetables as we walked into the peaceful kitchen. I watched Dr. Stanfield talking and laughing loudly with a handsome yogi. Deep serenity filled me as I ate the food which had been prepared in loving remembrance of God.

The sky was dark and crickets chirped cheerfully when everyone gathered later in the evening. A handsome man from Australia told his story about how he had gotten involved in Raja Yoga. He explained that he had been to India many times and talked to God through the medium. Even though he had not believed it was God at first, his faith had grown as he experienced positive changes in his life. Various yogis explained the benefits of their strict lifestyles. A kind, brunette woman named Lisa, who worked at the Vegetarian society, said that she disagreed with celibacy because she thought sex could be spiritual. When I told her I hated the place I lived in, she kindly responded that I could stay with her while I found a place and a job.

After the program, my room mate and I talked until my eyelids started closing. The fresh smelling sheets soothed me as I rested my head on my pillow and drifted into a deep, peaceful sleep.

When the alarm went off for four a.m. meditation, I turned it off, rolled over and went back to sleep. Luckily, I woke up and got myself to the six a.m. murli class. After running up a steep hill, I slumped in exhaustion onto a blanket on the ground. Sister Dianne read the murli in her beautiful, English accent. Now and then, she looked into my eyes with love. A warm feeling of hope spread through me. I relaxed into very deep peace.

Churning the knowledge, I hiked through the beautiful woods after murli class. I breathed deeply, feeling refreshed by the clean oxygen. Wild elk and deer roamed around peacefully. Their strange, loud mating calls intrigued me. I enjoyed the radiant, golden sun warming my face and body.

A while later, everyone gathered in the kitchen and ate a delicious, healthy breakfast. Dr. Stanfield put his arm on my shoulder and encouraged me to talk with my new family members when he noticed that I had withdrawn into my shell. I rejoined the celebration gratefully.

Later that night, the house came alive with fun and festivity. Several yogis performed a hilarious skit. Dr. Stanfield looked adorable as he danced and sang "Singin' In The Rain", swinging his umbrella playfully. After the festivities, everyone walked into the kitchen to get something to drink. A sweet Indian sister, named Jyoti, touched me on the shoulder and gazed gently into my eyes.

"Don't worry", she said.

As I looked into her love filled eyes, I wanted to fall into her arms and cry. I stood there smiling, enjoying the sensation of her hand holding mine. As I walked with my room mate to our room, I thought about how much I wanted to start enjoying my life. My soft pajamas comforted me as I pulled them on. Setting the alarm for four a.m., I hoped I would be there meditating with the others at Amrit Vela. But, at four a.m., I turned the alarm off, yawned drowsily and fell back to sleep.

As I ran up a hill to get to six a.m. murli class, I got hopelessly lost.

Luckily, Sister Dianne and Sister Carol stopped and gave me a ride in their car. I sat on a blanket on the ground. The singing of birds in the gorgeous, towering trees and the golden sunlight cascading through the shimmering, emerald foliage mesmerized me. A pretty, Indian sister read the murli.

"With your elevated attitude, make intense effort to make your vibrations and the atmosphere powerful; give blessings and receive blessings. Today, Baba, the ocean of love and power has come to meet his loving, long-lost and now found beloved children. All the children, through the attraction of love, have also reached here from far, far away to celebrate a meeting. Whether you are sitting personally in front of Baba or whether you are sitting in this land or abroad, you are celebrating a loving meeting. Baba is pleased to see all his loving children and totally co-operative companion children. Baba sees that the majority of the children have just the one thought in their heart: we will now very quickly reveal the Father. The Father says the enthusiasm of all the children is very good. However, you will only be able to reveal the Father when you first reveal yourselves as complete and perfect, the same as the Father. Have you fixed a date to become equal to the Father? You children must purify yourselves and others and help with this task of world transformation."

I wanted to stay in the enchanted forest when the retreat ended. A brother I saw regularly at the center gave me a ride home. His manner was detached but kind. He wished me the best of luck as he let me out in front of my miserable, tenement home.

A malevolent energy hung in the air like an omen as I walked up the gloomy, dark stairway and let myself into my stuffy, windowless room. Pulling my clothes off despondently, I tossed them onto the floor. I pulled a nightgown on and crawled into bed. As I pulled the covers over me I felt like a lotus flower surrounded by a stinking, filthy pond. I hated the city with all its poisonous air, evil people and endless sorrow.

Larry, my former house painting boss arrived in a torrent of urgency the next morning. I'd applied for a few jobs before I left for the retreat but nothing had materialized. I wanted to get another elderly care job but couldn't remember the name of the agency I had worked for. Painting houses was hell and I never wanted to see my pushy, rude boss again.

"Stop screwing and get your ass out of bed and off to work", his voice thundered down the hallway to Pam's slumbering, heroin using son.

I walked out into the hall nervously. Her son walked out and hurried down the stairs and out the front door to paint houses. His girlfriend came out in a drugged daze and walked to the kitchen. Her green, purple and pink hair was strewn haphazardly around her head. Pam walked out of her room, running her fingers through her hair and yawning. I listened in shocked horror as she launched into a cruel attack on me.

"Don't use my friends. Mrs. Lee was very kind to give you rides to the Buddhist meetings but you are not allowed to use her. I haven't been able to sleep all night and I've got to move all these boxes", she yelled, clenching her fists. I had ridden in Mrs. Lee's car once when I went with Pam to a Buddhist meeting.

"I don't know what you're talking about. I'm sorry…." She cut me off. I felt my knees wobble underneath me.

"I don't want your pity. Give me help, not pity. I have to move these boxes out of the hallway", she said angrily.

"Well, I don't know how to help you."

"Because you've got rocks in your head. You never stop, do you?", she said in a denigrating tone, imitating me running my fingers through my hair.

"Listen, I'm tired of you watching T.V. at two in the morning. I can't sleep. And you are not behaving in a very spiritual way. I just wonder if you've learned anything from Buddhism", I said, raising my voice in anger.

"I had surgery on my back and I get migraine headaches and I can't sleep. Watching T.V. is the only way I can get myself to fall asleep", she yelled.

"Well, don't ask me to help unless you're nice about it", I said.

"Just because I'm a Buddhist, that doesn't mean I can't beat the shit out of you", she said, glaring at me with hard eyes.

I walked down the stairs, out of the front door and down the chaotic, noisy street. I longed to sit with the counselors back at the halfway house more than ever. Rough looking winos watched me as I walked across the street and put a quarter into a newspaper box. Like a frightened deer, I hurried back to the safety of my gloomy room.

Longing for comfort, I called Dr. Stanfield to confirm my appointment with him. I was surprised when Sister Carol answered the phone.

"I'm calling to confirm my appointment with Dr. Stanfield", I said.

"There won't be any appointment. He's left his body", Sister Carol said in a detached voice. A choking sensation filled my throat and my eyes flooded with tears.

"Why don't you come and spend the night at the center?", she suggested in a softer voice.

"Okay. I will", I replied. I hung up the phone and sobbed uncontrollably.

Sister Carol welcomed me as I arrived at the center. She told me to sit in meditation. Memories of my happy times with Dr. Stanfield ran through my mind as I sat in silent solitude in the simple, white room. I filled myself up with God's love and, after meditating for an hour, I walked into the kitchen.

A sweet sister served me a delicious supper. Her beautiful, dark eyes glowed with love as she refilled my plate again and again.

"That is Baba or God", she said, pointing to a photograph on the wall.

An older Indian woman with other worldly, intense eyes smiled in the photo. I studied it with fascination.

"Baba speaks through her. You can go and talk with him", she said sweetly.

The delicious food and loving company lifted my spirits. I slept peacefully in a fresh smelling, comfortable bed. At four a.m. I meditated with the sisters, feeling a profound, unlimited love calm me. I rode with Sister Carol to Dr. Stanfield's funeral.

Beautiful organ music played as I walked to his casket and placed some red and white carnations on top of it. He had told me that they were his favorite flowers. As I sat in the pew listening to Sister Dianne speak to the crowd, tears rolled down my cheeks and a lump of grief blocked my throat. She said that death was just a new beginning. After the funeral, I went with Sister Carol to her small apartment. I told her I would like to go to India and talk with God. My parents would think I was crazy if I told them my plans, I laughed. They had locked me up in an institution, in the past, I told her shyly.

"No. Don't tell them that. They'll lock you up permanently."

We laughed together in a lighthearted way. She made me a cup of mint tea with honey. Her long, dark hair shone lustrously against her white sari. Her sweet energy soothed me as she sat down at the small table across from me.

"Be happy that you have a new family. You now have divine brothers and sisters all around the world. Dr. Stanfield had a very special love for you. He always spoke of you fondly", she said, looking at me with loving eyes.

"I'm going to start saving my money so I can go to India", I said with determination.

I gritted my teeth in anger over the way Pam had yelled at me as I rode the bus back to my miserable, tenement home. Depression overtook me as I put my belongings into boxes and plastic bags. Not mentioning a word to her, I called a cab and headed to Lisa's place at the Vegetarian society. Lisa had talked with me in a kind, gentle way at the Raja Yoga retreat and I missed her.

She welcomed me warmly and I enjoyed playing her piano and eating her delicious vegetarian food. With strong determination, I went on about ten interviews a week. We talked about mysticism and some of our life experiences in the evenings. We laughed about how crazy life could be. Her kindness deeply touched me.

About two weeks later I got hired to be a live-in nanny for a one year old girl in a well to do section of town near the Raja Yoga center. It would pay me four hundred dollars a month and I did not have to pay for food or rent. After a number of months I would have enough to buy a plane ticket to India.

I felt my spirits rise when I moved into my new employer's home. Taking care of her little girl was the best job I had ever had. She provided me with a comfortable, nicely decorated room with a private sun porch. Tranquility filled me as I pushed the adorable little girl, Kathy, in a stroller through the Golden Gate park, enjoying the October sun and cool air. She had a cherubic face with blue eyes surrounded with fine, golden hair. I loved filling her tiny hands with cookies and giving her a bottle.

I made plans to go home for Christmas. My brother sent me three hundred dollars for Christmas. He must have wanted to make up for his cruelty. I gave all my money to Sister Carol so she could buy me a plane ticket to India. October, November and December satisfied me as I gave love to little Kathy and got love back from her.

In early December, I told my employer that I was going to India. She felt disappointed and told me that I would have to give up the job. Even though I didn't want to lose the best job I had ever had, I decided it was worth it to go to India.

Soon, it was almost Christmas. Sister Carol gave me a big bag of murlis to read. I read them the entire flight home, feeling my heart expand from God's loving words. It seemed like no time had passed when the pilot announced that we would soon land in Atlanta. The motor screamed in fury as it pounded down onto the runway. Then, it slowed down and hummed as it coasted into the terminal with smooth ease. I surveyed the crowd as I walked into the crowded airport.

Suddenly, I noticed my father walking toward me, his tall body moving quickly, towering over the others.

"Hi. It's nice to have you home. Give me a hug", he said.

"I'm glad to be home. That was a long flight. How is everything going for you?", I asked.

"Oh, I'm still running the rat race. The rats are still winning", he said. His mind seemed to be a million miles away as I followed him through the crowded airport.

"How is Mom doing?", I asked.

"Oh, she's been doing a lot of painting. She's at the beach now. She flung a fit and left about a week ago. I've been trying to get her to come back, calling her on the phone and sending her letters. She got angry over some petty little thing and left in a huff. You know how she blows things out of proportion. She's the most selfish person I've ever known. I'm trying to help her by encouraging her painting. I got some of her paintings hung in different places. She's got some in the Mayor's office now. I thought some success would make her happy but it doesn't. She still complains all the time", he said.

"How is everything in San Francisco?"

"It's alright. My live-in nanny job is going well. The little girl I take care of is really cute. I'm going to go to India with my meditation group."

My father must have wondered how I could afford it but he didn't ask. There was a long awkward silence. I fidgeted nervously as I imagined that images of kooks walking on beds of nails and people dying of dysentery were flashing through his mind. Trucks and cars sped by with a deafening sound, delivering a brute force that almost blew us off the road.

"Dr. Stanfield, my psychologist, got me to take the course in spiritual knowledge from them. I've been going there every morning at six o'clock and meditating", I said nervously, fearing his disapproval.

"Oh, yes. I talked with him on the phone many times. He doesn't understand the true nature of your problems", he said.

"Well, he died. I really miss him. He was my best friend in San Francisco. I had some of the best experiences of my life because of him", I said, sighing with deep sadness.

"Yeah. You may have had some good experiences in San Francisco but you didn't get anywhere." The truth in his statement moved like a death toll through me. I had wasted a lot of time.

We arrived at the long, beautiful, curving road that I had begun to live on when I was eleven. Huge, shiny magnolia trees spread their welcoming arms and tall pines reached endlessly to the sky. Gravel grumbled under the tires as my father drove up the long driveway. I walked into the house and onto the porch. My father turned on the television set.

"What's on T.V?", I asked.

"This is the Time Life Series on nature", he replied.

"Oh, these nature shows are incredible. I love watching them", I said.

I wished we could have a heart to heart talk but he remained glued to the T.V. I sighed in frustration as I told him good night. Drowsiness overcame me as I walked up the stairs to go to sleep. I had been off of my medicine for four months now. After tossing and turning in my older sister's bed, I finally fell asleep with my arms wrapped around me.

Shimmering sunlight streamed through the yellow curtains and embraced me in a warm glow the next morning. I sat up in bed and meditated for an hour, drinking in the unlimited love of God. Excitement rushed through me as I contemplated the fact that I would soon be talking to God face to face.

That afternoon my mother arrived home from her condo at the beach. Her face glowed with health and she looked refreshed and relaxed. Even at her age, she was still gorgeous. I felt glad my trust fund money had helped her get her beach condo because it was definitely benefiting her. She had been stifled and oppressed by my father far too long and I was glad she now had her freedom. I smiled and reached out to hug her.

"Oh, you look so……..California", she said, looking at me as though she didn't quite know how to relate to my weirdness. She hugged me with the half hug which had always left me hungry for more. In this ambivalent, emotionally confusing gesture, she put one hand on my back and sort of patted it, while simultaneously pulling away from me as though I did not really deserve her love. She greeted my father distantly, wielding her power, enjoying knowing that she could leave him any time. I followed her onto the porch. As we talked, I felt happy to be home.

After a while, my sister arrived bubbling over with light hearted talk about the fun she had had going out of town with a friend. I envied her happiness and wished I was not so sad and damaged. We all went out to a Chinese restaurant that night. I felt like the invisible person as my mother talked on and on about seeing the Great Barrier Reef in Australia with my father. I felt angry that they had never taken me on any of their exotic trips.

Soon, it was the day before Christmas. My older brother, Bill, flew in from California. My older sister, Laura, arrived from Florida with her handsome, incredibly wealthy surgeon husband. Envy churned in my guts as everyone sat around the dining room table eating and talking. I listened to my brother talk with enthusiasm about his successes in journalism. My older sister looked gorgeous as she glowed with happiness, talking about scuba diving in Aruba. My younger sister, Dianne, said funny things and brought me out of my shell of fear luckily. She had listened with empathy and encouraged me to move home when I had called her in desperation from California. None of them knew anything about the hell I had been through. A silent scream built up inside me as I longed for someone to look into my eyes. I felt like no one even saw me.

Christmas day arrived. I longed to get back the feeling of enchantment it had given me as a child. I smiled and tried to hide the immense pain I was feeling as we sat on the floor around the decorated tree and opened presents. When I opened a card from my parents, I felt grateful that it contained a check for a hundred dollars. A little cash in my pocket would make my trip to India much easier.

CHAPTER 24 ——————— DECEMBER, 1983. JANUARY, FEBRUARY, MARCH, 1984

There's No Place Like Home

WE PILED INTO THE CAR to visit my father's parents. My grandparents greeted me warmly, as always. I sat on the sofa and flipped through a stack of magazines as I listened to my parents talk about their trip to Scotland. When my leg began kicking restlessly, I knew it was nature, in all her glory, calling me to get out and enjoy the wondrous woods. As I walked outside, I remembered the beautiful afternoons I had spent playing badminton with my cousins. Walking into the woods I looked for the place that my grandfather had said was an Indian burial place. Birds sang sweetly as I craned my neck back to look up at the tall pine trees. Fluffy, white clouds floated gently through the baby blue sky. Peace flowed through me like a waterfall as I remembered my simple childhood days.

Suddenly, my father appeared behind me. I was surprised when he said that he wanted to join me on my walk. My bold move across the country had gotten his attention, finally. He expressed great happiness over the fact that I was home and said that he hoped I would feel comfortable enough to talk about anything with him.

I wished I had opened up to him about my inability to be accepted by my peers who I lived with but I felt too shy. Later on, I decided to try to understand my social failures with my older brother.

"Do I make strange expressions on my face or is my behavior odd?", I asked my older brother.

SOPHIA MOON

"Yeah. Look at you now like you're saying "'I'm a good girl. Don't hit me.'"

His mockery hurt. I left his room and walked downstairs sadly. I sat on the living room sofa feeling invisible as I listened to my mother and father talk. My shoulders felt tense and tight as I looked through photos of their travels.

Later, I decided to try talking with my older sister. As I peered into her door, I heard her crying over a designer Gucci skirt that had gotten an ink stain on it. She yelled, over and over, that it made her sick. I slithered sheepishly into her room and sat down on her covered radiator. Feeling at a loss for words, I sat and waited for her to speak to me. She said nothing. I said a few words to console her over the loss of her designer skirt and then left. When I walked into the kitchen later on, I heard her complaining to my mother.

"She comes into my room and just sits there and doesn't say anything. I wish she would just leave me alone. She's not any fun to be around", she said in a disgusted tone of voice.

I retreated to my room feeling hopeless. Soon, Christmas ended. My brother returned to his journalism job in California. My older sister returned to life with her husband and my younger sister returned to her activities with friends.

My emotional torment reached its peak the next afternoon. I sat on the porch with my mother soaking up the peaceful stillness of the soothing, lush greenery outside. As she looked at a magazine, I approached her carefully, praying that we could have a nice conversation. I asked her about her recent trip with my father to the International Diabetes Convention in Toronto. She looked coldly out of the side of her eyes as though I was imposing on her.

"We had a wonderful time. Daddy was honored at a banquet and they treated us like big wheels." Her voice sounded disinterested, as though I was the last person on earth she wanted to talk to.

"Oh, I haven't heard from any of my grammar school friends for so long.

We used to write back and forth but now I've lost their addresses", I said wistfully.

"Oh yeah. I remember, when we went up there to visit, none of them would speak to you. You really drove all of your best friends away", she said in an accusing tone of voice.

"Don't start with me", I said firmly.

"You get out of here. I was having a perfectly nice afternoon until you came in and ruined it", she said coldly.

"Why are you treating me like this? I haven't done anything to you", I said, trying to connect with her reasonable, loving side.

"Oh, poor little spoiled brat". Haughty self-righteousness blazed on her scowling face as she started walking into the kitchen. I trembled fearfully as I followed her.

"What's going on Mom?" There was a good mother in there. She had just been buried beneath years of frustration. My abusive father had changed her from a sweet person into a monster I thought, feeling empathy for her. She avoided my eyes and walked quickly away from me. Then, she suddenly turned on her heels, glared at me with eyes like daggers and began yelling at a decibel level which went through the roof.

"The whole time I was working like a dog trying to get your older sister's wedding planned and I was losing my mind you didn't lift a finger to help. You come in here spewing venom trying to pick a fight with me. You just weren't worth the trouble", she snarled like a rabid dog.

"I've always tried to love you but you tell me what a horrible person I am all the time", I said, looking pleadingly into her eyes. I realized that it had been distressing to her to have a daughter who was always going to a psychiatrist and getting in some disastrous, miserable situation. I started to understand her anger toward me. I understood why my father got angry at me too. Worrying about me must be grueling.

"Come over here. Do you want to see what you look like? Come here and take a look at yourself in the mirror." I walked over and looked at myself briefly.

"You look like a big fake. You can wear a T-shirt that says, 'My mother thinks I'm a big shit.'"

"I'm just trying to talk to you." I knew I could find my good mother if I just kept trying.

"Oh, yeah. You're so pitiful", she mocked, making her face blank and pushing out her stomach in a cruel imitation of me.

"Why are you treating me like this? I don't think…..She cut me off sharply before I could finish.

"You don't think about anything. You're always saying something stupid", she snapped, cutting me down to size.

"Why are you doing this to me?", I pleaded as my heart splintered into bleeding fragments.

"Because you're following me around looking like a big shit".

She put a blank expression on her face, dropped her mouth open and stuck her stomach out, mocking me again.

"You would have had me aborted if you could have", I yelled, as humiliation burned me like a hot cattle prod.

"I want you out of this house by sundown", she demanded, erupting like a volcano spewing a hundred years of built up lava. Then she stormed up the stairs. I jumped as she slammed her bedroom door.

My legs felt weak as I left the house. I walked around the neighborhood for an hour or so, until I was too tired to go further. As I walked into the kitchen my father stood by the counter in his underwear, filling a glass with red wine. He swayed back and forth.

"Where have you been?", he asked with concern.

"Mom started yelling at me and ordered me to leave the house so I walked around the village for a while."

"Well, just act like nothing happened", he responded.

He fumbled awkwardly as he put the cork back into the wine bottle. I wished him a good night and retreated to my older sister's room.

I began staying in there, reading murlis most of the time, only leaving the house to apply at various temporary employment agencies.

My mother never meant it literally when she exploded suddenly. We both acted like nothing had happened and exchanged superficial greetings as we passed each other. I did my best to empathize with the loneliness she must be experiencing as she coped with her difficult relationship with my father.

My hopes rose when I landed a job filing medical records. I worked diligently through January, February and part of March, enjoying the peace and quiet. I built up a nice nest egg which I tucked safely away in a handbag. The time for my return flight to San Francisco was rapidly approaching. I started packing my things, looking forward to seeing Sister Carol and the rest of my spiritual family. I thought my mother had cooled off but she exploded like Mount Vesuvius the day before I left.

"You can't just keep coming back here blaming all your failures on Daddy and I. We have sacrificed all our lives for you", she yelled one day. I wasn't trying to blame her. She must have been triggered by Dr. Stanfield commenting that I had ambitions to be a professional singer.

The only way I knew how to handle her was to walk away. I walked to the kitchen telephone and called my aunt and uncle. My uncle, Fred, listened with attentive curiosity as I told him about my plan to travel to India. I beamed with self confidence as he called me a courageous world traveler.

I walked out onto the porch and sat next to my mother, hoping she had decided to forgive and forget. It was a shame that my father had made her so unhappy. I looked at her sitting there, like a bird trapped in a gilded cage. She had been meant to sing in the opera, to experience glory and to fly. However, like a powerless servant, she had been suffocated by my father's domination and cruelty.

"Are you just going to follow the guru for the rest of your life? Why don't you get your life together instead of always traipsing away on another crazy adventure? India is a wretchedly poor country. You could get a fatal disease. And why would you tell Uncle Fred about your trip? He doesn't have any investment in you", she said critically.

What was I? A stock that she had invested in?

"I don't understand why you are so upset about me going to India", I said.

"Yeah. You just don't understand. Well, let me explain. It's like you work your whole life growing a beautiful rose and then someone comes along and says, 'Let me take this rose and turn it into a cabbage.'"

I remembered times when she had called me common. Hanging out with the poor folks in India would at least seal my reputation, I thought angrily. I was going to India to get love which I desperately needed. She wasn't capable of giving it.

March ninth arrived and I prepared to take the plane to San Francisco. I sat in worried silence as my parents drove me to the airport. They walked me to my gate not saying much, as though they thought I was a hopeless case.

Soon, everyone boarded the flight. Looking out at the clouds floating below, like mounds of cotton candy from my childhood May Fair, I pondered about what it would be like to meet God. Dr. Stanfield's voice played warmly in my mind. "Baba has come to transform the world. He will give you everything." "See the doughnut and not the hole" his voice said, reminding me of his eternal love. Daydreaming, I lost track of the time.

I was surprised when, suddenly, the plane dropped down onto the runway in San Francisco. The motor roared as it sped toward the gate, gradually slowing down. Carrying my heavy suitcase, I waited as the long line of people filed off of the plane and down into the gate. Walking quickly, I found my way out to the front entrance, wanting to plug my ears as the loud voices of travelers pierced through them. A rain shower had just ended and the trees sparkled radiantly in the sun. Extending my arm, I signaled for a cab. As the driver sped through the streets, I told him that I was going on a spiritual pilgrimage to India. He talked about his faith in Jesus and eternal life, waving his hand in fast, jerky movements, sending cigarette smoke curling through the air.

Soon, he arrived in front of the Raja Yoga center. He smiled with appreciation and wished me the best of luck when I handed him a twenty dollar bill and told him to keep the change. I walked to the front door of the Raja Yoga center and rang the bell. Sister Carol had told me to go there on my return from Atlanta. A beautiful Indian woman with a face like an angel welcomed me. Her peaceful presence soothed me as she helped me carry my bags up the stairs. Her long, white sari looked as pure as snow.

I sat down at the kitchen table. Her dark, liquid eyes glowed with love as she placed a bowl of warm, vegetarian stew and some bread and butter in front of me. My mouth watered as the delicious, spicy aroma wafted into my nostrils. As I lifted my spoon to eat, I stared with fascination at a photograph of an Indian woman with intensely luminous eyes.

"That is Baba speaking through the body of the medium. We call the Supreme soul Baba to show our affection for him", she said in a gentle voice.

"The eyes are so intense. I have never seen so much light in anyone's eyes", I said in amazement.

There was a long pause while I ate my delicious vegetarian meal gratefully. I hadn't had such a satisfying meal in a long time.

"You must be tired after your long trip. You can lie down and take a nap", she said.

After my nap, I rode the bus and streetcar to Sister Carol's small apartment. Her warm hug relaxed me and I soaked up her motherly concern as she looked through my suitcase to see what I had and what I needed. She wrote out a list of things for me to buy and told me the names of some cheap places where I could shop for white clothes. The Yogis had to wear white at all spiritual gatherings. Curiosity and excitement rushed through me. I knew that my three and a half weeks stay in India would be a fascinating, life changing adventure.

I looked out of the window with curiosity as I rode the street car to the Mission District. The sun shone brightly as I walked down the street to Thrift Town. My mind wandered as I browsed through the endless racks of clothes. I bought several pairs of white pants and some white shirts. A Spanish clerk took my money and gave me change. I dodged passing pedestrians as I walked down the street to Woolworth's. I bought three pairs of long underwear and six pairs of thick socks. Then, I ducked into the Goodwill store and, after browsing through the dusty shelves for a while, found a sleeping bag for six dollars. Sun streamed brightly through the window as the clerk added up my purchases. The sound of clinking coins filled my ears as the clerk counted my change and handed it to me with a kind smile. I walked down the street to the Army Surplus store. After browsing for a while, I found a duffel bag for five dollars. All my shopping was finally done. Clattering noises filled my ears as a streetcar arrived. I climbed up onto it and relaxed into a window seat near the front. Suddenly, trees began swaying and torrents of rain pummeled the windows loudly.

The rain stopped just as the driver let me off at my departure point. I wished him a good day and stepped out onto the street which was slick with shiny wetness. I breathed deeply as I walked, watching drops of water glisten on the green, flowering trees as the brilliant sun broke out from behind the clouds. Peace flowed through me as I arrived, turned the key and unlocked the door to Sister Carol's apartment. She was gone. I enjoyed my privacy as I made myself a cup of licorice tea from natural bark like pieces she kept in a jar. Later, when she arrived, tired from work, she helped me pack. She told me that my cloth suitcase could be easily sliced through and asked her sassy teen aged daughter to lend me her suitcase.

When two of our spiritual brothers arrived the next morning to take us to the airport, I was too excited to speak. Watching the concrete, chaos and corruption of the dirty city flash by like a disappearing mirage, I sighed with gratitude. Three weeks in an ashram in India had come to me as a gift from God. Communing with God and the other yogis was just the medicine I needed to heal myself from my time in hell. My heart expanded with hope as we walked through the frenetic, noisy corridors of the airport to our gate. We sat at the gate for a short while and, soon, a voice announced that it was time to board. I followed the line of travelers to the steps of the airplane. When a beautiful Indian sister smiled sweetly at me I felt honored.

"Are you the new sister?", she asked, looking at me with respectful reverence. Love poured through me as she gave me a handful of tiny sugar granules mixed with anise seeds and almonds.

When the plane finally touched down in India, I followed the long line of people down into the gate. Swaying with jetlag, I looked all around as we walked through the airport. The promise of springtime vibrated in the clear air as we walked outside, past colorful trees in full bloom. I shook the stiffness out of my arms and legs.

A huge, steel vehicle transported us across the airport. We collected our bags and walked to the custom's office. A thin, Indian man stamped my passport and handed it to me.

We all crawled into a cab. The driver spoke quickly in a thick, Indian accent as fields and trees spun around me. A dizzy feeling came over me as I pondered the mysteries of Yogis who could sit in forty degrees below weather and not feel cold. When the driver let us out at the Raja Yoga meditation center my eyes grew wide with wonder. Laughing and talking with my brothers and sisters, I walked toward a beautiful, white house at the end of an expansive, spring green lawn. An elderly lady with white hair in a long, white sari, handed me a silver glass of warm, spicy tea and a silver bowl filled with a crunchy snack. After a while, she led me upstairs to my bedroom. The clean, white room had airy windows with flowers on the sills. I dropped my suitcase onto the floor and collapsed onto the large bed, sprawling out my legs and arms. As I drifted off, I experienced the sensation of being rocked back and forth like a baby in a crib. I had never felt such blissful comfort. I must have been swinging in the swing of super sensuous joy I had heard mentioned in the murlis. Being off of the medications for almost seven months had served me well.

The next day I told Sister Cynthia from Seattle about the strange sensations I had had.

"Baba was rocking you", she replied. I contemplated with wonder about the mysterious forces that were healing me.

In the early morning, we crawled into a cab to journey to Delhi. The energy of chaos swirled madly in the frenetic air as women carrying huge vases on their heads walked by. Tiny, three-wheeled vehicles filled with passengers sped by. Cows ambled along, looking like important foreign dignitaries with their flower garlands hanging around their necks. They seemed to be far above the silly, time-wasting activities of human beings.

Merchants tried to sell us vases, sculptures and various things as we observed the Red Fort and various historical landmarks. I looked in awe at the eternal flame which memorialized Mahatma Gandhi. Snake charmers in orange turbans played flutes as black cobras with expanded faces stood in rapt attention listening to them. Barefooted children in dirty, ragged clothes walked along. We took a cab to the train station. Some children made a makeshift home in a corner of the train platform.

We stepped on board and carried our bags to a small compartment. I settled down into a seat across from a sister who told me she was from Paris. She said that this was her second visit to the spiritual university. As I observed the wrinkles around her eyes, I wondered what difficult experiences her life had given her.

The San Francisco brother who had told me about putting cold rags on his head to stay awake at four a.m. sat across from me. The train sped past endless, barren fields which were dotted with dilapidated shacks. Barefoot mothers in worn saris carried their children in sacks on their backs. Elderly, decrepit people carried huge bundles of sticks on their hunched backs. I caught glimpses of words on a sign which flashed by. It said something about restoring dignity to the women of India. As I imagined them being raped and beaten I let go of all doubt that the world was in hell—the Kali Yuga.

We finally arrived at a transfer stop sixteen hours later. I stepped down onto the ground and watched some muscular men transfer our luggage to a huge bus. An elderly, emaciated man huddled in a corner of the train platform wearing only a loincloth. As I observed him wasting away, without food and without love, I wondered how he kept any will to stay alive. I climbed onto the bus and sat down next to a handsome brother from Scotland. He handed me some toli. As I munched on it I exchanged sweet words with him. He had a ruddy complexion and strawberry blond hair. His kind, respectful manner soothed me. The gears of the bus groaned as it began to climb a staggeringly steep mountain. As it wound around curve after curve, ascending higher and higher, it stayed very close to the edge of the mountain. My mouth dropped open in awe as I looked down into a deep, vast valley of green, lush trees.

When we finally reached the top of Mount Abu, a feeling of magical wonder filled me and I stepped down onto the holy soil. A thick blanket of fog hung in the cold March air mysteriously. Clean, white buildings that looked like dormitories shone in the moonlight. A smiling Indian man and white-haired, older woman approached us and hugged us warmly. The man handed me a warm, thick blanket

"It gets foggy before Baba comes", Sister Carol said sweetly.

I dragged my suitcase as we walked through the grounds to one of the clean, white buildings. I followed Sister Carol up some stairs and down a hall to our room. Collapsing onto the bed, I listened to the quiet conversations of my sisters from countries all around the world. The room had a row of five beds on each side. The clean, white walls were calming. My pillow felt good underneath my head and the fragrant sheets soothed me as I drifted peacefully away.

CHAPTER 25 ————————————————MARCH, 1984
The Forest Of Honey

I WAS WOKEN AT FOUR A.M. by loud, high pitched Hindi singing reverberating through the halls. Sister Carol instructed me to wash every morning before meditation. Following her down the hall, I listened intently as she told me to use only one bucket of water. Water gushed into the bucket as I stooped in the tiny cubicle. I shampooed my hair and body and then poured the bucket of water over my head. After drying off with a towel, I walked back to my room in my bathrobe. When a sister handed me a long, white sari I looked at her through half-closed eyes. I could barely tell my ass from a hole in the ground and I certainly couldn't dress myself. I felt grateful when Sister Carol helped me gather the endless, white material into pleats, wrap it around my waist and pin it into place.

I followed her down some stairs, through a courtyard and up the stairs into a room full of silent, meditating yogis. Looks of bliss shone on their faces as two older Indian women waved ornate, silver incense holders back and forth sending intoxicating fragrance through the love charged air. Focusing my attention on the middle of my forehead, I visualized myself as an eternal point of light. Waves of divine consciousness washed through me, relaxing and healing me until I felt I had entered another dimension—an exalted realm of pure, powerful, transforming love. The energy in the air was electrically intense, as though God was right in front of us. My mind became completely still and my entire body relaxed as I floated on a peaceful cloud. At five a.m. I followed my spiritual sisters back to the dormitory. I fell onto my bed and drifted into a deep sleep.

It was nearing six a.m. when a sister from England woke me gently and led me to a place where I was to perform my karma yoga duties. I sat in a circle with souls from around the world grating carrots and watching peelings fly into a huge bucket. Drinking a silver cup of delicious, spicy tea which I got from a beautiful, silver urn, I looked out over a majestically expansive valley.

Curiosity overcame me as I followed the others to the Universal Peace Hall. As I walked up the long stairway, I admired the simple, white, elegant building with an orange-red oval, representing God, at the top of its tower. Thousands of souls from many different countries listened as a heavy Indian woman read the words of God. I clutched my thick blanket tightly around my shoulders but couldn't stop shivering as I sat in the cold air, yawning and struggling to stay awake. My head kept dropping down to my chest.

After class, we went to the dining hall and ate a delicious breakfast. In the afternoon, I walked around enjoying the spring flowers and breathtaking views of the mountains and valleys with Sister Cynthia from Seattle. She bubbled with happiness as she spoke about the blessings she had received from Baba.

When I got back to my dormitory room I reclined on my bed. Sister Anne from Los Angeles began talking with me. Her kind voice comforted me as she asked me if I would like a back rub. Pleasure pulsated through every cell in my body as she massaged my neck, head and shoulders.

As I walked around the grounds, I saw love shining in the eyes of everyone. I drank it in thirstily, feeling myself come back to life. During our free time, we had fun walking to the nearby village, exploring tailor shops, sari shops and a variety of other stores. A sweet Indian tailor made me an outfit. In the afternoons, people gathered to sing and play guitars or play Frisbee. I had a wonderful time playing Frisbee with a brother from Australia one sunny afternoon. After classes, the head Yogis gave us toli, a sweet dessert. As they placed it in my hands they gazed into my eyes with deep love which melted my heart. At every meal, Indian servers put the delicious food on our plates and looked into our eyes with love and a smile.

I ate lunch on a sunny roof one day and a monkey grabbed a potato off of my plate and dashed away in the blink of an eye. I had a great laugh with my spiritual sisters.

One night there was a cultural program. I laughed with amusement as yogis performed skits full of clever humor. A beautiful Indian woman performed classical Indian dance. The graceful precision of her agile movements amazed me. A tiny Indian boy who couldn't have been more than six performed a dance entitled The Birth of Krishna inside a huge lotus flower that bloomed dramatically on the stage.

Everyone piled into buses and rode out to a huge field one afternoon. The white capped Himalayan mountains towered in the distance as brothers and sisters played badminton, threw Frisbees, danced and sang songs. As I enjoyed spicy, vegetarian food which was blessed with love I listened to my Indian brothers and sisters speak Hindi. I didn't know a word of what they were saying, yet it was a fascinating sound. I contemplated about how simple life would be in the Golden Age with everyone speaking the same language.

I spent another wonderful afternoon hiking with a sweet sister from Australia. Enjoying one another's company, we sat down to meditate on the rocks, looking out over the vast, green valley. As we walked back to the University her lighthearted cheerfulness lifted my mood. Wishing her well, I retreated to my room. Some yogis sang and played guitars outside my window. I listened to one of my all time favorite songs "Here Comes The Sun" as I enjoyed a pleasant cat nap on my bed.

The night finally came for God to descend. Sister Carol helped me wrap my sari around my waist and pin it into place. My palms sweated and I worried that God might turn away from me, because of my past sexual conduct, as we walked up the long stairs of the Universal Peace Hall. I followed her into the large room and we sat on the floor in front of the stage. High pitched Indian singing filled the air.

Suddenly, the music stopped and silence saturated the room. Everyone held their breath in anticipation as the trance medium, an Indian, middle-aged woman, sat down on a white chair. A far away, blank expression covered the medium's face as she went into a profoundly deep trance. Suddenly, her body jerked. A voice with a mesmerizing, whispering quality began to talk through the microphone. People from various countries put headphones over their ears to hear the translated words in their language.

"I, the Father-God am so delighted to see my children filled with such enthusiastic eagerness for working towards a new world. The ocean of peace and love has come to meet his children. Bapdada sees the one desire of all the souls of the world—the one desire of pure love. Bapdada has come to the children for this reason. The merciful father feels great mercy. You have claimed all rights. You became beggars. Some have even lost hope. You have been asking, "Is it impossible to have eternal peace in the world?" Baba himself has come to answer the questions, to give good news. The good news is that you, my children, ruled the world of happiness. Yesterday you were masters of the world of love. Tomorrow you will be in that world again. This will be the land of heaven with no trace of sorrow or peacelessness. Where there is no impurity nothing is unattainable. It is unmoveable, unshakeable—that which is destined. The new creation will definitely take place."

An electrifying current of divine love flowed through the room as God spoke for the next two hours. I flew in ecstasy when the translator announced that God would now speak with the individual groups. Trembling with emotion, I followed my brothers and sisters from San Francisco up onto the stage and sat down in front of God. My palms sweated and I listened in fascination as he talked with one person after another, in a hypnotic voice.

Suddenly, my name was called. I sat down in front of the medium. Floating euphorically into another dimension, I looked into the dark eyes which glowed with the most powerful, unlimited love I had ever seen. He looked at me like I was a great treasure, a priceless jewel.

"Do you feel as though you're new or as though you're an old one here?", he asked, transporting me to heaven with his eyes.

"I feel new", I replied.

"Do you experience that you've reached a place of peace? Do you know whose place this is? It's Baba's place, the Father's place. Is this what you understand? The Father's place means it's your place doesn't it? So where have you come? It's to your own home. So always be happy in that realization that I have reached my original, sweet home. Do you have this happiness? Do you worry about things? Do you think too much? What do you worry about?", he asked, his eyes glowing with compassion.

"I worry about getting along in the world", I replied.

"The special help that you have is the experience in the divine family. This is the instrument to help you get along in the world. It's no longer necessary for you to worry because you have this help. Stay happy. Have the happiness that you've come to your own true family", he whispered hypnotically as he reached out and squeezed my hand. Infinite love poured from his phenomenal eyes into my expanding heart. The love of this moment was all I wanted and the trappings of the world faded like cheap, junky trinkets. I floated in ecstasy, far above the ruined world.

As the next group was called, I left God reluctantly. After walking with my sweet sisters to the dormitory, I fell onto my bed and drifted into a profoundly peaceful sleep.

High pitched Hindi singing woke me up at four a.m. and I scrambled, bleary eyed, to the meditation hall. Divine love poured into me as I sat in the Lotus posture communing with the ocean of love, Baba. That afternoon, all the new yogis were given Raja Yoga rings by the two Indian, female heads of the University. They were called Dadis in affection. One of them had overcome cancer by meditating. She gazed at me with deep love as she slipped the silver and red ring onto my finger. I was now married to God, protected from harm by the most loving being in the universe.

The days passed quickly and, soon, my last chance to talk with God arrived. I chatted cheerfully with my sisters as I got dressed, with trembling hands. A sweet sister from Denmark helped me pin my sari into place. We looked like a band of angels as we walked through the grounds and up the long stairs of the Universal Peace Hall. I sat in a chair alongside my sisters.

Soon, the room was filled with enthusiastic souls who watched the medium sitting on the stage.

She sat in deep meditation on a white cushioned chair. A vase of beautiful flowers sat on a table next to her. Everyone sat in complete silence, focusing their attention on her. Her eyes got a far away look as she went deeper and deeper into a trance. Suddenly, her body jerked convulsively and her face became masculine. Then, the slow, hypnotic whisper of God vibrated through the room, electrifying the energy. The microphone made a loud noise as the translator adjusted it.

"Today, the Ocean of love has come to meet his children who are worthy of God's love. All of you have also arrived here in the subtle airplane of love, have you not? Did you fly here in an ordinary plane or in the plane of love? Waves of love are emerging in everyone's heart and love alone is the foundation of this Brahmin life. When all of you came here it was love that pulled you, was it not? You would never even have dreamt that you would become worthy of God's love. And what do you say now? That you have become that. This love is not ordinary love, it is love from the heart. It is soul-conscious love, it is true love, it is altruistic love. This love from God very easily gives you the experience of remembrance. Love is a subtle magnet. Love makes you an easy yogi. It liberates you from labor. Remembering with love doesn't require effort. You then eat the fruit of love. Look how children have come running here from ninety countries."

For the next couple of hours everyone listened with rapt concentration. Then, the translator announced that the individual groups could now speak with Baba. My heart bloomed with love as I followed my group onto the stage and sat in front of Baba. As my spiritual brothers and sisters talked with him their faces glowed with innocence. When my personal time came, emotion rolled in a cosmic wave through me. I kneeled in front of the medium, drinking in the unlimited ocean of love. Soothing sensations rippled through me as God's voice came through the microphone.

"You can attain great power", Baba said.

I could not imagine a lost soul like me being powerful.

"What will you remember?", he asked, as his intense, glowing eyes transformed me with love. I knew why he was called the master psychiatrist now.

"You're a Shiv Shakti", he said, squeezing my hand.

I wanted to stay with him forever, suspended in time, drinking in this nectar of love. Peace and love rolled through me in pleasant waves. I returned to my group reluctantly.

My time in the forest of honey had passed far too quickly. I only had a few days left. I watched my sweet sisters get undressed and into bed, lingering and clinging to their presence. I was definitely in the land of angels. Their kindness soothed me to the depths of my being.

Everyone celebrated with funny skits and singing the next night. My eyes widened with awe as I admired yogis from around the world dressed like Deities of the Golden Age. They looked gorgeous in their sparkling gowns and shining, gold crowns. After the performance, multi-colored fireworks were set off. I walked to the sun roof of the girls' dormitory with a sister from England. A spirit of joyful celebration filled the air as fireworks exploded loudly, spreading gorgeous colors through the velvet, black sky. A new world was being created. Hopeful happiness rushed through me as I stared at the bright stars, drinking in the purifying cosmic energy. A lump formed in my throat as I dreaded leaving this magical place, my own sweet home.

"The constellations are memorials to us", my loving sister said.

"Really? I feel honored", I replied.

"Baba said that the constellations were created in remembrance of us", she said.

"I've never seen the stars so bright. I don't want to leave here", I said sadly.

"Keep Baba with you all the time wherever you go. He wants to give you everything. You are very precious to him and he loves you endlessly. Whatever you're doing, always remember him and keep filling yourself with his love. If you have problems or worries tell him about them and he'll give you the answer. He is always there to give you everything you ask for.

There's no limit to the miracles he performs. Every second you spend in his remembrance is purifying you and building your fortune for the Golden Age. Always remember that you are a priceless treasure to him. You can eat lunch with him or take him for a ride on your bike."

"I want to stay with Baba all the time. I've never felt so much love. I feel like I'm being transformed", I said, my heart booming like a bass drum.

"You are. You're becoming a deity of the Golden Age."

The day to leave arrived and I cried. My heart sank as I hugged my divine brothers and sisters goodbye. I looked back at them as I climbed onto the bus and sat down in a seat. Majestic mountains and open fields which sparkled in the sun spun around me as the bus sped down the open road. I gazed out of the window, lost in thought, reliving the touching moments I had enjoyed with my sweet brothers and sisters.

After a long train ride, we arrived in a busy city. I tried to not stare as I watched beggars with no legs roll by on skateboards and starving people hold up cups asking for spare change. Ragged, barefoot children wandered aimlessly. Snake charmers played flutes for attentive, upright cobras. Struggling people sat on blankets trying to sell fruits, vegetables and various other things to pedestrians. Cows sauntered by peacefully as rickshaws zigzagged through the chaotic traffic. An emaciated man pulled a huge cart loaded with bricks. Several brothers waved their arms and, finally, two cabs pulled up. Half of the group went to one and the other half to the other. The driver spoke Hindi in a thick accent as he drove us to the airport.

I settled onto the plane in a window seat next to two sisters. The motor began to rev as I stared at the hard working, muscular men driving huge vehicles. Soon, it was roaring. The plane began to speed down the runway, accelerating faster and faster each second until it lifted into the air with a sudden jolt. My ears popped as we rose higher and higher. We chatted lightly, enjoying each other's company. Time passed quickly.

I resisted facing the ugly reality of life in the city as we landed in San Francisco. I rode a big bus into downtown San Francisco. Standing on the curb of a busy street, I waved my arm to hail a cab. Beggars stood aimlessly on street corners as cars and buses sped by spreading harmful fumes. Pimps and drug dealers killed for money as cripples and mentally ill people struggled to survive. This corrupt, materialistic civilization was gasping its last breath. A brunette cab driver pulled to the curb and I got in. When I told him I had no place to stay, he said I could stay for free in the Fort Mason shelter. I asked him to take me there.

After paying the cab driver, I had ten dollars to my name. I walked into the shelter, dragging my suitcase wearily. I had not stayed in it before and it was surprisingly clean, attractive and quiet. A friendly, overweight woman at the front desk gave me a voucher and said that I could stay for three nights. Brimming with gratitude, I lugged my suitcase down a hall and into a room with two bunk beds. I dropped it onto the floor and climbed the ladder quickly.

As I reclined on the top bunk and stared at the ceiling I worried. After a while, I couldn't stand thinking any longer. I climbed down the ladder and walked outside. As I passed a row of buildings, I recognized the one where I had attended sketching sessions. Seagulls cried out the loneliness in my heart as I walked around. After a while I sat down on a pier and stared at the ocean. Ships came and went like the strangers passing through my beggar's life as I hugged myself around the waist. Pelicans flapped their large wings and splashed down onto the water, catching big fish in their huge beaks. When I had worried until my head ached, I walked back up the hill. The city sprawled like a terrifying maze as I walked into a Safeway and bought a container of orange juice. A friendly clerk wished me a good night.

Desperation splintered me into pieces as I climbed the ladder and crawled into my lonely, bunk bed. I slept fitfully, worrying through the night.

Longing to escape from the pathetic planet forever, I headed out the next morning. I filled out applications in bookstores, cookie businesses, fast food restaurants and shops. I continued all day every day until my three nights at the shelter were gone.

Somehow, I wound up in a halfway house in the Haight Ashbury, after calling a counseling line to help me. I must have looked strange as I lugged my suitcase and duffel bag up the long stairway. Bored, spaced out people sat around lost in their drugged, unhappy worlds. A counselor led me into an office and spoke with me. She handed me some Stelazine and a small cup of water. I swallowed it obediently but, when she told me I needed to wash my clothes, I felt insulted. It had been seven months since I took medication and I felt fragile, raw and vulnerable.

"I'm sick of being ordered around by all of you California fucks", I yelled at the top of my lungs, spewing rage uncontrollably. The Yogis said I was not allowed to get angry but I was angry as hell and I couldn't hold it in any more.

They only put up with me at the halfway house for one night. The next day, I was roaming up and down the streets, lugging my suitcase and duffel bag, and wondering what to do next. Riding the bus downtown, I decided to stand around on Market street. Two guys started talking with me. When I told them my dilemma, one of them said I could stay with him for the night. Worry splintered my peace as I slept in his barren, ugly room in a high rise building. My uncomfortable, bare mattress was on the other side of the room from him and he didn't bother me luckily. It was a strange home and I wondered if he was a drug addict.

The next morning he began to rage at me, calling me a bitch. I lifted my suitcase and duffel bag and hurried away from him. My heart raced as I ran down the creepy corridor, onto an elevator. I sighed with relief as its steel doors closed, protecting me from my deranged sleep mate. Deep depression weighed me down as I dragged my things through the unfriendly streets all day. By the late afternoon, I had found myself shelter in a hotel in the Tenderloin District. When I told the aloof front desk clerk that I was homeless, he handed me a voucher for a three nights stay.

As I dragged my things up the dark, dirty stairway, the nauseating stench of cigarettes, alcohol and urine gave me an urge to vomit. Dirty syringes and trash were scattered here and there. My key clicked as I let myself in. Thoughts of drug addicts breaking down the door and raping me raced through my mind. I watched a cockroach crawl along the dirty, peeling wall like an omen of doom. Falling down onto the bed in despair, I clutched the tattered pillow tightly. My abdomen began to heave in and out as tears streamed down my face. An ocean of grief poured from my guts.

Pulling my clothes on and running my fingers through my hair the next morning, I felt like a mangy animal, too dirty and unattractive to show my face. Locking the door behind me, I headed down to the street, determined to find a job. The loud rush of traffic and the tough people walking down the dirty streets scraped my soul raw. I bought a newspaper from a corner box. Leaning on a post at the corner bus stop, I scanned the want adds.

A bus roared up to my stop. I climbed up the steps and sat down behind the driver. I tried to fight the desperate fear that was holding me in a tight grip. My mind raced with confusion as I tried to decide what to do and where to go.

When I saw the Public Library, I asked the bus driver to let me out. The door creaked open and I stepped out onto the sidewalk. My mouth dropped open in shock when I noticed a man sucking his lover's penis behind the library.

I walked into the library. Sitting down at a table, I thought and worried and thought and worried. Looking around suspiciously, I read a newspaper and began circling job listings. After a while, I began to kick my leg restlessly under the table. Walking quickly out of the library, I yearned for someone, anyone, to help me escape my unbearable loneliness. My stride became brisker and more frantic every second. After walking for a long time, I arrived on Market Street. Feeling my shoulders rise with fear, I observed X-rated movie theaters with their glaring neon lights. Liquor stores advertised the promise of pleasure yet I saw sorrow in the eyes of swaggering drunks. My cheeks burned with shame as I walked back to the shelter, watching the sun descend, casting pink streaks through the sky. The front desk clerk greeted me and I walked on trembling legs up the dirty stairway. Laying on my uncomfortable, torn mattress on the floor, too terrified to breath, I clutched the covers around me through another sleepless, dark night.

CHAPTER 26 ———————————————— APRIL, 1984
Last Days Of Boot Camp

PRIL 9, 1984, MY TWENTY seventh birthday, arrived. Sunlight streaming through the window of my Tenderloin shelter comforted me. Weakness pervaded me as I dressed myself, trying to decide what to do next. Facing the fires of the hell surrounding me felt overwhelming. I was easy prey for the drunks, addicts, murderers, rapists and mentally ill maniacs I would encounter throughout the day. A drunk, smelly man stumbled by me as I let myself out of my room and locked the door behind me. Bracing myself for another day of misery and loneliness, I walked down the stairs. The loud rush of traffic scraped my nerves raw as I stepped out onto the sidewalk. Hunger rumbled in my stomach as I crossed the street and walked into a Dunkin' Donuts. Looking around in suspicion, I felt lost in a void as I ordered a donut. I asked the employee for an application and filled it out while I ate. Confusion tossed my mind and I longed for some medication and a safe halfway house.

I left the application with an employee and began hurrying down the street. The sound of roaring traffic blasted through me as I approached a corner light. I craned my neck back and looked up at the tall glass and steel buildings surrounding me. They stood haughtily, looking down on me with the satisfaction that they had conquered their powerless prey. How foolish I had been to think that I could take on the world. Everywhere I turned, voices seemed to mock me, echoing in cruel finality that I had no power and never would have any. Staring at the sidewalk in shame, I hurried past the liquor stores and Triple-X movie theaters. A rough looking man who looked like he could kill someone in a minute without blinking an eye hurried by, sending chills up my spine.

I walked quickly, feeling disdain for the world of sorrow surrounding me. Endless rage flowed through me. My dreams had once shone like brilliant, sparkling jewels. Now, they lay shattered on grimy concrete as feelings of worthlessness crashed through me. After walking in a confused, frenzied rage through the chaotic, hostile streets for hours I returned to the shelter.

A lightning bolt of emotion struck me as I stared in disbelief. My father was standing there, glowing with benevolence like a true hero.

"I think it's time for you to come home", he said with empathy. I realized I couldn't afford to be proud.

"That's fine with me", I replied.

My father spoke in a business like tone as he directed the shelter manager to call a cab. Soon, a Yellow Cab arrived. The driver spoke in quick, short sentences in a Spanish accent. He sped through the traffic filled streets and let us out across from a huge hotel.

The Fairmont Hotel glittered in opulence as my father pulled the gold front door handle strongly. Sparkling chandeliers hung from the ceilings as elegantly dressed people walked through the lobby which was decorated with expensive furniture and paintings. My father told me he had enjoyed the medical convention he had attended at the hotel. A feeling of unreality filled me as we walked down the hall to our room. I walked into the bathroom and, as I soaked in a warm bubble bath, I dreamed of Baba's love.

I dried off with a fluffy towel and dressed. When I walked into the room, my father had fallen asleep and he looked innocent and sweet. As I watched his chest rise and fall with the rhythm of his breathing I forgave him for his harsh side. He had a loving side that was truly endearing. I felt sympathy for him as I pondered that he was a very sick man—an alcoholic and a diabetic. I crawled onto the far side of the King sized bed and fell into a deep sleep.

The next morning, my father treated me to delicious blueberry pancakes. I ate them with gusto, thoroughly enjoying every bite. He explained to me how he had asked someone if he had seen me. He had responded that he had and that I came into the shelter about three p.m. every day.

After breakfast, we took the elevator up to the room. My father called for a concierge. Soon, a smiling, handsome young man arrived. He carried my bags through the hall and called a cab to take us to the airport. The driver drove rapidly through the city and down the expressway. In just a short time, we arrived at the airport.

I contemplated most of the four hour flight. My ears popped as we began our descent into Atlanta. The motor roared noisily as we landed. We talked a little bit as we walked to the baggage claim. It took us a long time to find the car in the dark, crowded parking lot.

My life in hell had ended. Grateful joy moved through me as my father sped down the freeway. Soon, he was driving up the long driveway of my childhood. He parked the car and turned off the motor. Picking up my suitcase and duffel bag, I carried them into the kitchen, feeling disoriented and dizzy from jet lag. I followed him upstairs to the master bedroom tensely, hoping my mother would be civil to me this time. A lamp glowed on the table beside her as she sat in bed reading a magazine. I smiled as I greeted her. She looked at me with bemused scrutiny as I told her my trip to India had been wonderful.

"God is pure love and he wants to transform the world and make everyone happy", I said, beaming with joy.

"I learned that in kindergarten", she replied, bursting my bubble.

My father crawled into the bed beside her. Wishing them a good night, I slithered self-consciously down the hall to my older sister's room. Affection rose in me as I thought about my time in the forest of honey. A peaceful reverie came over me as the aroma of fresh linens soothed me and, soon, I drifted into dreamland.

A radiant sun poured in the window and woke me the next morning. My father said I could set up my home in the garage apartment behind the house. A medical student had fixed it up and lived there for a while. As I sat eating breakfast with my parents my father commented that he would never forget the way I ate those pancakes in the fancy hotel. My mother looked concerned when my father said he had found me in the most dangerous section of San Francisco. She praised me for my bravery and talked with deep emotion about how happy she was that I was home. With no rent to pay and the fortress of my father's house keeping me safe, I felt ecstatic. My father was very proud of me for surviving my time on the streets. He took my sister, mother and I to see a moving play about struggle, which formerly homeless people acted in.

I furnished my home with a small futon, a writing desk and a typewriter my father bought for me. With its large windows surrounded by trees, it felt like a tree house. The rolling hills of the golf course down below looked as beautiful as the English countryside. I got hired at a shop two blocks away. I woke up at four a.m. every morning and meditated, filling myself up with the ocean of love and sending love to my parents. Then, I read a murli, looking forward to seeing my kind co-workers.

"With your elevated attitude, make intense effort to make your vibrations and the atmosphere powerful; give blessings and receive blessings."

"Today, Bapdada, the Ocean of love and power, has come to meet his loving, long-lost and now-found, beloved children. All the children, through the attraction of love, have also reached here from far, far away to celebrate a meeting. Whether you are sitting personally in front of Baba, or whether you are sitting in this land or abroad, you are celebrating a living meeting. BapDada is pleased to see all his loving children and totally co-operative companion children. BapDada is seeing that the majority of the children have just the one thought in their heart: We will now very quickly reveal the father. The Father says: The enthusiasm of the children is very good. However, you will only be able to reveal the Father when you first of all reveal yourselves as perfect and complete, the same as the Father. So, have you fixed a date to become equal to the Father? BapDada hears the heart to heart conversation of every child everywhere. You are making effort but there has to be intense effort. Each one of you must check yourself. Many papers will come, however, an intense effort maker is not troubled by problems. Just as the rockets of science fly very fast, in the same way, your spiritual attitude of good wishes and pure feelings will change your vision and your world.

To all the intense effort making children from everywhere who create a spiritual and powerful atmosphere with their attitude, to those who always give an experience of powerful vibrations through their place and stage, to the elevated souls who have determined thoughts, to the merciful souls who always give blessings and receive blessings, to the double-light souls who always experience themselves to be in the flying stage, BapDada's love, remembrance and namaste.